NATIONAL SUICIDE

NATIONAL SUICIDE:
Military Aid
to the
Soviet Union

Antony C. Sutton

Arlington House   New Rochelle, N.Y.

Library of Congress Catalog Card Number 73-11977

ISBN 0–87000–207–4

MANUFACTURED IN THE UNITED STATES OF AMERICA

Library of Congress Cataloging in Publication Data

Sutton, Anthony C
    National suicide.

    Bibliography: p.
    1. Technical assistance, American—Russia.
2. Military assistance, American—Russia.
3. Russia—Defenses. 4. United States—Defenses.
I. Title.
HC336.24.S97   355.03'2'47   73-11977
ISBN 0-87000-207-4

Dedicated to the memory of the 35 million individuals killed by Soviet statism between 1917 and 1972.

> This business of lending blood money is one of the most thoroughly sordid, cold blooded, and criminal that was ever carried on, to any considerable extent, amongst human beings. It is like lending money to slave traders, or to common robbers and pirates, to be repaid out of their plunder. And the men who loan money to governments, so called, for the purpose of enabling the latter to rob, enslave and murder their people, are among the greatest villains that the world has ever seen.
>
> LYSANDER SPOONER, No Treason (Boston, 1870)

CONTENTS

PREFACE

The evidence and the argument in *National Suicide: Military Aid to the Soviet Union* will come as a surprise—and perhaps as an unwelcome shock—to almost all readers. It is a first attempt to penetrate what may ultimately turn out to be one of the most tragic stories in the 200-year history of the American republic.

The 100,000 Americans killed in Korea and Vietnam were killed by our own technology. This tragedy was brought about by irrational policies, based on unsupportable premises and reflecting grossly inaccurate analyses of the available information.

I make no claim for completeness. Sometime ago I planned a detailed academic treatment of our military assistance to the Soviet Union. Regrettably, the Administration has been unwilling to declassify sufficient file material for that purpose. The related exchange of correspondence is printed here as Appendix A.

Consequently, where information is still censored, the book is incomplete. Continued censorship of the Operation Keelhaul files by the U.S. Army is a similar example of big words and little action when it comes to providing the American public with the basic facts about recent history. In presenting this preliminary version of *National Suicide,* which reflects most of the available open evidence, it is my hope that the public reaction will blast loose enough government files for me to research and write the definitive academic study.

The views and interpretation expressed in this book are those of the author alone. In no way does this book reflect the views or interpretation of any organization otherwise associated, or to be associated, with the author.

November 1972   ANTONY C. SUTTON

CHAPTER ONE
The "Detente"-Aggression Cycle

Russia remains today, more than ever, an enigma for the Western world. Simple American minds imagine that this is because we don't know the truth about it. They are wrong. It is not our lack of knowledge which causes us to be puzzled by Russia. It is that we are incapable of understanding the truth about Russia when we see it ...

GEORGE KENNAN, Memorandum in the State Department files, dated September 1944

As the reader opens this book he may well have one thought in mind: "Military aid to the Soviets? Impossible! How can *that* be?"

The impatient, or unduly skeptical, reader will find an instant overview of the evidence in Appendix C, which lists, from an authentic Soviet source, the technical specifications of the ninety-six ships used by the Soviet Union to transport weapons and supplies to Haiphong for use in South Vietnam against the United States and its allies. A glance at this appendix will verify with hard precision that while the ships on the Haiphong run may fly the Soviet flag, most of them are certainly not Soviet in construction. Moreover, all their propulsion systems originated outside the Soviet Union.

A full understanding of the extent and nature of our military aid to the USSR must be based on an understanding of the extent and nature of the trade conducted by the United States and the Western world with the Soviet Union, the role of technology in this trade, and specifically the contribution of transferred Western technology to the development of the Soviet military-industrial complex. The Haiphong-run ships and their engines originated in the West and came to the Soviet Union through "peaceful trade." This kind of observation and evidence is the key to the argument in this book.

The History of "Peaceful Trade"

From time to time in the last fifty years, both Democratic and Republican administrations have declared a "new" policy of "peaceful trade" with the Soviet Union as the road to a world at peace.

Bridge-building to the Soviets began in 1918 under President Woodrow Wilson, before the Bolsheviks had physically gained control of more than a fraction of Russia. As a result of this trade, the Bolsheviks were able to consolidate their totalitarian regime. Edwin Gay, then a member of the U.S. War Trade Board, later dean of the Harvard Business School and a long-time member of the Council on Foreign Relations, is the most likely originator of "bridge-building." He is on record as follows in the State Department's files for 1918:

> Mr. Gay stated the opinion that it was doubtful whether the policy of blockade and economic isolation of these portions of Russia which were under Bolshevik control was the best policy for bringing about the establishment of a stable and proper government in Russia. Mr. Gay suggested to the Board that if the people in the Bolshevik sections of Russia were given the opportunity to enjoy improved economic conditions, they would themselves bring about the establishment of a moderate and stable social order.[1]

[1] Minutes of the War Trade Board, 1918.

Fifty years of trade with the Soviet Union by the United States and its European allies have, through the transfer of free enterprise technology, created a formidable economic and military power.

All this is well known in Washington, although the official version for public consumption sidesteps the historical realities, which are not incorporated into our policies vis-à-vis the Soviet Union. The real story has been told elsewhere in profuse technical detail.[2] More briefly, in June 1944, W. Averell Harriman, reporting to the State Department on a discussion with Stalin, made the following statement:

> Stalin paid tribute to the assistance rendered by the United States to Soviet industry before and during the war. He said that about two-thirds of all the large industrial enterprises in the Soviet Union had been built with United States help or technical assistance.[3]

Stalin could have added that the remaining third of Russia's large industrial enterprises and military plants had been built with German, French, British, Swedish, Italian, Danish, Finnish, Czech, and Japanese "help or technical assistance."

Official Washington also knows that Soviet industrialization has been preeminently Soviet militarization. The first priority in Soviet industrial plans was given to the military departments. Indeed, the original drive behind Russia's industrialization was military. This objective was clearly stated in 1929 by Unashlicht, vice president of the Revolutionary Military Soviet, *before* American firms went into Russia to carry out the Five-Year Plans:

> We must try to ensure that industry can as quickly as possible be adapted to serving military needs . . . [therefore,] it is necessary to carefully structure the Five-Year Plan for maximum cooperation and interrela-

[2] See Bibliography.

[3] U.S. State Department Decimal File, 033.1161 Johnston, Eric/ 6–3044: Telegram June 30, 1944.

tionship between military and civilian industry. It is
necessary to plan for duplication of technological
processes and absorb foreign assistance . . . such are
the fundamental objectives.[4]

Even after the massive U.S.-Soviet trade agreements of 1972,
which will obviously further enlarge the Soviet military-industrial complex (if this is not obvious to the reader now, it will be
at the end of this book), Secretary of State Rogers could
claim that these new trade agreements would create a "climate
for peace," unknowingly reiterating the still unfulfilled claims
that Edwin Gay made fifty-four years ago. Just how this "climate
for peace" is to be achieved is not stated. For good reason! The
historical evidence goes the other way.

What is "peaceful trade"? It is an essential but ignored truth
that peaceful trade can only flow from a world at peace. Trade
cannot *create* peace. The blunt, unwelcome fact is that "peaceful trade" with statist countries is a non sequitur. Statist systems create wars and internal oppression; this was as true of
Hitler's Germany as it is of Soviet Russia. For peaceful trade
you must first have a world at peace. Trade is a symptom of
peace, not a cause of peace.

The reader may counter-argue, "Well, some goods are peaceful; what's wrong with exporting sugar or soap powder or
automobile gasoline?"

The problem with this argument is that almost all products
have some military use. An effective formula for Molotov cock-
tails is one-third sugar and two-thirds gasoline; another formula
is one-third soap powder, two-thirds gasoline, and a dash of oil.
So whether the sugar, soap powder, and automobile gasoline
supplied by "peaceful trade" are used in the kitchen and
garage or in a civil war depends on the *intent* of the recipient.
Intent is the primary question. But Soviet intent is not considered by Washington policymakers in this context, as will be
discussed further in Chapter Two.

[4] *Pravda,* April 28, 1929.

More important than Soviet military use of imported civilian goods is the use of imported technology to produce military goods. Rather than sell machine guns, we are selling the machines with which to fabricate machine guns.

History teaches the lesson that statist systems are inherently aggressive. Moreover, statist systems have little ability to push forward the frontiers of technology. Thus, any technology transferred to a statist system will more than likely be used for military or oppressive purposes. The record of the last fifty years provides the evidence that the United States has received back its own technology on the battlefield from both national socialists (Nazis) and international socialists (Soviets). This is the simple, tragic, but ignored lesson of modern history.

Technological Transfer Is the Critical Issue

Before we present the evidence and press our argument, we must clear the decks. What precisely is the relationship between military assistance to the Soviet Union and "peaceful trade"?

Our military assistance to the Soviet Union has taken two forms. First, direct assistance through the transfer of military information, weapons, and technology; second, and more important in recent years, the transfer of the technology required for the building of a gigantic military-industrial complex. "Peaceful trade" is the carrier vehicle by which equipment, technology, and skills are transferred from the West, mainly the United States, to the Soviet Union.

Free trade is eminently desirable in a free world of non-coercive societies, but free trade with a statist system is not neutral. The question at issue is: If we can show that trade is a carrier for self-destruction, then is free trade desirable? There are laws on the books to prevent such technical transfers. They are virtually ineffective. In practice the policymakers and the bureaucrats in the Executive Branch act almost as if such laws did not exist, and if the reader thinks this a rash statement, he must explain the evidence presented in the chapters that follow.

This evidence is well known in Washington. Is it ignored because it is uncomfortable? Or because it interferes with some other policy objectives? In the conduct of economic relations with the Soviet Union, the ambitions and objectives of influential financial and business groups play a central role. Many prominent businessmen—Maurice Stans, Peter G. Peterson, Peter Flanigan, Averell Harriman, Robert McNamara—have exercised significant roles in developing our commercial policy towards the USSR. Publicized political labels may differ for election purposes, but they fade away once such men attain office, and our national policies remain fundamentally the same.

Further, quasi-governmental institutions such as the Committee for Economic Development (CED) play a discreet but obviously important role in policymaking. If the reports issued by such organizations ignore national security factors, then one can be sure that these factors are not reflected among prominent business appointees to political office. We therefore have a major problem regarding the interaction of "big business" and state policy and the influence of business on state decisions, particularly if the objectives of the business-financial group require the downgrading of technological transfers.

The Mystical Foundations of Policy

The mystical* approach to research for foreign-policy determination, and the intimate interest of some elements of big business in specific policies, is well exemplified in a recent report by the Committee for Economic Development, *A New Trade Policy towards Communist Countries*. CED is a prestigious organization with trustees from the highest levels of American industry and with research conducted by prominent academicians. Undoubtedly, CED is a persuasive influence in

---

* By *mystical* we mean a policy not based on empirical observations and rational deductions from these observations.

current policymaking. Peter G. Peterson, former Secretary of Commerce and one of the prime architects of current "detente" policy, is listed as a CED "Trustee on leave for Government Service," and other trustees of CED will be prime beneficiaries of our "new" trade policy towards the USSR.

The paramount factor in the strategic aspects of trade with Communist countries is technology and technological transfers through trade—specifically, the use of our technology by the Soviets for military purposes and the demonstrated inability of the Soviet Union, as a typical statist country, to push forward the technological horizon. Far from coming to grips with this fundamental problem, the CED report suggests only that it is a "very troublesome issue" and then evades the topic as follows, "The fact that the transfer of a technology will strengthen the economy of a potential enemy is not necessarily a sufficient reason to deny the transfer" (p. 28).

Then, without further ado about the "very troublesome issue," the CED report recommends what it so urgently set out to prove:

> We recommend that the United States remove all restrictions on exports to communist countries with the exception of military equipment and the kind of advanced technology that would be particularly useful in producing such equipment. (p. 28)

This means little, for we have never had meaningful restrictions on trade with Communist countries that *could* be removed: (The evidence for this statement will be presented further on in this book.) It should be noted that CED only wants to ban "particularly useful" military technology: presumably military trucks are okay, but atomic warheads taboo.

Now why did the CED report hastily abandon the obvious research path: that is, to investigate technological transfers to the USSR and their effect on the Soviet military-industrial complex? The scientific method is known to CED's academic research staff, and it suggests that a "very troublesome issue" requires thorough exploration and detailed investigation. Of course, if the CED staff had explored and investigated the "very troublesome issue," it would have found the same story that is outlined in this book—but then CED would not have been able to prove the conclusion it had set out to prove.

Our military assistance to the Soviets is not what the Committee for Economic Development wants to discuss—or even to consider as part of the evidence. CED is apparently determined to prove, come what may, that expanded trade with the USSR can only be beneficial. Only one member of the committee, Philip Sporn of New York, submitted a strongly dissenting opinion. He concluded, "This report has left me wondering why a group of hardheaded businessmen can so easily be beguiled by shallow philosophical shibboleths" (p. 46).

It may leave others wondering too.

Assume what you set out to prove. Sweep contrary evidence under the carpet. Put the dissents in the footnotes or in the back of the report. Stack the committee. Stack the research staff. And, no doubt, complain if someone calls the Committee for Economic Development an organization of mystics.

This mystical approach to making policy recommendations bears strange fruit. One of the CED trustees is Ellison L. Hazard, a director of Kennecott Copper Corporation. In July 1971, the Marxist Allende government of Chile seized the Kennecott mines in Chile and the firm has now reported a related loss of $50.4 million. Nowhere in the CED report is there any sign of protest by Mr. Hazard. Nowhere in the CED report is there any indication that our transfer of technology will encourage further Marxist takeovers and further Marxist expropriations, if not for Kennecott, then for some other U.S. company.

Lenin once averred that capitalists would supply the rope to hang themselves, and no truer words have ever been spoken. If the directors of Kennecott Copper and the trustees of CED want to hang themselves, that's fine! But the rest of us may well get hanged alongside these myopic mystics and their policy-

making friends in Washington.* That is the prime raison
d'être for this book.

The "Detente"-Aggression Cycle

The Soviet Union has made masterly use of a cycle of "detente"
and aggression to first delude and then plunder the West, and
particularly the United States. Within this secular cycle the
Soviets sometimes use "detente" and aggression simultaneously:
for example, they will preach detente in Washington to gain
American technology while simultaneously using American
technology to provide arms for North Vietnam to kill Americans. Contradiction is fundamental to the Russian mind and is
an important operational weapon for the Communists, but
the American mind has difficulty in understanding this. Washington policymakers, therefore, push aside as irrelevant those
aspects of Soviet policy that are contradictory and do not fit
their preconceptions.

In the early 1920s, when socialist ineptness brought famine to
Russia, former President Hoover and the American Relief
Administration organized the import into Russia of vast quantities of food and clothing. The Soviets were simultaneously exporting wheat to help German revolutionaries. A contradiction
to American observers, this went largely unnoticed at the time,
but it was a harbinger of the ability of the Soviets to conduct
hostilities against the West while holding out the hand of
friendship.

The life-saving assistance of the American Relief Administration did not inhibit the Soviets from espionage and subversion
in the United States in the 1920s, or from arming Chinese
revolutionaries, or from exporting revolution to Europe and
the Far East.

Then, in the 1930s, American firms planned and constructed

* Ellison L. Hazard is not one of the more prominent of these
business mystics. Irwin J. Miller (Cummins Engine) and Eugene R.
Black (Chase Manhattan Bank) are considerably more prominent—
and more vocal.

the largest units of the Five-Year Plans. President Roosevelt made an agreement with Russia only to find that the Soviets had broken their political promises within a month of signature. However, American assistance in technology and credits continued to flow.

This assistance weathered Soviet involvement in the Spanish Civil War and massive Soviet espionage in the United States. In fact, altruistic detente was so powerful a force within the Roosevelt Administration that a secret military-information agreement between Stalin and Roosevelt, known to only four persons in the United States, averred that democratic America and totalitarian Russia had a commonality of interests.

During World War II the United States gave the Soviets top priority in supplies. One-third of the Lend-Lease shipments to Russia comprised industrial supplies for postwar reconstruction. Lend-Lease continued to flow after the war up to the end of 1946 under twenty-year credit terms at $2\frac{3}{8}$ percent interest—a far better interest rate than returning GIs could obtain.

The Soviets used their enlarged military-industrial complex, which had been expanded with Lend-Lease assistance, to foment the invasion of South Korea and supply their allies throughout the disastrous Korean war.

After a decade of further Soviet intervention abroad and repeated assertions of their peaceful intent—the latter emphasized by the State Department and promoted by "liberal" academics—we had the fiasco of Vietnam. By now the altruistic mystics in Washington were in full control. Instead of clamping down on technological exports to the Soviet Union, they *expanded* assistance and so guaranteed a ten-year war of attrition.

Persecution of Russian Jews, Russian Baptists, and Lithuanian Catholics

Economic assistance to the Soviet Union is usually justified on the grounds that it will "mellow" the Soviets and induce the regime to gradually relax totalitarianism. This has been the argument for fifty years. Since there have never been any signs of fundamental change, and since this economic assistance is precisely the means by which the Soviet military establishment is maintained, it is well to emphasize both the continuation of repression by the Soviet authorities and the absence of "mellowing."

Internal actions confirm that the Soviet government is acting exactly as we would expect a statist regime to act. Anatoly Marchenko, in *My Testimony*,[5] illustrates that the change in Soviet prison camps is only quantitative but certainly not qualitative. The camps do not hold the tens of millions that were incarcerated under Stalin, but there are still tens, probably hundreds of thousands in Russian concentration camps.

The repression takes several forms. Firstly, religious groups are brutally oppressed for no more than their wish to practice the natural right of worship. The Jews have recently been in the news, but the Baptists have long suffered persecution, as have the Catholics in Lithuania.

The case of the Jewish scientist Vladimir Slepak has aroused considerable interest in Great Britain (but not in the United States, where the wire services are indifferent to details of Soviet persecution). The case caused so much concern in Great Britain that a prayer book signed by the British Prime Minister, the leader of the Opposition in the House of Commons, and 200 members of Parliament was sent to Slepak as a token of British esteem and sympathy. (It is difficult to imagine, in the present pro-Soviet euphoria, that 200 members of Congress would so express their esteem for an imprisoned Russian.) The Soviet authorities refused to allow Slepak to accept the prayer book, and it was returned to Great Britain. Released after his most recent arrest, he was contacted on October 7, 1972, by a British member of Parliament (Greville Janner, also a Queen's counsel). The following is an extract from Janner's conversation with Slepak concerning his arrest and brutal treatment by the Soviets:

[5] London: Pall Mall Press, 1969.

Slepak: On the 19th September, I was arrested in the street and kept in the police station from 10 a.m. until 7 p.m. Then I was released and I went to the Central Telegraph, where there was a group of Jews who were on hunger strike in protest [against the ransom tax]. Then I went to my friend's place, where I had a telephone conversation . . . After the conversation, I was arrested again in front of my house.

For three days, I was kept in a cell in the police station, where I had to sleep on the bare floor. I was alone.

Janner: Any blankets?

Slepak: Without.

Janner: Anything to read?

Slepak: No.

Janner: Anything to eat?

Slepak: Something. Then I was removed to the prison of Matroska Yeshena where, before that, Nashpits and Shapira [young Jewish activists, each now serving 12 months' corrective labour] were kept. There, for 20 hours, I was kept in a box one metre by half a metre [about 3 ft. x less than 2 ft.].

Janner: What sort of box was that?

Slepak: A little room.

Janner: Of course in that one metre by half a metre, there was not room to lie down?

Slepak: No. There was no place to sit or to lean against the wall. The walls were covered with thorns. The box was very dirty. (A friend of Slepak explained to me that these "thorns" were in fact spikes or nails protruding from the cement, which had the effect of preventing lice from mounting the wall, but which also prevented the occupant of the "box" from leaning against the sides.)

Janner: Did you have a bucket?

Slepak: I was twice allowed out for that. Then for four days I was in a cell without any heating or glass in the window. It was very cold. There I had to sleep on the bare boards. The temperature outside was about zero.

Janner: Near freezing point.

Slepak: Yes. I had no warm clothing and I was freezing. The prison authorities gave no permission for my family to pass me any warm things. By the end of the eighth day, I was moved to the cell where Manievich, my friend, was kept. I was there for eight days. In all the term of imprisonment, we have had hot food only every other day. The day when we were not given hot food we had about a pound of rye bread and water.

Janner: Were you interrogated?

Slepak: In the police station only. They said that I must be in prison for 15 days. All 15 days we did not smoke. We had no books to read. We had newspapers five days before we were released. On the second day of my being in prison, I heard the chief of the prison telling the guard by my cell: "This is an enemy, a real enemy." The chief of the prison said this to the guard, near my cell.[6]

The treatment of Russian Christians is as bad or perhaps even worse than the treatment of Russian Jews. There are available in the United States translations of Russian underground books that portray the almost unbelievable persecution of these Christians. The trial of Baptists in Odessa on February 2–7, 1967, is described in a booklet, *Russian Christians on Trial*.[7] The charge against the Baptists was practicing religion in a manner inconsistent with Soviet law on "religious cults." The defendants would not accept state-appointed preachers but

[6] Text provided by courtesy of the Bay Area Council on Soviet Jewry, San Francisco.

[7] Glendale, Calif.: Diane Books, 1971.

wanted to form their own congregations. They were found guilty. Five defendants (N. P. Shevchenko, G. G. Borushko, Y. N. Krivoi, S. P. Solovyova, and V. I. Alexeeva) were sentenced to three years each in "ordinary regime" (forced labor) camps.

Swedish sources estimate that an "important" portion of the 3 million prisoners held in Russian "ordinary regime" camps are Christians and Jews persecuted only for their religious beliefs.

Another volume, *Before Death* by G. M. Shimanov,[8] which was published by *samizdat* (a Russian colloquial term for the underground circulation of mimeographed or typewritten copies of works that cannot be formally published because of government censorship), details the use of special psychiatric institutions in Kazan, Sychevka, Leningrad, Cherniakovsk, Minsk, and Dniepropetrovsk to treat Christians as insane. The drug Aminazon is used to break down personality.

It is obvious that the Soviets are no more a part of the civilized world than was Ivan the Terrible.

In 1969 President Nixon resurrected Gay's idea of "peaceful trade" with the Soviet Union. In January 1970 came the jailing of dissidents Gabai and Zhemilyev, followed by revocation of Svetlana's citizenship. Then the clergy was persecuted by the Soviet state. In May 1970 Amalrik was arrested. Then Medvedev was arrested. In August 1970 Joffe was placed in a mental hospital, soon after an American newsman was expelled, and the general pattern of charge and countercharge continued through the end of the year.

In 1971 we had the disgraceful case of the Lithuanian seaman Kudirka. U.S. Coast Guard officials stood by while Soviet sailors boarded a United States ship in U.S. territorial waters and removed a Soviet subject who had previously requested

---

[8] The American version, which is abridged, is: G. M. Shimanov, *Notes from the Red House: An Eyewitness Account of the Communist Torture of Sane People in Psychiatric Institutions* (Glendale, Calif.: Diane Books, 1971).

asylum. Probably no other single incident in recent years illustrates the moral degeneracy of those who make our foreign policy.

Apparently nothing has changed since 1945 when, under President Roosevelt, the United States and Great Britain cooperated in the forcible and brutal return of unwilling Russians to Stalin's tyranny. According to the *Wall Street Journal* (Nov. 24, 1972), the United States and Russia in 1945 "signed a special convention for forcibly repatriating to the USSR some four million anti-Communist Soviet subjects who had fled to the West." This agreement (known as Operation Keelhaul) was a violation not only of the traditional American spirit of freedom, but also of the Geneva Convention.

American military police "forcibly herded thousands of displaced persons into the waiting arms of the Russians." Even worse, in June 1945 at Fort Dix, New Jersey, some 200 Russian prisoners were drugged and, according to the *Wall Street Journal,* U.S. authorities ". . . allowed them to be taken unconscious aboard a Russian ship in New Jersey. Elsewhere, many refugees drowned themselves, slashed their throats and otherwise committed suicide rather than return to the brutal death they knew awaited them." In 1973, as this book goes to press, the Keelhaul file is still classified.

Such cases, ranging from 1917 to the present day, shock and horrify any decent person. Unfortunately, these incidents have no impact at all on the policymakers in Washington, where an effort is made to keep all the files locked and sealed.

External Soviet Aggression

In 1962 the Russians attempted to move long-range missiles into Cuba, thus precipitating the Cuban Missile Crisis and bringing the United States and the Soviet Union to the brink of hostilities. This strategic move shows that the Soviets had not abandoned their international ambitions. Yet the following year came the "wheat deal," again touted as a device to "mellow" the Soviets. It cost the American taxpayer at least $75 million in subsidies. Did the wheat giveaway mellow the Soviets? In the following year, 1964, they vigorously expanded their logistical support for North Vietnam in its efforts to take over the South, and so stoked up what was to become an eight-year nightmare.

The Korean and Vietnam wars are discussed in Chapter Two, but as we look around the world today, do we see any meaningful evidence of detente by the Soviet Union?

The Soviets currently have a ship of some 30,000–35,000 tons under construction at the Nikolayev yards on the Black Sea. It is an aircraft carrier, a type of vessel the Soviets do not as yet possess, although they have two helicopter carriers. If the Soviets want detente, why build an aircraft carrier? As *Human Events* commented (Oct. 28, 1972), "The Soviets clearly want to be able to project themselves into political situations anywhere on the globe."

The Soviet Union currently maintains a naval task force in the Indian Ocean. It is reportedly building a base at Socotra in the Red Sea. It supports insurgent groups in Portuguese Guinea, Angola, Mozambique, Zambia, Tanzania, and elsewhere. It attempts political penetration of Mauritius, Somalia, Tanzania, Zambia, and the Malagasy Republic. Arab terrorists are armed with modern Soviet weapons. A naval base is under construction at Cienfuegos, Cuba, to support Soviet naval operations in the Caribbean.

Moreover, the North Vietnamese attack on the South in the spring of 1972 was made possible only by new heavy weapons imported from the Soviet Union, including Soviet T-54 tanks, T-56 tanks, and PT-76 amphibian tanks. Hanoi's total tank force—all Soviet supplied—was estimated at 1,000. Even Henry Kissinger admitted on May 9, 1972, that these weapons were supplied "in quantities and of a type that . . . in many respects, especially artillery and heavy tanks, tipped the balance in the North Vietnamese direction" (*U.S. News & World Report*, May 22, 1972). Nor is the Soviet Union shy about claiming the credit for shooting down 4,018 American aircraft in Vietnam: "Thanks to Soviet assistance, the Democratic Republic of Vietnam is equipped with up to date means of air defense, such as electronically controlled anti-aircraft missiles, radar and jets" (*San Jose Mercury*, Aug. 19, 1971).

The Soviet withdrawal from Egypt made headlines. Where did the Russians go? Some of them went to Iraq to participate in another buildup, and simultaneously there was a less publicized buildup in Syria. Moreover, 1,000 Russian military instructors remain in Algeria, at least 1,200 in Iraq, 2,000 in Syria, and about 1,000 in the Yemens. The Soviets have recently built a naval base at Berbera in Somaliland on the Red Sea and in early 1973 were building a naval base at one of the most strategic locations in the Middle East—Um Qasr, Iraq, near the head of the Persian Gulf.

In 1971, the British expelled 105 Soviet "diplomats" for espionage. Moreover, it was revealed that the Soviets had infiltrated British trade unions and provided financial strength for crippling strikes throughout the United Kingdom.

Finally, in July of 1972 Mikhail Suslov, the longtime Communist theoretician, reminded the Russian Communist party that nothing has changed: The United States remains the prime enemy; internal dissent will not be tolerated. This flat, authoritative statement flies in the face of the "peaceful trade" propagandists in the United States, who have argued steadily for fifty years, and vehemently for a decade, that trade will bring world peace. Nothing the Soviets do or say will change the minds of these propagandists. The mystic is convinced by his fantasy. He has no time for reality. Thus, representatives of the State Department peddle their party line that the Suslov statement is only for public consumption and that the Soviets have *really* changed. State Department said that a decade ago. Since then another 50,000 Americans and countless allies have lost their lives.

The Soviets mean exactly what they say, and they will act in accordance with their statements.

Always in the past the pundits and the prophets hailed "detente" as permanent, as a sign of a new world order and a signal of lasting friendship with totalitarian states. They have always been wrong. "Detente" has cost us 100,000 men killed in Korea and Vietnam. The mystics will be wrong again. The empirical evidence and Soviet statements are just not consistent with true detente. All the secret agreements stashed away in White House safes only delude the policymakers. And the price for their delusions is paid in the blood and taxes of American citizens.

Soviet strategy therefore employs an exquisite combination of policies to gain its objectives. The most important is this two-phase cycle of "detente" and aggression. "Detente" to gain technological and economic sustenance from the West. Then, when strength is built up, or if possible simultaneously, "detente" vanishes, to be replaced by renewed territorial expansion.

The Western world, under pressure from its business-financial community, has never yet failed to take the bait. It has responded only reluctantly to subsequent territorial aggression, and with so much delay that the original Soviet assault is only halted at enormous cost. The West responds reluctantly, because policymakers are locked into an illusion that a statist system can be peaceful, and that Soviet "detente" genuinely implies peace. The high cost of response is also to the Soviets' advantage for it demoralizes the West and establishes the psychological groundwork for the next "detente" phase.

Once again we are about to expand the Soviet military-industrial complex. Once again we will be disillusioned. Once again we will pay the cost in human suffering. There can be no peace with statist systems. Perpetual war is the only outcome of statism. This is the tragic lesson we have yet to learn.

CHAPTER TWO
More Trade, More Casualties

History has shown that where there is increasing trade between countries ... there is a tendency toward increasing understanding.
MAURICE STANS, former Secretary of Commerce, 1972

Unfortunately for Maurice Stans's credibility, no historian or politician has ever produced evidence that trade necessarily and automatically leads to increased understanding.

Why not? Because no such evidence exists. While it is true that peace encourages trade, this does not mean that trade encourages peace. In fact, trade has often enabled aggressive countries to go to war—witness the aviation gasoline and steel scrap shipments to Japan and Standard Oil's agreements on hydrogenation patents with I. G. Farben of Germany prior to World War II.

The blunt truth is that trade with the Soviet Union from 1917 to the present has built the Free World an enemy of the first order. Moreover, the technological component of this continuing trade enables the Soviet Union to pursue its programs of world conquest and, more to the point at the present stage of history, to supply the North Vietnamese invasion of the South. It costs the American taxpayer $80 billion a year to counter this Soviet threat.

The chart illustrates the increase in trade between the United States and the Soviet Union from 1963 to 1971. The figures for

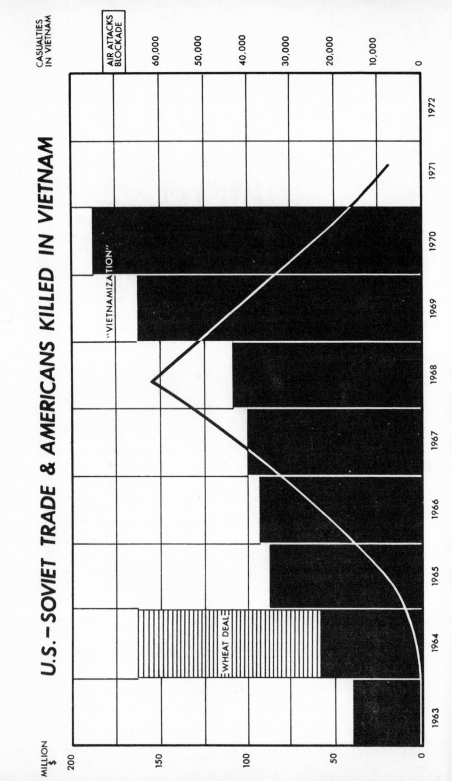

U.S.—SOVIET TRADE & AMERICANS KILLED IN VIETNAM

CASUALTIES IN VIETNAM

AIR ATTACKS BLOCKADE

60,000
50,000
40,000
30,000
20,000
10,000
0

MILLION $
200
150
100
50
0

1963 1964 1965 1966 1967 1968 1969 1970 1971 1972

WHEAT DEAL

"VIETNAMIZATION"

casualties (killed and wounded) in Vietnam are superimposed on the U.S.-Russian trade figures. As trade increases, so do casualties—up to the point when the United States began its Vietnamization program and placed the burden on South Vietnam.

Obviously, claims that increasing trade is accompanied by increasing understanding are false. A more accurate characterization appears to be that increasing trade is accompanied by increasing conflict (i.e., misunderstanding). The concept of "peaceful trade" with Communist countries assumes some positive causal link between trade and peace. It is a false assumption. On the contrary, the figures demonstrate that there may well be some relationship between trade and casualties.

The Causal Link between U.S.-Soviet Trade and U.S. Casualties in Vietnam

The overlooked causal link—that is, the relationship between trade and casualties—is contained in one word: *technology.*

From the Soviet viewpoint, the benefit of U.S.-Soviet trade is the acquisition from the United States of the technology required for building and maintaining the Russian economy. This subsidized technology is the basis of the Soviet military structure, as is proved by the Soviets' own statements.[1] The armaments produced by Russia's American-subsidized military-industrial complex are used to promote Soviet global expansion.

There are four logical steps in this process:[2]

1. Trade between the United States and the USSR (with its key technological component).

2. Consequent buildup of the Soviet military-industrial complex.

[1] See Chapter Four.

[2] Steps 1 and 2 have been fully demonstrated in the author's three-volume study, *Western Technology and Soviet Economic Development.* See Bibliography.

36

3. Use of the U.S.-subsidized Soviet military-industrial complex to provide inputs for Soviet armaments production.
4. Use of these armaments against the United States and its allies.

This is the "trade–technology–armaments–war" cycle; it suggests that the "peaceful trade" promoted by successive administrations should more realistically be entitled "war trade."

If any of the links in this cycle can be broken (or shown to be false), the argument would collapse. However, no link is demonstrably false. Indeed, there is evidence that the trade–casualties link is stronger than even the most pessimistic have envisaged. The information that would have enabled the "trade–war cycle" to be widely known at an earlier date has been deliberately classified and blacked out.[3]

We trade freely with European nations because these nations have no deceitful intent to use the technological component of this trade against the United States. Nor has the United States any hostile intent towards these European countries. Free trade is vital and necessary, and both sides benefit from its advantages. However, gains from free trade ultimately depend on intent. Where countries are potentially hostile and make hostile use of imported technology, the gains from free trade must be modified by the hostile intent of the trading partner. In other wards, "peaceful trade" is only peaceful if Soviet intent is peaceful.

What then *is* Soviet intent?

The Soviet Version of Soviet Intent

The Soviets have always been explict about their intentions—so was Hitler in *Mein Kampf*.

Objective truth has no place in Communist morality. Any statement that will advance the cause of world communism is regarded as truthful, acceptable, and perfectly moral. As far

[3] See Chapter Three.

back as 1919, Zinoviev put it well in a statement that applies to the Viet Cong as much as to the revolutionary Bolsheviks:

> We are willing to sign an unfavorable peace. It would only mean we should put no trust whatever in the piece of paper we should sign. We should use the breathing space so obtained in order to gather our strength.[4]

This immoral dogma—which is moral in Communist ideology—was emphasized by Joseph Stalin:

> Words must have no relations to actions—otherwise what kind of diplomacy is it? Words are one thing, actions another. Good words are a mask for concealment of bad deeds. Sincere diplomacy is no more possible than dry water or wooden iron.[5]

In 1955 the staff of the U.S. Senate Committee on the Judiciary examined the Soviets' historical record and, not unexpectedly in the light of the foregoing statements, came to the following conclusion:

> The staff studied *nearly a thousand treaties*[6] and agreements . . . both bilateral and multilateral, which the Soviets have entered into not only with the United States, but with countries all over the world. The staff found that in the 38 short years since the Soviet Union came into existence, its Government had broken its word to virtually every country to which it ever gave a signed promise. It signed treaties of nonaggression with neighboring states and then absorbed those states.

[4] *Congressional Record,* vol. 74, p. 7049.

[5] David J. Dallin, quoted in *The Real Soviet Russia* (New Haven: Yale University Press, 1971), p. 71.

[6] Italics added.

It signed promises to refrain from revolutionary activity inside the countries with which it sought "friendship" and then cynically broke those promises. It was violating the first agreement it ever signed with the United States at the very moment the Soviet envoy, Litvinov, was putting his signature to that agreement, and it is still violating the same agreement in 1955. It broke the promises it made to the Western nations during previous meetings "at the summit" in Teheran and Yalta. It broke lend-lease agreements offered to it by the United States in order to keep Stalin from surrendering to the Nazis. It violated the charter of the United Nations. It keeps no international promises at all unless doing so is clearly advantageous to the Soviet Union.

[We] seriously doubt whether during the whole history of civilization any great nation has ever made as perfidious a record as this in so short a time.[7]

Consequently, the history of Soviet foreign relations from 1917 to the present suggests, for those who can interpret history, two conclusions:

1. The Soviets will not keep their word in any foreign agreement.
2. Their intent is self-admittedly aggressive, with world conquest as the ultimate goal.

Current moves by the United States massively to increase U.S.-Soviet trade, though designed to lower tensions, are entirely contrary to historical observation and rational deduction. Mikhail Suslov, longtime Russian Communist party theoretician, stated in 1972 that the U.S.-Soviet detente is temporary and that, so far as the Soviet Union is concerned, it is merely an interlude to gain strength for the next stage of the battle against "imperialist aggression." Suslov in 1972 repeated and

---

[7] U.S. Senate, Committee on the Judiciary, *Soviet Political Agreements and Results*, 4th printing (Washington, 1964).

reinforced Zinoviev's 1919 statement; there is no change of heart or direction.

The Soviet Record of Aggression and War

A review of the human cost of Soviet double-dealing will emphasize the risk we run by such attempts to mellow Soviet statism.

In every year since the Bolshevik Revolution the Soviets have murdered their own citizens for political reasons: that is, for alleged or real opposition to the Soviet state. The AFL-CIO has mapped Soviet forced labor camps of the 1960s. Moreover, in every year since 1917 the Soviets have attacked other countries or interfered massively in their internal affairs.[8]

The human cost of the Bolshevik Revolution and the ensuing civil war in Russia has been estimated at 7 million Russians. Between 1930 and 1950 more than 20 million Russians died in forced labor camps. Khrushchev personally supervised the massacre of more than 10,000 Ukrainians at Vinnitsa; twenty years later he was photographed in an embrace with Governor Nelson Rockefeller of New York.

Soviet agents were in Spain before the Spanish Civil War of 1936 and unquestionably had some role in starting it (cost: 275,000 killed).

The supply of Soviet armaments to the Spanish Republic is known from material in the records of the German military attaché at Ankara, Turkey.[9] Soviet arms shipments began in September 1936. Soviet intelligence agents, operating in Spain

[8] For the early years there is a State Department Staff report: *Interference of Representatives or Employees of the Soviet Government Abroad in the Internal Affairs of the Countries in Which They Are Stationed.*

[9] D. C. Warr, "Soviet Military Aid to the Spanish Republic in the Civil War 1936–1938," *Slavonic and East European Review,* June 1960, pp. 536–41. Also see: Uri Ra'anan, *The USSR Arms the Third World* (Cambridge, Mass.: MIT Press, 1956).

before the war broke out, were under General Ulansky, who was also responsible for logistics. In addition to supplies, the Soviets sent 920 military "advisers": 70 air force officers, 100 other officers (as early as September 1936), and 750 enlisted men. From September 1936 to March 1938 about 110 shiploads of Russian military supplies left Odessa en route to Spain. Foreshadowing the situation when the USSR supplied Cuba and North Vietnam, only thirty-two of these ships were under the Soviet flag—and most of these Soviet-flag vessels were foreign-built. Thirty-seven ships were British-flag vessels, twenty-three were Spanish, and seventeen were Greek; others were under the Mexican, French, and U.S. flags.

These 110 vessels carried the following armaments to Spain from the new Western-built Soviet plants:

Tanks and armored cars	731
Planes (mostly fighter aircraft)	242
Guns	707
Antiaircraft Guns	27
Trucks	1,386

What was the U.S. technical component of these arms?

The tanks sent to Spain in 1936 were based on British Vickers or U.S. Christie designs. Soviet aviation technology was mainly American (except for French Potez and Italian seaplane designs).[10] The guns were Krupp, but the trucks were Ford, Hercules, and Brandt—all from plants built by American firms five years previously.

After this, in 1937, Stalin's Red Army purge killed 30,000—the cream of the Soviet military.

Two years later, in 1939, Russia attacked Finland. Cost: 273,000 Finns and Russians killed. In 1939 or 1940, the Soviets murdered 30,000 Polish officers at Katyn.

Persecution of Russians and the peoples of Eastern Europe continued after World War II, assisted by the British-American

---

[10] See the chapters that follow.

Operation Keelhaul (file still classified in 1972). In 1946 the Ukrainians tried unsuccessfully to fight for independence, after having fought the Germans for four years. One after another the East European peoples attempted to overthrow domestic communism, which survived only with Russian help and American inaction. In 1956 there was another Polish revolt and a major outbreak in Hungary in which 25,000 Hungarians and 7,000 Russians lost their lives.

In the early 1960s the Soviets began to look beyond the satellites, secure in the knowledge that the United States would not intervene to protect human rights in these countries. There was the Cuban Missile Crisis of 1962: the missile-carrying Soviet ships had engines manufactured by Denmark. Then came the airborne Congo adventure. Then the Vietnamese War, which Soviet advisers, as in the Spanish Civil War in 1936, entered at an early stage; in 1965, the year 1,369 Americans were killed in South Vietnam, 2,500 Russian engineers and experts were at work in North Vietnam,[11] and Russian arms were even then in widespread use by the Viet Cong and the North Vietnamese. These arms included the standard 82-millimeter recoiless rifle, the RP-46 light machine gun, and other types of military equipment. This was also the year in which President Johnson decided to expand trade with the Soviets in the guise of "building bridges for peace."

The continuing crisis in the Middle East has been directly dependent upon the supply of Soviet arms to militant Arab countries and guerillas. In the ten years from 1958 to 1968, Soviet arms supply was as follows:

Algeria	200 jets, plus tanks and ships
Egypt	800 jets, 1,200 tanks, 15 warships
Iraq	200 jets, 500 tanks, some ships
Syria	250 jets, 500 tanks, some ships[12]

[11] *Los Angeles Times,* Aug. 18, 1965.

[12] Geoffrey Kemp, "Strategy and Arms Levels," *Proceedings of the Academy of Political Science,* 29:3(1960), 24.

In subsequent pages it will be shown that the MiG-15 uses copies of Rolls-Royce and German engines, that Soviet tanks derive heavily from Western assistance and technology, and that two-thirds of Russia's merchant ships and four-fifths of the main diesel engines of these ships have been built outside the USSR.

The Korean War (1950–1953)

The American casualty roll in the Korean War was 33,730 killed and 103,284 wounded. Of the 10,218 American prisoners taken by the Communist forces, only 3,746 returned to the United States: 21 men refused repatriation and 6,451 American servicemen are listed as "murdered or died."[13]

This massive casualty toll does not include America's allies. Altogether 118,515 United Nations soldiers were killed, in addition to 70,000 South Korean soldiers and over 3,000,000 South Korean civilians.

The 130,000-man North Korean Army, which crossed the South Korean border in June 1950, was trained, supported, and equipped by the Soviet Union. This army included a brigade of Soviet T-34 medium tanks (with U.S. Christie suspensions).[14] The artillery tractors that pulled the guns were direct metric copies of Caterpillar tractors. The trucks were either from the Henry Ford–Gorki plant or the ZIL plant. The North Korean Air Force had 180 Yak planes built in plants with U.S. Lend-Lease equipment; these Yaks were later replaced by MiG-15s powered by Russian copies of Rolls-Royce jet engines sold to the Soviet Union in 1947.

American casualties from Soviet action did not cease between the Korean and Vietnamese wars. Between January 1950 and

[13] R. Ernest Dupuy and Trevor N. Dupuy, *Encyclopaedia of Military History* (New York: Harper & Row, 1970), p. 1219.

[14] Antony C. Sutton, *Western Technology and Soviet Economic Development, 1930–1945* (see Bibliography).

May 1964, when the Vietnamese War entered its full-scale ground stage, the U.S. Air Force lost 108 airmen killed or missing from various hostile Soviet actions, in addition to twenty-six aircraft shot down.

The Vietnamese War (1961–1973)

Between 1961 and 1964 the American casualty roll in Vietnam was relatively light.[15] Killed and wounded among American forces as result of hostile action were as follows:

1961	11 killed	2 wounded
1962	31 killed	41 wounded
1963	78 killed	218 wounded
1964	147 killed	522 wounded

Then in 1965 the Soviets stepped up the flow of supplies to North Vietnam, President Johnson stepped up the flow of technology to the Soviets, and the American toll mounted rapidly:

1965	1,369 killed	3,308 wounded
1966	5,008 killed	16,526 wounded
1967	9,378 killed	32,371 wounded
1968	14,592 killed	46,799 wounded

After President Nixon took office in 1969 the American toll was as follows:

1969	9,414 killed	32,940 wounded
1970	4,221 killed	15,211 wounded
1971	1,380 killed	4,767 wounded
1972	300 killed	587 wounded

[15] All casualty data are from the Directorate for Statistical Services, Office of the Secretary of Defense.

About 80 percent of the armaments and supplies for the Vietnamese War came from the Soviet Union, and a key part of President Nixon's policy is the transfer of technology to the USSR.

Soviet military aid has of course been fundamental for the North Viets. In September 1967 the Institute for Strategic Studies in London reported that the Soviets had sent large numbers of MiG-17 and MiG-21 fighters, Ilyushin-28 light bombers, transport aircraft, helicopters, 6,000 antiaircraft guns (one-half radar controlled), surface-to-air (guideline) missiles, 200–250 missile launchers, several thousand air defense machine guns, and a training mission of about 1,000 men to North Vietnam.

This aid was confirmed in April 1967 in the testimony of former Assistant Secretary of Defense John T. McNaughton to the effect that the Soviet had supplied the "sophisticated equipment in the field of anti-aircraft defense." The loss of 915 U.S. planes over North Vietnam between February 1965 (the date of the first U.S. air operations over North Vietnam) and the bombing halt of November 1, 1968 testifies to the accuracy and utility of the Soviet equipment. After President Nixon took office in January 1969 and expanded technical transfers, losses mounted, rising to a total of more than 4,000 U.S. aircraft by the end of 1972. It would appear from this statistic alone that increased trade leads to increased aircraft losses. Another testimonial is the 539 U.S. Air Force personnel killed between 1965 and 1968 in Vietnam. Further Soviet military assistance was confirmed in an agreement signed by Kosygin and Deputy Premier Nghi in July 1968.

Support by the Soviet Union for North Vietnamese aggression in South Vietnam has been no secret. Brezhnev, on the occasion of his visit to Bulgaria on May 12, 1967, demonstrated the solidarity of supposedly polycentralist-socialist East Europe on the question of Vietnam:

> You know well, comrades, that the Soviet Union is rendering great economic, military and political

assistance to fighting Vietnam. This assistance is merged with the assistance coming from Bulgaria and other fraternal socialist countries. We are rendering it in response to a command of the heart, as people reared by the Communist party in a spirit of proletarian internationalism, in a spirit of high understanding of class tasks. And let the aggressors know this: fighting Vietnam will never be left without the help of its true friends. Our answer has been and will continue to be commensurate with the requirements of an effective rebuff to the unbridled imperialist interventionists.[16]

Soviet political support is of course well founded in Leninist philosophy. Since the days of Lenin, Soviet objectives have only changed in the imagination of Washington policymakers.

The Soviet Union provided both the military and the economic means for the North Vietnamese invasion of South Vietnam and the trade figures measure this assistance. In the mid-1950s the value of Soviet exports to North Vietnam came to no more than $3 million per year. By 1966 this had rocketed to $68.2 million, and a year later the figure doubled to $148 million. In return the North Viets shipped to Soviet Russia only $25.3 million worth of goods in 1966 and 1967. While imports from the USSR doubled, Vietnamese exports slumped even further to $20.9 million. Thus, at the key juncture of the Vietnamese War, the Soviets were not only rapidly increasing their supplies but were receiving in return less than one-seventh the value of the supplies in Vietnamese products. The balance was Soviet "Lend-Lease" for the takeover of South Vietnam.

The Soviet Union has truly been the "arsenal for revolution" in Vietnam, and as Shirley Sheibla wrote in *Barron's*

[16] *Pravda,* May 13, 1967.

Weekly, the United States has been the "arsenal for communism" in the Soviet Union.[17]

Each year in the spring the North Vietnamese have attempted to conquer the South. In 1972, in their latest attempt, a full-scale invasion was launched with various kinds of heavy equipment they had not previously used. The tanks, guns, and trucks came from the Soviet Union—and were produced in plants erected and equipped by American and European companies.

The T-54 tank was used in force in early 1972. The T-54 has a modified Christie-type suspension. The GAZ trucks on the Ho Chi Minh trail came from the Ford-built Gorki plant. The ZIL trucks on the Ho Chi Minh trail came from the Brandt-built plant. Both plants were equipped with new American machinery while the Vietnamese War was in progress. The amphibious PT-76 tank is manufactured at Volgograd—in a factory built by eighty U.S. firms. This is called "peaceful trade" by the mystics in Washington.

As the material presented in this book will show, the "arsenal for revolution" was built by Western firms and has been kept in operation with "peaceful trade." When all the rhetoric about "peaceful trade" is boiled out, it comes down to a single inescapable fact—the guns, the ammunition, the weapons, the transportation systems that killed Americans in Vietnam came from the American-subsidized economy of the Soviet Union. The trucks that carried these weapons down the Ho Chi Minh trail came from American-built plants. The ships that carried the supplies to Sihanoukville and Haiphong came from NATO allies and used propulsion systems that our State Department could have kept out of Soviet hands—indeed, the Export Control Act and the Battle Act, ignored by State, required exactly such action. The only other route for these supplies was by rail across Siberia and China. But Soviet locomotives and railroad-operating equipment have also been traced to U.S. and European origins.

Whichever way we cut the cake, there is only one logical and

[17] Jan. 4, 1971.

inescapable conclusion: The technical capability to wage the Korean and Vietnamese wars originated *on both sides* in Western, mainly American, technology, and the political illusion of "peaceful trade" was the carrier for this war-making technology.

As U.S. casualties in Vietnam mounted, the lessons of history were clear for those with eyes to see—reduce trade with the USSR and all suppliers to North Vietnam, and so provide an incentive for the other side to decelerate the conflict. (This is not hindsight; the writer made this argument, in print, in the mid-1960s.) Both the Johnson and Nixon administrations irrationally and illogically chose to expand trade—the carrier for the technology required to fuel the North Vietnamese side of the war—and so voted to continue the war.

The more Hanoi stoked up the war, the more Soviet Russia received from the United States. American policy—wittingly or unwittingly—was guaranteed not only to maintain the Vietnamese War but to expand it, increase our losses, and compound the problem of preserving South Vietnam.

CHAPTER THREE
Censorship and Our Military Assistance to the Soviet Union

> The Department of State is not interested in devices to withhold information from the Congress. We fully understand that the Congress must have information if it is to perform its constitutional role in the field of foreign relations. . . .
>
> WILLIAM B. MACOMBER, JR., Deputy Under Secretary for Administration, Department of State, July 13, 1971

The ability of the Soviet Union to present a credible military threat is the result of past and present technical assistance by the United States and its allies. Much of the American evidence substantiating this statement is still in classified government files. Consequently, the reader may justifiably ask how it was possible to write this book. Furthermore, if the evidence is classified, how does the writer even know that it exists?

Information for this book was obtained from three main sources: declassified U.S. government files (in some cases declassified with the assistance of, and intervention by, members of Congress); congressional investigations, reports, hearings, and "unscheduled information leaks"; and, finally, information from Soviet sources. It is a paradox, and a sad commentary on the state of freedom of information in the United States, that considerably more detailed information came from "censored" Soviet sources than from U.S. government sources.

Let's look at each of these information sources in more detail.

Declassified U.S. Government Files as a Source of Information

Classification is freely undertaken by thousands of government officials under President Eisenhower's 1953 executive order, but declassification is a slow and intermittent process—even for documents with no relation at all to national security. Documents with significant political implications are apparently not declassified.

According to National Archives public-relations releases, almost all government documents more than twenty-five years old are open for research. This is not the situation in practice, however. The files of the State Department contain numerous documents dated earlier than 1947 (i.e., over twenty-five years old) that are still classified. Indeed, whole sections of records with no present national security import, which are well over twenty-five years old, are under complete prohibition for nonofficial research. For example, in May 1964 Donald J. Simon of the Department of State sent a letter to Wayne C. Grover of the National Archives requesting a seventy-five-year restriction on the following files: *Records of the Office of the Counselor and Office of the Chief Special Agent 1916–1928* (National Archives Job III-NLD-105, signed on March 31, 1955). These records have no relation to national security and are between forty-four and fifty-six years old: that is, well over the twenty-five-year limit. This section of documents may contain information on American residents and citizens who went to Russia in 1917 to overthrow the Provisional Government and install the Bolsheviks—an interesting topic for academic investigation. Personal investigative records of U.S. citizens should, of course, be subject to careful restriction, but this hardly applies to revolutionaries who voluntarily left the United States to become

Bolsheviks, or to persons who have acted on behalf of foreign governments, when these actions have major historical significance.[1]

Information suppression concerning Soviet relations with the United States may be found in all administrations, Democrat and Republican, from President Wilson to President Nixon. For example, on November 28, 1917, just a few weeks after the Petrograd and Moscow Bolsheviks had overthrown the democratic and constitutional government of Russia, "Colonel" House (then in Paris) intervened on behalf of the Bolsheviks and cabled President Wilson and the Secretary of State in the "Special Green" cipher of the State Department as follows:

> There has been cabled over and published here [Paris] statements made by American papers to the effect that Russia should be treated as an enemy. It is exceedingly important that such criticisms should be suppressed . . .[2]

Suppression of information critical of the Bolsheviks and the Soviet Union may be traced in the State Department files from this 1917 House cable down to the present day, when export licenses issued for admittedly military equipment exports to the USSR are not available for public information.[3] In fact, Soviet sources must be used to trace the impact of American technology on Soviet economic and military development. The Soviet Register of Shipping, for example, publishes the technical specifications of main engines in Russian vessels (including country of manufacture): this information is not available from U.S. official sources. In November 1971, *Krasnaya Zvezda* published an article with specific reference to the contribution of the basic Soviet industrial structure to the Soviet military power—a contribution that representatives of the U.S. Execu-

[1] On April 8, 1971, the writer was refused access to this record group by the National Archives.

[2] See p. 52.

[3] See p. 134.

tive Branch have implicitly and explicitly denied to the public and to Congress.

U.S. assistance to the Soviet military-industrial complex and its weapons systems cannot be documented from open U.S. sources alone because export license memoranda and instructions are classified data. Unless the technical nature of our shipments to the USSR is known, it is impossible to determine their contribution to the Soviet military complex. This technical information is not declassified (see Appendix A) and thus the facts must come from Soviet sources (see the prolific detail in Appendix C). The national security argument is not acceptable as a defense for classification because the Soviets know what they are buying. So does the United States government. So do U.S. firms. The groups left out in the cold are the American taxpayer-voter and independent researchers.

From time to time bills have been introduced in Congress to make such export-license information freely available. These bills have never received Administration support.[4] The nonavailability of current information means that decisions affecting all Americans are made by a relatively few government officials without impartial outside scrutiny. In many cases these decisions would not be sustained if subjected to public examination and criticism. It is argued by the policymakers that decisions affecting national security and international relations cannot be made in a goldfish bowl. The obvious answer to this is the history of the past fifty years: we have had one catastrophic international problem after another—and, in fact, in the light of history the outcome would have been far less costly if the decisions *had* been made in a goldfish bowl.

[4] The late Congressman Glenard P. Lipscomb was a strong supporter of such bills. The latest bill to require publication of such data was introduced by Congressman Schmitz as H.R. 8300 of May 11, 1971 and referred to the Committee on Banking and Currency: "... to require the publication of lists on a quarterly basis of individuals and firms who export any goods or services valued at $1,000 or more in any calendar quarter to any Communist-dominated nation."

One such example has already been given. On November 28, 1917, Colonel House, who had no official position in the U.S. government and had never been elected to office, cabled President Wilson just two weeks after the start of the Russian Revolution to suppress newspaper criticism of the emerging Bolsheviks: "... it is [cabled House] exceedingly important that such criticism should be suppressed."[5] This comment was placed in the "confidential file" and was not declassified until the 1960s. Open public discussion in 1917 of Colonel House's instructions and intentions might well have changed the history of the world.

Little more than a decade after House's appeal to Wilson, Senator Smoot inquired of the State Department about the possible military end-uses of an aluminum powder plant to be erected in the Soviet Union by W. Hahn, an American engineer. According to William Macomber (opening paragraph), the department did not withhold information from Congress, but State Department files contain a recently declassified document which states why no reply was ever given to Senator Smoot:

> No reply was made to Senator Smoot by the Department as the Secretary did not desire to indicate that the Department had no objection to the rendering by Mr. Hahn of technical assistance to the Soviet authorities in the production of aluminum powder, in view of the possibility of its use as war material, and preferred to take no position at the time in regard to the matter.[6]

Aluminum powder is used, among other military applications, to raise the explosive force of ammunition.

The Operation Keelhaul file, presently classified by the Department of the Army, is a prominent example of politically motivated censorship. The 1945 file, classified secret in 1972,

---

[5] See p. 50.

[6] U.S. State Dept. Decimal File, 861.659-Du Pont de Nemours & Co/5.

relates to the forced and brutal repatriation of 4 million Russians to the Soviet Union by the United States and Britain after World War II. It is probably the greatest single blot of all time on British and American diplomacy. The question has no possible relation to current national security, yet declassification has been repeatedly refused. Julius Epstein and the American Civil Liberties Union sued the Secretary of the Army under the Freedom of Information Act, but a U.S. District Court of Appeals upheld continued classification as not "arbitrary or capricious."[7] The Supreme Court denied review.

In brief, declassified government files are not sufficient to substantiate the argument of this book. The key documents, and in many cases whole sections of files, are completely off limits to Congress, the independent researcher, and the general public. Congressional action in the Freedom of Information Act and administrative claims of speedy declassification have not changed this basic situation. The major significant documents covering the history of the past fifty years are buried, and they will remain buried until an outraged public opinion puts some pressure on Congress.

Congressional Investigations and Unscheduled Leaks

From time to time congressional investigations have unearthed caches of relevant data that would not normally be released. These data have been supplemented by corporate and individual investigations. For example, in 1970 the import of presumably embargoed Rhodesian chrome ore as "Soviet" chrome ore prompted Crucible Steel Company to undertake a technical investigation of the real origin of the so-called Soviet ore.

Government files from Great Britain, Canada, France, and, especially, pre-1945 Germany have provided data not obtainable from U.S. government files. Finally, we have leaks such as the Major Jordan records on the precise nature of U.S. Lend-Lease

[7] 421 *Federal Reporter,* 2d Series, p. 930.

to the USSR—confirmed twenty years later by declassified government files.

Congress has investigated and subsequently published reports on the export of strategic materials to the Soviet Union. One such instance, called "a life and death matter" by Congress, was a 1961 case concerning the proposed shipment of ball bearing machines to the USSR.[8] The Bryant Chucking Grinder Company accepted a Soviet order for thirty-five Centalign-B machines for processing miniature ball bearings. All such precision ball bearings in the United States, used by the Department of Defense for missile guidance systems, were processed on seventy-two Bryant Centalign Model-B machines.

In 1961 the Department of Commerce approved export of thirty-five such machines to the USSR, which would have given the Soviets capability about equal to 50 percent of the U.S. capability.

The Soviets had no equipment for such mass-production processing, and neither the USSR nor any European manufacturer could manufacture such equipment in the near future. A Department of Commerce statement that there were other manufacturers was shown to be inaccurate. Commerce proposed to give the Soviet Union an ability to use its higher-thrust rockets with much greater accuracy and so pull ahead of the United States. Subsequently, a congressional investigation yielded accurate information not otherwise available to independent nongovernment researchers and the general public.

Congressional investigations have also unearthed extraordinary "errors" of judgment by high officials. For example, in 1961 a dispute arose in U.S. government circles over the "Transfermatic case"—a proposal to ship to the USSR two transfer lines (with a total value of $4.3 million) for the production of truck engines.

In a statement dated February 23, 1961, representatives of the Department of Defense went on record against shipment of

[8] U.S. Senate, Committee on the Judiciary, *Proposed Shipment of Ball Bearing Machines to the U.S.S.R.* (Washington, 1961).

the transfer lines on the grounds that "the technology contained in these Transfermatic machines produced in the United States is the most advanced in the world," and that "so far as this department knows the USSR has not installed this type of machinery. The receipt of this equipment by the USSR will contribute to the Soviet military and economic warfare potential."

This argument was arbitrarily overturned by incoming Secretary of Defense Robert McNamara. In response to a later inquiry from the congressional investigating committee, he stated:

> I concluded that the Defense Department should not oppose export licenses for the transfermatic machines in question . . . My decision was based solely on the merits of the case as I saw them from the point of view of alternative sources and availability of comparable machinery and was in no part dictated by political or other policy considerations. My decision in this case was based on my own knowledge of this type of machinery and of its alternative sources of supply . . . As you know, the transfermatic machines were not to be used for manufacture of military vehicles, but rather for the production of medium priced or high priced passenger cars.
>
> Your letter asks whether I consulted with other knowledgeable persons before making my April decision on transfermatic machines. The answer is that I reviewed this case thoroughly myself. I did not consult formally with other automotive experts as I had had the benefit of recent and direct experience with the equipment concerned in private industry.

Secretary McNamara did not point out that most Soviet military trucks came from two American-built plants even then receiving equipment from the United States. The Transfermatic machines approved by McNamara had clear and obvious military uses—as the Department of Defense had previously argued.

The Soviet Union as a Source of Information

In practice the Soviet Union is a more prolific source of hard information—information that can be blended with declassified U.S. files.

The availability of data on the origin of the main engines of Soviet ships used on the Haiphong supply run and in the Cuban Missile Crisis is a prime example of the Soviet Union publishing detailed information not available from U.S. government sources and directly conflicting with official statements made by U.S. government officials.[9]

This case of the origin of Soviet vessels, for which ample and accurate hard data are available, is worth exploring. For most of the period since 1949, the Battle Act and the Export Control Act have supposedly prohibited the export of transportation technology for military purposes. However, the specific case-by-case determinations made by State, Commerce, and CoCom within the framework of these laws are classified. It is not possible to obtain free access to the relevant decision papers to examine the manner in which the intent of Congress has been administered. We *do* know, however, that any member of the Cocom (Coordinating Committee; the operating arm of the Consultative Group established by NATO and Japan in 1950 to coordinate the export controls of the major industrial nations) group of nations has veto power and that no shipment has ever been made to the Soviet Union without the unanimous approval of all members. Thus, the transfer of Danish marine technology in 1959 had implicit or explicit State Department approval.

Some years ago research strongly suggested that the Soviets had no indigenous military transport technology: neither motor vehicles nor marine diesel engines. Yet about 80 percent of the weapons and supplies for the North Vietnamese were transported by some means from the Soviet Union. The greater part of these Soviet weapons went to Vietnam by Soviet freighter

[9] See Appendix C and p. 158 for the related case of the transport of Russian missiles to Cuba.

and then along the Ho Chi Minh trail on Soviet-built trucks.

By using data of Russian origin it is possible to make an accurate analysis of the origins of this equipment. It was found that all the main diesel and steam-turbine propulsion systems of the ninety-six Soviet ships on the Haiphong supply run that could be identified (i.e., eighty-four out of the ninety-six) originated in design or construction outside the USSR. We can conclude, therefore, that if the State and Commerce departments, in the 1950s and 1960s, had consistently enforced the legislation passed by Congress in 1949, the Soviets would not have had the ability to supply the Vietnamese War—and 50,000 more Americans and countless Vietnamese would be alive today. The names of the ninety-six Soviet ships used on the Haiphong run were gleaned from *Morskoi Flot* and similar Russian maritime publications.[10] The specifications of the main engines were obtained from *Registrovaya Kniga Morskikh Sudov Soyuza SSR* and other Russian sources. This hard information came from *censored* Soviet sources. The same information is only available in the West in classified government files; and it is therefore totally censored to the independent researcher and to Congress. In this case—not the only such case—Soviet censorship is far less restrictive than that of the United States.

U.S. classification of information also conceals another fundamental problem—that illegal or inefficient administration of the export control laws in the 1950s and 1960s gave the Soviets the ability to supply the North Vietnamese in the 1960s.

The Practical Effect of Censorship

The real reasons for concealment of information or, to put it more bluntly, censorship, are twofold:

1. Washington officials do not want detailed public knowledge of policies that cannot be empirically defended.

[10] Acknowledgment is gratefully made to Joseph Gwyer of Washington, D.C., for his assistance.

2. Firms trading with the Soviets do not want public knowledge of such sales because public knowledge might lead to adverse criticism, boycotts, and loss of domestic sales.

Censorship has enabled appointed officials and the permanent Washington bureaucracy to make almost unbelievably inaccurate statements without fear of challenge in Congress or by the American public.

The State Department files are crammed with information concerning U.S. technical and economic assistance to the Soviet Union. The author of this book required three substantial volumes (see Bibliography) just to summarize this assistance. Yet Dean Rusk, presumably acting on the advice of State Department researchers, could state in 1961, "It would seem clear that the Soviet Union derives only the most marginal help in its economic development from the amount of U.S. goods it receives." This statement is flatly contradictory to the empirical evidence available in departmental files.

In 1968 Nicholas de B. Katzenbach, Assistant Secretary of State, made a statement that was similarly inconsistent with observable fact, and displayed a fundamental lack of common-sense reasoning:

> We should have no illusions. If we do not sell peaceful goods to the nations of Eastern Europe, others will. If we erect barriers to our trade with Eastern Europe, we will lose the trade and Eastern Europe will buy elsewhere. But we will not make any easier our task of stopping aggression in Vietnam nor in building security for the United States.[11]

In fact, aggression in South Vietnam would have been impossible without U.S. assistance to the Soviet Union. Much of the key "European" technology derives from U.S. subsidiaries.

[11] House of Representatives, *To Amend the Export-Import Bank Act of 1945* (Washington, 1968), p. 64.

The United States has veto power within CoCom. Moreover, the United States holds the umbrella of security over Europe and has an excellent bargaining weapon. Looking at the evidence, it is more to the point that U.S. officials such as Katzenbach are not concerned with the national interest.

Jack N. Behrman, former Deputy Assistant Secretary for International Affairs at the Department of Commerce, repeated the same Alice in Wonderland theme on behalf of the Commerce Department:

> This is the old problem of economic dependency. However, I do not believe that Russia would in fact permit herself to become dependent upon imported sources of strategic goods. Rather she would import amounts additional to her strategic needs thereby relieving the pressure on her economy by not risking dependence.[12]

In fact, Jack Behrman to the contrary notwithstanding, Soviet Russia is the most dependent large nation in modern history, for wheat as well as technology.

Behind this smoke-screen of misleading information, the most extraordinary government operations can be, and have been, conducted. Take the relatively harmless but still expensive escapades first.

In 1966 the U.S. Department of State produced a beautiful, extravagantly illustrated brochure of American hand tools. This was printed in Russian, for distribution in Russia, with a preface—in Russian—by Lyndon Johnson. Requests to the State Department for a copy of this brochure went unanswered. It is not listed in official catalogues of government publications. It is not available or even known to the general public. No printer's name appears on the back cover. The publisher is not listed.[13]

[12] House of Representatives, *Investigation and Study of the Administration, Operation and Enforcement of the Export Control Act of 1949, and Related Acts* (Washington, 1962), p. 428.

[13] The author obtained a copy direct from Russia.

60

HAND TOOLS—USA*

Welcome to the "Hand Tools—USA" exhibit—the eighth consecutive exhibit arranged for citizens of the Soviet Union.

At this exhibit you will see samples of various hand tools currently manufactured in the United States—tools that facilitate manual work and make it possible to produce better-quality industrial goods at a much lower cost.

Since the very early days of the history of our country, Americans of all ages have worked with hand tools. In industry and at home, in factories and on farms, in workshops and schools, the hand tool has become indispensable in our lives. Some of these tools have retained their original simplicity of design; others have acquired entirely new forms and are now used to perform new functions.

We sincerely hope that this exhibit will lead you to a better understanding of the American people and their way of life.

/s/ Lyndon B. Johnson

Why all the secrecy? What would have been the public reaction in 1966, when the Soviets were supplying the North Viets with weapons to kill Americans (over 5,000 were killed that year), if it had become known that the State Department had published lavish booklets in Russian for free distribution in Russia at the taxpayers' expense?

However, the point at issue is not the wisdom of publication but the wisdom of concealment. The public is not told because the public might protest. In other words, the public cannot be trusted to see things in the same light as the policymakers, and the policymakers are unwilling to defend their positions. This is dictatorship.

Further, what would be the domestic political consequences if it had been known that a U.S. President had signed a document in Russian, lavishly produced at the taxpayers' expense for free distribution in Russia, while Russian weapons were

* Author's translation from Russian of brochure for "Hand Tools—USA" exhibit.

killing Americans in Vietnam? The citizen-taxpayer does not share the expensive illusions of the Washington elite. The political reaction by the taxpayer, and his few supporters in Congress, would have been harsh and very much to the point.

The other party interested in the concealment of information about our exports to the Soviet Union is the relatively small group of American firms and individuals prominently associated with such exports.

In general, the American public has a basic right to know what is being shipped and who is shipping it, if the Soviets are using the material to our disadvantage. The public also has a right to know about the personal interests of presidential appointees and their previous employment with firms prominent in trade with the USSR.

Until now, the businesses involved could claim ignorance of the use to which the Soviets put imported Western technology. It is not a good claim but it can be made. But from now on, ignorance of end-use is not a valid claim. The evidence is now clear, overwhelming, and readily available: The Soviets have used American technology to kill Americans and their allies.

The claim that publication of license information would give undue advantage to competitors is not the kind of argument that a competent businessman would make. It is only necessary to publish certain basic and elementary information—date, name of firm, amount, destination in the USSR, and a brief statement of the technical aspects. Every industry has a "grapevine," and potential business in an industry is always common knowledge. Unfortunately for independent researchers and the Congress, the grapevine is limited to the industry.

In any event, suppose there *was* adverse comment about a particular sale to the Soviets. Is this a bad thing? If our policies are indeed viable, why fear public opinion? Or are certain sectors of our society to be immune from public criticism? If certain firms and individuals fear public comment, they should take another look at the situation.

Soviet dependency on our technology, and their use of this technology for military purposes, could have been known to Congress on a continuing basis in the 1950s and 1960s if current export license information had been freely available. The problem was suspected but the compilation of the proof had to wait several decades until the evidence became available from Soviet sources. In the meantime, Administration and business spokesmen were able to make absurd statements to Congress without fear of challenge: *In general, only those who had already made up their minds that Soviet trade was desirable had access to license information.*

In 1968 the Gleason Company of Rochester, New York, reportedly shipped equipment to the Gorki automobile plant in Russia, a plant previously built by the Ford Motor Company. The information about the shipment did not come from the censored licenses but from press sources. Knowledge of license application for any equipment to be used at Gorki would have elicited vigorous protests to Congress. Why? Because the Gorki plant produces a wide range of military vehicles and equipment. Many of the trucks used on the Ho Chi Minh trail are GAZ vehicles from Gorki. The rocket-launchers used against Israel are mounted on GAZ-69 chassis made at Gorki. They have Ford-type engines made at Gorki.

The American scientific community also has a double standard when it comes to helping the Soviet Union.

The scientific community, or at least an important segment of it, distinguishes between types of totalitarian rule, favoring one form but not another. In 1939 a group of prominent U.S. physicists, including Einstein and Weisskopf, agreed to limit publication of information on atomic energy and its military applications. This censorship was prompted by the threat of Hitler's self-proclaimed propensity for aggression and his brutal anti-Semitism. It was an eminently acceptable decision. However, when it comes to the Soviet Union, with its equal propensity for aggression and anti-Semitism, the scientific community (including Wiesskopf) argues *for* publication of information on atomic energy and *for* major technical assistance. The Soviet Serpukhov linear accelerator, to give one example, was only made possible with assistance promoted by Weisskopf, chairman of the High Energy Physics Advisory Panel of the Atomic Energy Commission. There is an element of self-interest in this, because if the Soviets have a large accelerator (which they cannot build themselves), U.S. scientists have a useful means of prodding Congress into building yet bigger machines in the United States. Sure enough, in 1970 Congress appropriated $250 million for the 200-GeV unit at Weston, Illinois. Obviously the scientists will now push for more technical assistance to the Soviets and then go back to Congress and, pointing at the "extraordinary progress" of the Soviets, claim that the United States must not "fall behind." And so it goes, always at the expense of the taxpayer and of national security.

Thus, a screen of censorship compounded by self-seeking promoters has withheld knowledge of a major shift in direction of U.S. foreign policy, a shift likely to generate considerable criticism. This shift can be summarized as follows:

1. Our long-run technical assistance to the Soviet Union has built a first-order military threat to our very existance—or, at least, we believe there to be a first-order threat, which in practice amounts to the same thing.
2. Our lengthy history of technical assistance to the Soviet military structure was known to successive administrations but has not been admitted to Congress or to the American public.
3. Current military assistance is also known, but is admitted only on a case-by-case basis when information to formulate a question can be obtained from nongovernment sources.
4. As a general rule, detailed data on export licenses, which are required to establish the *continuing* and long-run dependence of the Soviet military-industrial complex on the United States, have been made available to Congress only by special request, and have been denied completely to the American public at large.

In brief, all presidential administrations, from that of Woodrow Wilson to that of Richard Nixon, have followed a bipartisan foreign policy of building up the Soivet Union. This policy is censored. It is a policy of national suicide. The reasons for it are not known.

CHAPTER FOUR
Construction of the Soviet Military-Industrial Complex

Trade with the West as a general matter, must necessarily be a marginal factor in the performance and potentialities of the Soviet economy.

JACOB JAVITS, U.S. Senator from New York, 1966

The Soviet View of the Soviet Military-Industrial Complex

While Western policymakers persist in the delusion that the Soviet economy is neatly packaged into military and civilian sectors, the dependence of Soviet military strength on the Soviet industrial base is repeatedly stressed in Soviet literature and practice.

In November 1971, for example, *Krasnaya Zvezda* ("Red Star," organ of the Red Army) stated: "In this era of complex weapons systems, all of heavy industry—from steel to electronics—and not only the pure defense industries producing military end products, represents the foundation of military power."[1]

In other words, Soviet military power depends on Soviet

[1] Paraphrased from *Krasnaya Zvezda,* Nov. 17, 1971.

economic power. A moment's reflection will suggest to the reader that all military products are made from industrial products. No army has a machine that by itself can produce complete missiles or complete tanks. Industrial plants produce the armor-plate, the stainless steel, the aluminum castings, the nuts and bolts, and so on, all of which can be used, with minor changes in analysis or specification, for military *or* civilian products.

The interdependence of the Soviet military and civilian sectors is in fact greater than the above quotation from *Krasnaya Zvezda* suggests. In fact, the Soviet economy is primarily a military economy—again as shown by Soviet statements—and only secondarily a civilian economy. One of the great successes of Soviet planning has been the priority diversion of resources to armaments production and the associated militarization of industrial sectors. Konstantin Krylov sums up the picture in a recent article in *Military Review*: "All work relating to national economic planning is inseparably tied to national defense requirements."[2]

Consequently, since the late 1920s all Soviet industrial plants have been designed first to produce end-products for military use and only second for civilian output. Searches of the Wehrmacht intelligence files have failed to reveal a single Soviet plant in 1937–38 that was not devoting part of its capacity to war purposes. The German intelligence lists of plants producing war equipment were at the same time, in fact, comprehensive lists of all Soviet plants.

This objective for Soviet industry was clearly stated in 1929 by Unashlicht, vice president of the Revolutionary Military Soviet:

> We must try to ensure that industry can as quickly as possible be adapted to serving military needs . . . [therefore,] it is necessary to carefully structure the

[2] Konstantin K. Krylov, "Soviet Military-Industrial Complex," *Military Review*, Nov. 1971.

66

Five-Year Plan for maximum co-operation and inter-
relationship between military and civilian industry.
It is necessary to plan for duplication of technological
processes and absorb foreign assistance . . . such are the
fundamental objectives.[3]

After Unashlicht's proposal, Soviet military industry was as-
signed to Group A—the favored-priority industry group—and,
even further, military production was given absolute priority
for labor and materials within Group A industry. This absolute
priority continues down to the present day. Krylov in 1971
cites, for example, a musical instrument factory, "where the
main shop . . . was planned and constructed for possible use as a
small arms ammunition plant," and a high school has been
planned for quick conversion to a military hospital.[4]

This absolute priority for military work enables the Soviets
to mobilize with extreme rapidity, although their economy is
always geared to maximum output and consequently lacks
significant flexibility. This emphasis on military production
also enables the Soviets to equal U.S. military production with
an economy only half as productive as the American economy.
Every Russian plant has a Special Section, "entrusted with
planning the conversion of civilian industrial establishments to
military production in time of mobilization,"[5] and, Krylov esti-
mates, "about 70 to 75 percent of . . . resources are spent by the
armed forces for the purchase of armaments from industry."[6]

The percentage is much larger than in the United States,
partly because the Soviet armed forces, except for the privileged
high ranks, are paid pitifully low wages. In the U.S. defense
budget, labor absorbs about half of the total.

Finally, the ability of Soviet military production to progress
in new weapons systems depends on progress in "civilian" industrial technologies, which are in turn maintained by Western

[3] *Pravda,* April 28, 1929.
[4] Krylov, *op. cit.,* p. 92.
[5] *Ibid.*
[6] *Ibid.,* p. 93.

technology. The *Krasnaya Zvezda* article previously quoted goes on to state:

> The creation of modern armaments now requires the production of high-grade special metals and plastics, the most modern instruments, computers and communication systems . . . the interdependence of industries is now so great that almost all branches of heavy industry play a role in the manufacture of any complex mechanism or device.

These statements from Soviet sources and by Konstantin Krylov, a Western observer, are directly contrary to statements to the Congress and the American public made by the spokesmen of successive administrations, and are also in direct contrast to the illusion that Soviet military production takes place in some kind of industrial vacuum. In brief, Soviet weapons production draws its inputs on a priority basis from Soviet industry. This is a well-known long-term planned arrangement. Therefore, any technology injected by the West into Soviet "civilian" industry is, pari passu, technology injected into Soviet weapons production.

The American View of the Soviet Military-Industrial Complex

The American view of the Soviet military-industrial complex is quite different from the Soviet view of it. Instead of a unified whole, the American observer sees two almost distinct complexes, one of which is a self-supporting military structure. The sheer logic of industrial production refutes such a view. Obviously no country would erect steel mills or aluminum rolling plants or fastener factories just for its military sector.

However, this misinterpretation does enable official Washington to identify or at least try to identify "strategic products"—that is, those for military end-uses—and to draw up regulations designed to forbid their export while permitting exports of nonmilitary products. As there is in fact no such distinction, it is not surprising that in the past two decades the definition of a strategic product has eroded under constant political and business pressures.

This spurious dichotomy has also enabled State Department representatives to go before Congress and make statements such as, "The United States government does not authorize trade in strategic goods or technologies with the Soviet Union and the Communist countries of East Europe." It should be noted that once official Washington admits that the industrial and military sectors are inseparably united (in line with the Soviets' own interpretation of the structure of their economy), the whole argument for "strategic" products becomes meaningless.

Under the Soviet definition *all* trade and *all* technological export becomes strategic. If we wish to deny exports of military value to the USSR, the only policy we can logically adopt is one of complete embargo. The only exceptions to the embargo would be products, such as wheat, with no technological component.

Evidence that *any* modern industrial economy has a major role in war production is not hard to find. For example, the American experience in World War II is valid:

> It is ironic and remarkable that the two mainstays of Patton's supply lifeline—the C-47 airplane and the 2½-ton truck—were designed and developed for civilian use, not for war; without them the extent of American achievement in World War II might have been far less impressive than it was and far more costly in time and casualties.[7]

Fortune magazine provided an excellent overview of the "Military-Industrial Complex—Russian style":

> The Soviet heavy weapons plants for tanks, trucks and artillery are still located mainly in the Ural complex that Stalin and Ustinov set up from Sverdlovsk south

[7] *Warrior: The Story of General George S. Patton,* by the editors of the *Army Times* (New York: G. P. Putman's Sons, 1967), p. 145.

to Chelyabinsk and Magnitogorsk feeding off the steel
that is produced there in great quantity from Ural ore.
This steel triangle is still out of bounds to all Western visitors.[8]

The Ural complex was built by American firms, not by Stalin
and Ustinov. But the key observation that the military-industrial complex is an integral unit is accurate. The *Fortune* article
then points out that this complex is "the pride of the Polit-
buro," the members of which take frequent trips to see latest
automated lines and "high-precision tools from Switzerland."

Western Construction of the Soviet Military-Industrial Complex

We must, therefore, focus our attention on the construction of
the Soviet industrial economy, with its special sections for
military production, as well as the construction of plants specifically engineered for production of weapons systems, such as
tanks and fighter aircraft, from semimanufactured inputs from
the industrial plants.[9] For example:

Organization methods and most of the machinery are
either German or American. The steel mill MORN-
ING near Moscow, is said to be one of the most modern establishments of its kind in the world. Constructed, organized and started by highly paid American specialists, it employs 17,000 workers and produces
steel used by motor plants, naval shipyards and arms
factories.[10]

[8] Aug. 1, 1969.

[9] The author's three-volume study, *Western Technology and
Soviet Economic Development,* describes with extensive technical
detail the construction of the industrial portion of the Soviet
military-industrial complex (see Bibliography).

[10] U.S. State Dept. Decimal File, 861.5017, Living Conditions/456,
Report No. 665, Helsingfors, April 2, 1932.

The construction of weapons-assembly plants will be discussed in subsequent chapters. The fundamental construction agreement creating the Soviet military-industrial complex was made in February 1930 with Albert Kahn, Inc., of Detroit, builders of the Ford River Rouge, General Motors, Packard, and other large plants in the United States. The Kahn group undertook design, architectural, and engineering work for all heavy and light industrial units projected by Gosplan. Kahn's chief engineer in the USSR, Scrymgoeur, was also chairman of the Vesenkha building committee.

The units designed and started in 1929–32 under the Kahn plan were of truly gigantic size—far larger than units designed and built by the same construction firm in the rest of the world—and, in addition, had separate shops or plants for the manufacture of inputs and spare parts. The Urals Elmash plant in Stalin's "steel triangle" (see p. 69) multiplied Soviet electrical-equipment manufacturing capacity by a factor of seven. The KHEMZ plant at Kharkov, designed by the General Electric Company, had a turbine-manufacturing capacity two and one-half times greater than GE's main plant in Schenectady. Magnitogorsk, also in the "steel triangle" (see p. 69), a replica of the U.S. Steel plant at Gary, Indiana, was the biggest iron and steel plant ever built. The Soviets do not exaggerate when they claim that these units are the "largest in the world."

In the early 1930s there was a massive infusion of foreign technology, engineers, and equipment to build the military-industrial complex wanted by the Soviets (see p. 69, n. 9). Most of these engineers left by 1932, but they left behind a gigantic productive capacity.

Major new units built from 1936 to 1940 were again planned and constructed by Western companies. Petroleum-cracking, particularly for aviation gasoline, as well as all the refineries in the Second Baku and elsewhere were built by Universal Oil Products, Badger Corporation, Lummus Company, Petroleum Engineering Corporation, Alco Products, McKee Corporation, and Kellogg Company.

Advanced steel-rolling mills were supplied under the United Engineering agreement, and in 1938–39 the Tube Reducing

Company installed a modern tube mill at Nikopol and supplied equipment for another mill. In 1937 the Vultee Corporation built an aircraft plant outside Moscow.

In 1940, as a reaction to the Nazi-Soviet agreement and the subsequent attack on Finland, assistance from the United States tapered off for a year. The Nazi-Soviet pact replaced this assistance and gave another boost to the Soviet military-industrial complex. The Soviets emphasized modern machine tools, and the Germans had problems in designing, producing, and shipping the large quantities of advanced military equipment on order. The German occupation of Czechoslovakia was indirectly beneficial to the Soviet Union, as large shipments of Czech machine tools were then channeled to the USSR.

The real bonanza was Lend-Lease; about one-third of the equipment supplied under the master agreements had reconstruction potential. These deliveries continued under the little-known "pipeline agreement" of October 1945, so that Lend-Lease supplies actually continued through 1947. There is no question that the Soviets, in spite of the war damage, ended World War II with greater capacity than in 1940 and on a technical parity with the United States.

Another source of increased capacity and military technology was the World War II reparations agreements. The Soviets received the lion's share of reparations. Germany (both zones), Austria, Manchuria, Finland, Rumania, Hungary, Italy, and other countries made a heavy contribution to the Soviet military-industrial complex.

Western construction of the Soviet military machine is detailed in other chapters. At this point, the history of two companies, General Electric and Radio Corporation of America, will suffice to exemplify the early and basic contribution of many individual firms.

In the field of electrical equipment, which is fundamental to the development of any military-industrial complex, we can trace a great deal of Soviet technology, either directly or through European subsidiaries, to these two American corporations.

In 1927, the Radio Corporation of America concluded an

agreement with the Soviet Union for extensive provision of technical assistance and equipment in the radio communications field. In 1935 the Soviets proposed another general agreement whereby RCA would furnish "engineering, technical and manufacturing information in those portions of the radio field in which RCA is or may be engaged." On September 30, 1935, RCA concluded the agreement[11] and approached the State Department for permission, using the conventional argument that if the agreement were not made with RCA, the Soviets would go to RCA's European competitors. The departmental reply indicated that the "proposed agreement will not be contrary to any policy of our government."[12] The extensive contract emphasized technical assistance and included "the entire field of manufacturing and experimental activities of RCA and its subsidiaries."[13] The fields of technology involved included both radio and television transmission and reception, electro-vacuum apparatus, sound recording, sound motion-picture equipment, measuring apparatus, and remote-control apparatus. RCA made a related agreement with the People's Commissariat of Heavy Industry, and Soviet personnel were sent to the United States for training. A payment of $2.9 million was made to RCA and it was further agreed that the Soviets would purchase large quantities of equipment from the company.

In 1939 the RCA agreement was extended to September 30, 1944.[14]

On May 24, 1929, the Soviet Union ratified an agreement with the International General Electric Company—by far the most important agreement in the development of the Soviet electrical-equipment industries. The contract provided for a

[11] A copy of the agreement is in U.S. State Dept. Decimal File, 861.74 Radio Corporation of America/30 and in 811.20161/52.

[12] U.S. State Dept. Decimal File, 861.74 Radio Corporation of America/21.

[13] U.S. State Dept. Decimal File, 861.74 Radio Corporation of America/30, Nov. 26, 1940.

[14] U.S. State Dept. Decimal File, 861.74 Radio Corporation of America/28 Memorandum, Division of Controls, Aug. 3, 1939.

"broad exchange of patents as well as exchange of designing, engineering and manufacturing information." The diffusion of General Electric technology within the Soviet Union was extraordinarily extensive. According to GE engineers working in the Soviet Union, the Soviets had "full rights to all patents and working drawings of the American concern." Amtorg noted that "much of the American equipment purchased in past years is used by the Soviets as models for the construction of similar machinery in their own plants." The 1929 agreement was followed by a long-term technical-assistance agreement signed in 1930, under which "vast amounts" of technical, design, and manufacturing information flowed from GE in Schenectady to the Soviet Union.

Subsequent chapters will present evidence that General Electric and Radio Corporation of America assistance for the Soviet military-industrial complex, assistance which is typical of U.S. companies in other sectors, continues down to the present day either through direct sales from the United States or through the European subsidiaries of these two firms.

The release of domestic resources is one of the most important effects of such technical transfers from one country to another, and it may be the effect most difficult for the layman to appreciate. Whenever assistance is provided from outside the Soviet economic system, internal resources are released, and by substitutions at the margin the Soviet Union is enabled to devote the released resources to other objectives, including military objectives.

This substitution is of major importance to military objectives, because while domestic resources are being devoted to military development, the broader industrial base is being updated and fortified from abroad. The industrial base is the prime determinant of military strength and therefore of success in military operations. The United States military does not produce its own weapons: research, development, and production are largely handled by private industry. The flexibility and efficiency of American private industry is the basic resource upon which the American military structure depends.

The Soviet military is equally dependent on Soviet industry and thus indirectly on Western industry. It has been estimated that 70–75 percent of the annual Soviet military expenditure goes to Soviet industry for the purchase of armaments materials. The military has top priority. Flexibility and innovation for Soviet industry are imported from the West. Thus, ironically, the prime forces making for efficiency in Soviet military production are imported Western initiative and efficiency.

Consequently, we cannot make any meaningful distinction between military and civilian goods. Every industrial plant directly or indirectly affords some military capability. It is Western technology, particularly U.S. technology, that makes the Soviet military-industrial complex more efficient. The import of technology releases resources for military efforts and also makes it possible for the Soviet industrial-military complex to incorporate the latest Western manufacturing techniques.

CHAPTER FIVE
Direct Supply of Weapons and Military Assistance to the Soviets

Finally, when the class war is about to be fought to a finish, disintegration of the ruling class and the old order of society becomes so active, so acute, that a small part of the ruling class breaks away to make common cause with the revolutionary class, the class which holds the future in its hands.

KARL MARX, FRIEDRICH ENGELS, The Communist Manifesto

From the Bolshevik Revolution to the Five-Year Plans

While the final story of American participation in the Bolshevik Revolution will have to await the release of the official files, some interesting glimpses of the activities of the American Red Cross Mission in Petrograd during the Provisional Government period are available. The doctors with the Red Cross Mission quit and returned to the United States in September 1917, protesting the overtly political actions of the more prominent members. Consequently, in November 1917, at the time of the Bolshevik Revolution, the mission comprised only the "political members"; and the actions of this group were, to say the least, extraordinary.

According to Clemenceau's papers, Red Cross "Colonel" Raymond Robins, a wealthy Wall Street operator, "was able to send a subversive mission of Russian Bolsheviks to Germany to start a revolution there" (Panouse to Clemenceau, Feb. 9, 1918).[1] Red Cross "Colonel" William B. Thompson, a director of the Federal Reserve Bank of New York, according to his own current press releases (*Washington Post,* Feb. 2, 1918), delivered $1 million to assist the Bolsheviks. Subsequently, General William V. Judson of the U.S. Army, who was also in Russia in 1917, recommended both Robins and Thompson for the Distinguished Service Medal, "for their effective work with Bolshevism" (U.S. Adjutant Generals Office A.G. 095 Thompson, Wm b 6/18/19).

In early 1918 American munitions were shipped to the Bolsheviks under some form of credit arrangement:

> Munitions that are being evacuated from Archangel are sent to Moscow, the Urals and Siberian towns. Soviet government desires to take up the matter of payment for these munitions, and expects to pay for them in raw materials, but asks for time to organize the economic resources of the country. [Robins to Ambassador Francis, April 4, 1918]

A few weeks previously, Trotsky had requested "five American army officers to act as inspectors of the organization, drill and equipment of the Soviet Army" (Robins to Francis, March 19, 1918). A little later we find that both the Murmansk and the Siberian interventions, recorded in modern history books as hostile interventions, were undertaken by the Western Allies with the express permission and cooperation of the Soviets. Clearly the whole story of American participation in the Bolshevik Revolution is yet to be uncovered.

[1] John Bradley, *Allied Intervention in Russia 1917–1920* (London: Weidenfeld & Nicolson, 1968), p. 19.

Subsequently, in the early 1920s and again in the late 1930s, it was Germany that provided military assistance to the Soviet Union. General von Seeckt, chief of the German General Staff, made contact with the Soviets even before the Treaty of Versailles was signed. In April 1921, Menshevik Victor Kopp visited the Krupp, Blohm und Voss, and Albatross Werke armaments plants and found these firms ready to supply Russia with equipment and technical assistance for the manufacture of war materials. Post-Rapallo negotiations widened this visit into full-blown cooperation for joint military production. Purely military production was under the control of Gesellschaft für Förderung Gewerblicher Unternehmungen (or GEFU), with a capital of 75 million reichmarks that was partly funded by an appropriation from the Ruhrfond (the Relief Fund for Ruhr Workers).

Lipetsk was used as a base for the final training of Russian military pilots and the testing and development of new planes. At the end of 1924, about sixty German pilots and close to a hundred other technical personnel, known collectively as the Fourth Squadron of the Red Air Force, were stationed at Lipetsk. Moreover, in accordance with the terms of the German-Russian military agreement, 1,200 German naval instructors were later sent to Russia to train the Red Navy.

The first Soviet-German cooperation in military production took place in 1921, when Junkers requested assistance from the German government for establishment of an aircraft plant in Russia. Special Group R of the German War Ministry was formed for this military collaboration and provided political guarantees and financial assistance to Junkers. A branch office of Group R, known as Zentrale Moskau, was established in Moscow.

The major task of GEFU was to supervise the construction of factories at Tula, Leningrad, and Schlesselburg for production of artillery shells at the rate of 300,000 per year. In 1927 it was reported that seventeen plants for artillery manufacture were being built by Krupp in Soviet Central Asia. The existence of such a large number of shell and artillery plants is credible in the light of the Russian counterattack in the winter of 1941 before Western aid began flowing to Russia in quantity. The counterattack utilized large fronts of massed artillery and tanks of a single model.

Both the Soviets and the Germans initially expected great benefits from the Soviet-Nazi military alliance of 1939. Stalin asked for a great deal and was anxious to acquire prototypes and the secret manufacturing processes of certain German weapons, but the Soviet Union did not receive anything near its expectations. Machine tools, up to the very largest sizes, formed a considerable part of the German deliveries. Armaments, such as optical supplies and armor-plate, were supplied in smaller amounts.[2]

American firms and engineers also played an intimate role in the establishment of Soviet military industries. In the early 1930s Soviet military industry was built largely by Soviet construction organizations under OGPU supervision and control. American engineers occupied prominent positions in these construction organizations. For example SOYUZSTROI (All-Union Construction Trust) was headed by Sergei Nemetz, a Russian-American who had formerly been an engineer with the Stone and Webster Company of Philadelphia. This unit supervised construction of plants in the "secret industries," which were defined as "having to do with the production or storage of war materials or secret equipment."[3]

One of the most prominent American engineers in the Soviet Union was Zara Witkin, who worked for SOYUZSTROI on its program for integration of the construction goals of the Second Five-Year Plan with those of the First Five-Year Plan. Zara Witkin, a former Communist who had previously worked for Bernard Baruch, had built the Hollywood Bowl and by the State Department's own assessment was an "unusually intelligent and competent engineer" (861.50 Five-Year Plan/276).

[2] U.S. State Dept., *Nazi-Soviet Relations 1939–1941*, p. 83.

[3] This information comes from an unpublished Witkin manuscript in the archives of the Hoover Institution.

Witkin supervised construction of numerous military installations, including a major facility for the storage of military planes at Lubertsi. Over 100 buildings were erected and, said Witkin, they would cover three miles if placed end to end. Witkin also supervised construction of an "enormous" aviation school at Mai, north of Moscow; a large airplane plant at Fili, outside Moscow; an aircraft plant and aviation school at Tsiam; and other units.

Individual firms, such as Vultee Aircraft, Consolidated Aircraft, Seversky, and Martin, either supplied military aircraft and assistance or erected plants for their production (these efforts are described in subsequent chapters).

Purchase of Armaments in the United States

Soviet armaments purchases and military technical-assistance agreements were expanded after 1936 and a determined effort was made to acquire advanced armaments systems and plants to manufacture such systems in the United States. For this purpose the Soviets established the Carp Export and Import Corporation on Fifth Avenue in New York City as a Soviet-front company. The president was Sam Carp, whose sister was married to V. M. Molotov, president of the Council of People's Commissars of the USSR and a member of the Roosevelt-Stalin "inner group" under the 1938 secret military agreement (see p. 81). The staff of Carp Export and Import was American. It included former officers of the U.S. Army and Navy, and consequently the corporation had considerable influence in American industry.

In November 1936, for example, the Soviet Embassy asked the State Department to intercede with the Navy Department for permission to purchase heavy armor-plate for battleships and cruisers from several American steel companies. This was followed by a visit to the State Department by a group of Carp officials, who were assured by the department that the proposed purchase of unassembled battleships would not be illegal or contrary to U.S. policy.

In a subsequent letter to Carp, the State Department indicated that it would not be possible to supply "designs, plans, working drawings and specifications of such vessels as the U.S.S. *Lexington, Colorado,* and *Mississippi,*" but there was no regulation to prevent U.S. naval architects from preparing such designs on behalf of the Soviet Union (see p. 151 for the details of such an agreement).

Purchases of war materials were made directly from American manufacturers. Thus, in 1938 the William Sellers Company of Philadelphia received a contract for heavy machinery for the manufacture of 12-inch steel-plate for armor-plate manufacture. In March 1939 the State Department approved a proposal (already approved by the Navy Department) under which the Electric Boat Company of Groton, Connecticut, would furnish plans, specifications, and construction services to the Soviet Union for a submarine. This weapons-acquisition process of the 1930s culminated in the 1941 Lend-Lease program, under which large quantities of war materials were transferred to the Soviet Union.

President Roosevelt's Secret Military Information Agreement with the Soviet Union

In mid-1938, while the Soviets were pouring arms and men into Spain to stoke up the raging civil war, President Roosevelt made a secret military-information agreement with Stalin and Molotov. Knowledge of this agreement was limited to four persons in the United States and their opposite numbers in the Soviet Union.

A strictly confidential report in the State Department files (800.51 W 89.U.S.S.R./247) was made on January 17, 1939 by Ambassador Joseph E. Davies to summarize the negotiations preceding the Roosevelt-Stalin agreement. Davies stated that he was initially "authorized to procure the advice and counsel of a prominent New York banker, Mr. Sidney Weinberg." This counsel was to decide how the Soviet Union could be granted "compensating credits . . . [at] low rates of interest" that would make it possible for the Soviet Union to settle the Kerensky debts. The context of the Davies report suggests some relationships between the credits and the proposed secret agreement, for according to the ambassador:

> In January 1938, and prior to my departure for the Soviet Union, the President directed me to explore the possibility of securing a liaison between the military and naval authorities of the United States and the Soviet Union with a view to the inter-change of information as to the facts with reference to the military and naval situations of the United States and the Soviet Union vis-a-vis Japan and the general Far Eastern and Pacific problem.

The reason given by President Roosevelt for this agreement with a totalitarian power then actively engaged in a European war was:

> it would be the part of prudence and wisdom on the part of each government to familiarize the other with facts which might be of substantial value in the future by reason of similarity of purposes and necessities even though each power were pursuing separate and independent courses.

An interesting question may be posed: Exactly *what* "similarity of purposes and necessities" did President Roosevelt envisage with a ruthlessly totalitarian Soviet Union ruled by a contemporary rival to Ivan the Terrible?

Ambassador Davies also reported that "the suggestion was most favorably received by both Messrs Stalin and Molotov." Davies proposed that the military information should be known to only four men in the United States: the President, the Secretary of State, the Under Secretary of State, and the liaison officer. Stalin and Molotov "spoke very highly" of the proposed liaison officer—Lieutenant Colonel Philip R. Faymonville.*

American Lend-Lease Supplies to the Soviet Union: 1941–1946

Soviet requests under the Lend-Lease program were more than amply fulfilled.[4] The Soviet Union was given priority over all other American and Allied fronts during World War II. The first Soviet request—for 3,000 pursuit planes—was sizable, but it resulted in a combined U.S. and British offer of 2,700 pursuit planes, which were obtained by stripping every other Allied front. An initial Soviet request for 9,900 light and medium tanks yielded a combined U.S. and British supply of 4,700 tanks. Other requests were overfilled; for example, the Soviets initially requested 20,000 submachine guns—and were offered 98,220 under the First Protocol alone.

The following military equipment was supplied to the Soviet Union under the master Lend-Lease agreement:

> *Category I* included aircraft and aircraft equipment. A total of 14,018 aircraft were shipped, including pursuit planes, light bombers, medium bombers, one heavy bomber, transport planes, flying boats, observation planes, and advanced trainers. In addition, link-trainers, and a considerable quantity of aircraft landing mats and communications equipment were shipped.

* An interesting commentary on the career of Lieutenant Colonel, later General, Faymonville is contained in Anthony Kubek, *How the Far East Was Lost* (Chicago: Regnery, 1963), p. 264, n. 12.

[4] Data from U.S. State Dept., *Report on War Aid Furnished by the United States to the U.S.S.R.* (Office of Foreign Liquidation, Washington, 1945), pp. 19–28.

Category II comprised military supplies of all types. Some 466,968 individual vehicle units were supplied. Combat vehicles included 1,239 light tanks, 4,957 medium tanks, about 2,000 self-propelled guns, 1,104 half-tracks, and 2,054 armored scout cars. The 2,293 ordnance service vehicles included 1,534 field-repair trucks and 629 tank-transporters. Trucks included 47,728 jeeps, 24,564 $\frac{3}{4}$-ton trucks, 148,664 $1\frac{1}{2}$-ton trucks, 182,938 $2\frac{1}{2}$-ton trucks, and smaller quantities of $2\frac{1}{2}$-ton amphibian trucks, 5-ton trucks, and special-purpose trucks. Also shipped were 32,200 motorcycles and 7,570 track-laying tractors with 3,216 spare tractor engines. All equipment was provided with spare parts and ammunition in accordance with U.S. Army standards.

A total of 325,784 tons of explosives was sent, which included 129,667 tons of smokeless powder and 129,138 tons of TNT. Wireless communication equipment included no less than 35,779 radio stations (one kilowatt and less) and related equipment, including radio stations of higher power, radio locators, 705 radio direction finders, 528 radio altimeters, 800 radio compasses, 63 radio beacons, and large quantities of radio tubes, component parts, accessories, and measuring and testing equipment. Construction machinery valued at over $10 million included $5,599,000 worth of road- and aircraft-construction equipment, $2,459,000 in tractor-mounted equipment, $2,099,000 of mixers and pavers, and $635,000 of railroad-construction equipment. Railroad equipment included 1,900 steam locomotives, 66 diesel-electric locomotives, 9,920 flat cars, 1,000 dump cars, 120 tank cars, and 35 heavy-machinery cars, for a total of 13,041 railroad units. Other military items shipped included 15 cableway bridges, 5 portable pipelines, 62 portable storage tanks, 100,000 flashlights with dry cells, and 13 pontoon bridges.

Category III comprised naval and marine equipment. The noncombat ships included 90 dry-cargo vessels, 10 oceangoing tankers, 9 Wye tankers, 3 icebreakers, 20 tugboats, 1 steam schooner, 2,398 pneumatic floats, 1 motor launch, and 2 floating repair shops. Combat ships sent to the Soviet Union comprised 46 110-foot submarine chasers, 57 65-foot submarine chasers, 175 torpedo boats, 77 minesweepers, 28 frigates, 52 small landing craft, 8 tank-landing craft, and 6 cargo barges. The marine-propulsion machinery included 3,320 marine diesel engines, 4,297 marine gasoline engines, 108 wooden gas engines, 2,150 outboard motors, $254,000 worth of shafting and ship propellers, $50,000 worth of steering gear, 40 storage batteries for submarines, and parts and equipment (valued at $2,744,000) for marine-propulsion machinery. Special marine equipment included $1,047,000 worth of salvage stations and diving gear, $109,000 worth of jetting apparatus, a submarine rescue chamber, distilling apparatus valued at $36,000, and miscellaneous special shipping valued at $44,000. Also sent were trawling equipment for minesweepers valued at $3,778,000, mechanical and electrical equipment for tugboats valued at $545,000, and mechanical and electrical equipment for ferry boats valued at $1,717,000. A large quantity of naval artillery and ammunition included 1,849 Oerlikon guns and $2,692,000 worth of equipment for naval guns.

In addition construction programs were subordinated to the main Lend-Lease supply protocols. These included an Arctic program for the supply of Soviet arctic ports, the Outpost program for construction of ports in the Soviet Far East, and the highly important Northern Siberian Air Route Program, as well as Project Milepost in support of Soviet Far Eastern operations.

The Northern Siberian Air Route program to establish a

trans-Siberian airways system was initially suggested by Ray Ellis, director of the Radio and Radar Division of the War Production Board, and was handled separately from the main Supply Protocol arrangements. Equipment comprising transmitters, receivers, and range equipment for eight major and fifty minor stations, valued at $12 million, was requested and substantially assigned by March 30, 1945, for 7,000 miles of airways with five 200-mile feeder lines.

Over 4.2 million tons of foodstuffs were consigned in Category IV. These supplies included 1,154,180 tons of wheat, wheat flour, grain mill products, and seed; over 672,000 tons of sugar; 782,973 tons of canned meat, including 265,569 tons of *tushonka* (Russian equivalent of Spam); 730,902 tons of sausage, fats, butter, and lard; 517,522 tons of vegeable oil; 362,421 tons of dried milk, eggs, cheese, and dehydrated products; 9,000 tons of soap; and 61,483 tons of miscellaneous food products.

Lend-Lease was, of course, a significant source of weapons technology for the USSR. Numerous items supplied under Lend-Lease later became prototypes for standard Soviet military equipment. For example, the BTR-40 Soviet armored personnel carrier is an almost exact copy of the U.S. M-3 A1 scout car. Although the skills of German scientists were used after the war to develop military electronics, including missile guidance systems, much technology in military electronics came from the United States. Soviet search radar was based on U.S. Navy type-SJ radar sets powered by magnetron tubes and received under Lend-Lease. Gun-laying radar was based on the British Mark-II, and the RUS-1 and RUS-11 radar units were also based on Lend-Lease equipment.

Quantities of industrial equipment, including thousands of specialized machine tools for military production, were shipped to Russia under the postwar October 1945 "pipeline agreement" and became the base of the Soviet postwar military construction program. This equipment, far more advanced than anything the Soviets had at that time, was the peak of U.S. technical achievement in 1945–46. It became the basis for future Soviet development. In 1954 it was reported, for example, that the Soviets had established a number of automated lines at ZIL (which produces military vehicles) for mass production of truck components.[5] Although this was not strictly automation in our sense of the word, the interesting aspect is that these were not new machine tools, for "many of the multi-spindle automatics were not only old—they had been in use for 20 years or so—but were of several different makes. These machines were completely rebuilt, and in the course of their reconstruction equipment for automatic loading and unloading was incorporated."[6]

Plants for Production of Military Vehicles

Any automobile or tractor plant can be used to produce tanks and armored cars, military trucks, and other military vehicles. Indeed, one of the major conclusions reached by a U.S. interagency committee formed to study the war-making potential of the U.S. and German automotive industries was that a motor vehicle industry has enormous military potential. "The Committee recognized without dissent that [Germany's] motor vehicle industry was an important factor in her waging of war during the period just ended." On the basis of its findings, the committee recommended that the manufacture of complete automobiles in Germany be prohibited, that the manufacture of certain parts and subassemblies be "specifically prohibited," and that Germany "should not be permitted to retain in her possession any types of vehicles of particular military application, such as track-laying vehicles, multi-axle vehicles, etc."

The committee further listed more than 300 "war products manufactured by the automotive industry." These conclusions have been ignored with respect to the Soviet automobile industry. The military vehicles manufactured at Gorki are

[5] David Scott, "Russians Apply Automation to 20 Year Old Machines," *American Machinist,* Oct. 11, 1954, p. 164.
[6] *Ibid.*

basically the product of Ford Motor Company technology. The Gorki plant was designed by Ford in the early 1930s, and additional foreign equipment has been installed down to the present day. Among the numerous civilian and military models now produced by this Ford plant is the GAZ-69, in its civilian version a medical-aid vehicle, but in its military version a 1-ton military truck, a scout vehicle, a command car, and a rocket-launcher.

Thus, individual parts and the overall design of present-day Soviet military vehicles, including those used for weapons systems (e.g., the GAZ-69 Shmel rocket-carrier), may be traced to American automobile technology sent to the Soviet Union as "peaceful trade."

The more recent Togliatti technical-assistance of the late sixties affords an excellent illustration of the military capabilities of allegedly civilian units. The engine to be produced at Togliatti belongs to "the small and medium" European size-class (engine displacement, respectively, 73 and 85 cubic inches). This is approximately the 1,500-cubic-centimeter class of engine. Does such an engine have any military usefulness? This is an important question, since this plant has a capacity of 600,000 vehicles per year, or more than twice the 1968 Soviet production of automobiles. In other words, over half the total Soviet automobile output will come from this single plant and three-quarters of the plant's equipment came from the United States as "peaceful trade."

The military possibilities for such a small engine include use as a main engine on a special-purpose small military vehicle (like the American jeep), or as a propulsive unit for a specially designed vehicle for carrying either personnel or weapons. Soviet strategy is currently toward supply of wars of "national liberation." The Togliatti vehicle would be an excellent replacement for the bicycle used in Vietnam. The GAZ-46 is the Soviet version of the U.S. jeep, and we know that such a vehicle figures in Soviet strategic thinking. General G. I. Prokovskii has commented on the advantage of the jeep as a weapons carrier, "Even relatively powerful recoilless artillery systems can, at the present time, be mounted on light automobiles, without reducing the number of men who can be accommodated."

It may be argued that a U.S. jeep engine is more powerful than the engine to be built at Togliatti. The unit is about two-thirds as powerful as the jeep engine, but a proven vehicle of excellent capabilities utilizing a 1,500-cc. engine already exists— and the Soviets have the performance and manufacturing data. During World War II the Germans developed the N.S.U. three-quarter-track vehicle, which weighed 3,100 pounds fully loaded, including three men. The ground pressure was only 4.5 psi. and with a turning circle of thirteen feet it was capable of fifty miles per hour. The Germans found this tracked vehicle "invaluable in wooded country impassable to a vehicle of normal size." The propulsion unit was a 1,500-cc. 4-cylinder Opel engine developing 36 horsepower: this same engine later powered the Moskvitch-401 and the Moskvitch-402 (Moskva) military cross-country 4-wheel drive version of the 401, produced at the MZMA in Moscow.

In brief, there already exists a tested and usable military vehicle capable of transporting men or adaptable for weapons use and powered by a 1,500-cc. engine. Therefore the statements by U.S. officials to the effect that the Togliatti plant can have no military capabilities are erroneous.

U.S. Assistance for the Skoda Armaments Plant

The largest outside supplier of weapons to the Soviet Union is Czechoslovakia. The largest weapons manufacturer in Czecho-slovakia is the Skoda (Lenin) Works at Pilsen, which produces everything from small arms to MiG-21s. Skoda provides an excellent example of U.S. assistance for armaments production via an East European Communist country.

Skoda has an agreement with the Simmons Machine Tool Corporation of Albany, New York, an old, established company specializing in the design of large automatic and numerically controlled special-purpose machine tools. Under the agreement, Simmons equipment is built by Skoda in Czechoslovakia. It is marketed under the Simmons name and specification in the United States and elsewhere as a joint Simmons-Skoda line. Included in the Simmons-Skoda line are such machine tools as heavy-duty lathes (40-inch- to 13-foot-diameter swing), vertical boring mills (53-inch- to 60-foot-diameter swing), horizontal boring mills (5-, 6-, 8-, and 10-inch bar diameter), rotary tables from 78.74 by 78.74 inches to 14.9 by 18 feet, planer-type milling machines, and roll and shaft grinders.

All these machines have obvious military end-uses. Thus it may be seen that a prominent East European Communist organization, supplying armaments to Vietnam and specialized heavy equipment to the Soviet Union, is able to take direct advantage of the most advanced U.S. technology.

American Accelerometers for Soviet Missiles

Accelerometers are small but vital instruments used in missiles and aircraft to measure gravitational pull. In 1965–68 the Soviets were displaying an extracurricular interest in American accelerometers, and a Soviet United Nations diplomat was forced to hurriedly leave the United States before being picked up for espionage involving acquisitions of U.S. accelerometers.

The testimony of Leonard I. Epstein, vice president of Trans-American Machinery and Equipment Corporation of New Jersey, to the House Un-American Activities Committee detailed Soviet interest in this American technology. Mr. Epstein related to the committee how he met Vadim Isakov, a Russian employee of UNICEF (United Nations International Children's Emergency Fund) on July 15, 1965, and how Isakov later visited Epstein's plant in New Jersey with a list of four items for purchase, including "an accelerometer made by American Bosch Arma Corporation or similar company. The accelerometer is an intricate device which measures the pull of gravity on any vehicle such as a missile or space-orbiting device. The device costs about $6,000." Mr. Epstein, under intsructions from the FBI, met several times with Isakov to "find out what he wanted."

In October 1965, "Isakov began to push for delivery on the accelerometer. [Epstein] surmised that the urgency had something to do with the fact that the Soviets had smashed three vehicles onto the surface of the moon." Although Epstein was able to stall for "quite some time" on various grounds, Isakov later became "quite anxious to obtain an accelerometer." When Epstein pleaded export problems, Isakov suggested he would use the Soviet diplomatic pouch.

Eighteen months later, in August 1967, another Russian, intensively interested in accelerometers, turned up in the United States, this time under the auspices of the State Department Academic Exchange Program. From August 1967 to June 1968, Anatoliy K. Kochev of the Kalinin Polytechnical Institute of Leningrad was at Catholic University in the United States working on "construction methods of equipment to measure small accelerations and displacements," that is, the manufacture of accelerometers.

Is there any connection between Isakov's unsuccessful espionage attempts to purchase accelerometers and Kochev's "academic" work on accelerometer manufacture in the United States, which was arranged by the State Department? There are indeed obsolete accelerometers and sophisticated accelerometers. The Soviets know the difference. They know how to make the obsolete versions but do not (or did not in 1966) have the technical ability to make more sophisticated instruments. The trick is in the manufacturing process—that is, in knowing how to build into the instrument the sensitivity necessary to measure small gravitational pulls quickly and accurately. *It is the manufacturing technique that was important to the Soviets—much more important than a boatful of purchased accelerometers.*

Why did Kochev come to the United States in 1967? The State Department reports the title of his project as "construction methods of equipment to measure small accelerations." Ten months would be sufficient time to determine the most modern methods in this field, and given the rather careless manner in which advanced accelerometers have found their way into used electronic equipment stores, it is unlikely that Kochev had major problems in adding to his knowledge of the state of the art.

Why did the State Department make an agreement in 1966 to allow a Soviet engineer into the United States to study the *manufacture* of accelerometers only a few months after another Soviet national had been foiled by the FBI in attempting to *purchase* an accelerometer?

American Ball Bearings for Soviet Missiles

Ball bearings are an integral part of many weapons systems; there is no substitute. The entire ball bearing production capability of the Soviet Union is of Western origin—utilizing equipment from the United States, Sweden, Germany, and Italy. This transfer has been fully documented elsewhere (see Bibliography). All Soviet tanks and military vehicles run on bearings manufactured on Western equipment or copies of Western equipment. All Soviet missiles and related systems including guidance systems have bearings manufactured on Western equipment or Soviet duplicates of this equipment.

One firm in particular, the Bryant Chucking Grinder Company of Springfield, Vermont, has been an outstanding supplier of ball bearing processing equipment to the Soviets. In 1931 Bryant shipped 32.2 percent of its output to the USSR. In 1934 55.3 percent of its output went to Russia. There were no further shipments until 1938, when the Soviets again bought one-quarter of Bryant's annual output. Major shipments were also made under Lend-Lease. Soviet dependence on the West for ball bearings technology peaked after the years 1959–61, when the Soviets required a capability for mass production, rather than laboratory or batch production, of miniature precision ball bearings for weapons systems. The only company in the world that could supply the required machine for a key operation in processing the races for precision bearings (the Centalign-B) was the Bryant Chucking Grinder Company. The Soviet Union had no such mass-production capability. Its miniature ball bearings in 1951 were either imported or made in small lots on Italian and other imported equipment.

In 1960 there were sixty-six such Centalign machines in the United States. Twenty-five of these machines were operated by the Miniature Precision Bearing Company, Inc., the largest manufacturer of precision ball bearings, and 85 percent of Miniature Precision's output went to military applications. In 1960 the USSR entered an order with Bryant Chucking for forty-five similar machines. Bryant consulted the Department of Commerce. When the department indicated its willingness to grant a license, Bryant accepted the order.

The Commerce Department's argument for granting a license turned on the following points: (1) the process achieved by the Centalign was only a single process among several required for ball bearing production, (2) the machine could be bought elsewhere, and (3) the Russians were already able to make ball bearings.

The Department of Defense entered a strong objection to the export of the machines on the following grounds:

> In the specific case of the granting of the export license for high-frequency grinders manufactured by Bryant Chucking Grinder, after receiving the request for DOD's opinion from the Department of Commerce, it was determined that all of the machines of this type currently available in the United States were being utilized for the production of bearings utilized in strategic components for military end items. It was also determined from information that was available to us that the Soviets did not produce a machine of this type or one that would be comparable in enabling the production of miniature ball bearings of the tolerances and precision required. A further consideration

was whether machines of comparable capacity and size can be made available from Western Europe. In this connection, our investigation revealed that none was in production that would meet the specifications that had been established by the Russians for these machines. In the light of these considerations it was our opinion that the license should not be granted.

The Inter-Departmental Advisory Committee on Export Control, which includes members from the Commerce and State departments as well as the CIA, overruled the Department of Defense opinion, and "a decision was made to approve the granting of the license." The Department of Defense made further protests, demanding proof that either the USSR or Western Europe was capable of producing such machines. No such proof was forthcoming.

The following is a summary of the objections of the Department of Defense:

(a) I expressed dissatisfaction and suggested that the Department of Defense not concur in the initial request of the Department of Commerce.

(b) The official member of the Department of Defense in this connection concurred and, at a series of meetings of the Advisory Committee on Export Control, spoke against the proposal that an export license be granted.

(c) The Deputy Assistant Secretary of Defense Supply and Logistics, after reviewing some of the circumstances, requested that I do whatever was possible to stop the shipment of these machines.

(d) A letter was transmitted from the Office of the Secretary of Defense to the Secretary of Commerce, approximately November 1, 1960, saying it [sic] spoke to the Department of Defense and requesting a further review.

(e) At two meetings where the matter was reviewed,

> the Department of Defense maintained nonconcurrence in the shipment of the equipment.
>
> As of this writing I am still convinced that it would be a tragic mistake to ship this equipment.

The reference to a "tragic mistake" refers to the known fact that miniature precision ball bearings are essential for missiles. Granting the license would give the USSR a miniature ball bearing production capability equal to two-thirds that of the United States.

In 1961 a Senate subcommittee investigated the grant of this license to Bryant. Its final report stated:

> The Senate Subcommittee on Internal Security has undertaken its investigation of this matter not in any desire to find scapegoats, but because *we felt that the larger issue involved in the Bryant case was, potentially, of life-or-death importance to America and the free world.* We are now convinced, for reasons that are set forth below, that the decision to grant the license was a grave error.[7]

The testimony of Horace Gilbert to the Senate summarizes the position on the Centalign machines:

> Mr. Chairman, I am Horace D. Gilbert, of Keene, N.H., and I am president of Miniature Precision Bearings, Inc., and I would like to express my appreciation for having an opportunity to be here with you and come particularly at this time, when I know that everyone is so busy, and at such short notice. As the name implies, my company produces miniature ball bearings of precision quality, 85 percent of which are used in the national defense effort. All but 1 percent of our sales are within the United States, and most of these

[7] U.S. Senate, *Proposed Export of Ball-Bearing Machines to U.S.S.R.* (Washington, 1961).

bearings are produced by machines manufactured by Bryant Chucking Grinder Co., of Springfield, Vt.

Our company owns about 25 of these machines out of the 66 which, I believe, presently exist in the United States. This machine was developed over a long period of years, and much of the know-how, Mr. Chairman, in the latest model, was contributed by our company.

Several months ago Russia ordered 45 of these machines from Bryant, and the Department of Commerce has granted an export license.

I was very much disturbed when I learned of this, and I and Mr. Patterson over there—whom I will further identify as one of the developers of this machine—we have attempted to demonstrate to the Department of Commerce the tragedy of these machines being sold to Russia.

Unfortunately, we have not met with success, and I would like to assure you, Mr. Chairman, that if these machines are sold it means absolutely no commercial or financial difference to us as a company or to me as an individual.

I have no fear as far as Russia selling in our markets is concerned, and our company does not do any significant amount of bearing business in their markets. I am here because I think that this is folly which would undermine our defenses.

The Department of Commerce has attempted to justify its decision with four or five arguments, none of which, in our opinion, appears to be valid, and I would like to touch on these.

First, they say these machines could be purchased in Europe, and consequently, Bryant might as well benefit by their sale here.

I am thoroughly familiar with the machines which are in production in Europe. Part of my knowledge has been gained by three trips to Europe in the last 11 months, and I can assure you that no European manufacturer in fact does produce comparable machines with the accuracy of that which is used by Bryant. I would suggest that, if the Russians could buy this machine in any other market, they would indeed do so. In fact, an American competitor of Bryant, Heald Machine Co., of Worcester, has been attempting for 3 years to imitate and produce a comparable machine, and they have not been successful.

Secondly, the Department of Commerce has pointed out that 45 of these machines which have been ordered by the Russians are only a small part of the total number in existence. The number in existence is a matter of record, and, as of the end of September, there were only 66 machines in the United States, and now Russia has ordered 45 for their own needs, and I understand that not all 66 of these are in production. They are in experimental facilities, they would have almost the equivalent of the entire U.S. capacity for production.

Thirdly, the Department of Commerce has suggested that these machines require skilled operators who need substantial training; and I can assure you this is not true, sir. Even if it were, I am confident that the Russians have skilled technicians who, in a short time, would be able to master the operation of this machine, were it complicated, which it is not, and that is part of the magic of the machine, that it is not complicated. There is a certain amount of skill required to set up the machine, but under a contract with Bryant, I understand that the machine must be disassembled and reassembled in the presence of Russian inspectors who are not at their doorstep. Consequently, they will have whatever knowledge they need to put this machine into immediate operation.

The case for Bryant Chucking Grinder Company is expressed in the following portions of a letter sent to Senator Dodd on

January 27, 1961 by N. A. Leyds, Bryant's vice president and general manager:

We appreciate the opportunity to make the following remarks concerning the testimony of December 21, 1960 and January 24, 1961, received by your Committee relative to the license granted to us by the Department of Commerce for the shipment of 45 of our Model "B" Centalign machines to Russia . . .

There was no objection by any of the dissenters to the shipment of the J&L machines, and we certainly have no objection. But it has been readily admitted that these machines will quite probably be used in the production of miniature bearings . . .

We were not surprised at the objection by the Department of Defense as it is well known that their technical expert, who could not appear, is, and has been, against the shipment of most, if not all, machine tools to Russia. We do not question his sincerity nor wish at this time to discuss the validity of this person's opinion, but, whether this opinion described the policy of U.S. Government in this area is highly questionable. To our knowledge, the top technicians from the Defense Department have not seen our Model "B" machine . . .

We, along with other machine tool builders, are not restricted from producing any of the machines, not on the international control list, in our foreign subsidiaries. Our Company has subsidiaries producing machine tools in England and West Germany and presently regulations permit us to manufacture Model "B"s with spindle speeds up to 120,000 r.p.m. in these subsidiaries and ship them to Russia . . .

We notice in comments made before your committee that certain people purport to be experts as to the competition which exists for the Model "B." Perhaps it should be pointed out that we certainly should be qualified to comment on this subject. It is known that some of the features on the Model "B" are available from other machine tool builders in the Free World, and we think our designs can and will be duplicated in many respects in a matter of months . . .

Our leadership in technology in this area is so slight that we must continually utilize our forces and talents at the maximum, to maintain the slightest gap which exists. We must be permitted to compete with our foreign competitors and maintain a healthy posture, or we must rapidly lose the race to maintain superior technology. A few other key machine tool builders with a similar problem can create a situation with far-reaching consequences to the nation's security. It is only when a company is strong that it can support the financial burden necessary to maintain research and development activities at their proper level.

In general we believe that in the matter of trade with the Soviet bloc, similar restrictions should apply to identical industries in each and all of the Free World countries. Our hands must not be tied.

The Senate subcommittee's conclusions were overwhelmingly in favor of denying the export license and raised major unanswered questions concerning the intentions of Leyds, the Bryant Chucking Grinder Company, and the Department of Commerce. These were the subcommittee's conclusions:

We believe that this testimony gives overwhelming support to the stand taken by the Department of Defense in this matter, and to the arguments presented by Miniature Precision Bearing in opposing shipment.

This testimony establishes conclusively (1) that the miniature bearings produced with the help of the Bryant machine are used primarily for defense purposes; (2) that the function performed by the Bryant machine is of critical importance; (3) that no comparable machines can at present be obtained from other sources; (4) that Soviet industry has not been able to master the problems involved in mass producing high precision miniature bearings; that the industry is in fact plagued by poor quality and obsolete equipment; that with its own resources, it would probably take a number of years to develop the capability; (5) that the possession of these machines would greatly accelerate Soviet mastery of the art of miniaturization.

... we think it would be helpful if we briefly summarized some of the high points of this testimony and recapitulated some of the essential facts.

1. *At least 85 percent of the bearings manufactured with the help of the Bryant machine are used by defense industries:*

> Subject machine is a key factor in the economical production of the highest precision for many important Department of Defense applications, such as the latest guidance systems, navigation, fire control, computer, synchro and servo mechanisms used for aircraft, ordnance, ships, missiles and other space vehicles (statement of Mr. J. R. Tomlinson, president, and Mr. B. L. Mims, vice president in charge of engineering, the Barden Corp., Danbury, Conn.).

2. *The function performed by the Bryant machine is of critical importance:*

> The outer ball track grinding operation is one of the last and most vital of those performed on the bearing outer ring. It is the operation which, until the advent of this machine, could probably be called the bottleneck opposing the precision performance of miniature bearings. The necessary perfection of other operations had been achieved 5 to 20 years ago (statement by Mr. H. B. Van Dorn, vice president in charge of engineering, Fafnir Bearing Co., New Britain, Conn.).

3. *The Bryant machine is unique in its field;* Secre-

tary Mueller in his letter of January 18, 1961, to Senator Dodd, said that "substantially comparable" machines could be obtained from other sources. Mr. Bradley Fisk, Assistant Secretary of Commerce for International Affairs, in his testimony before the subcommittee on January 24 said that there are "five factories outside of Russia that could make similar machines." It was not clear from his statement whether the companies he named do, in fact, make such machines, or whether they are theoretically capable of making them. A careful check has revealed that none of the companies named by Mr. Fisk produce machines that can be considered equal or "substantially comparable" to the Bryant machine.

For the Soviets and Bryant Chucking Grinder Company the matter did not end in 1961.

In 1972, just before the presidential election, Nicholaas Leyds, general manager of the Bryant Chucking Grinder Company, announced a contract with the Soviets for 164 grinding machines. Anatoliy I. Kostousov, Minister of the Machine Tool Industry in the Soviet Union, then said they had waited twelve years for these machines, which included mostly the banned models: "We are using more and more instruments of all kinds and our needs for bearings for these instruments is very great. In all, we need to manufacture five times more bearings than 12 years ago."

That makes sense—the Soviets have five times more missiles than they did twelve years ago.

Once again, no doubt, Nicholaas Leyds and the Department of Commerce will talk about "civilian uses"—without citing any. Once again national security will be ignored.

Where is Congress? Where is the press? We are so far down the road to committing national suicide that we now supply bearings for Soviet missile guidance systems and no one even bothers to protest.

CHAPTER SIX
American-Built Plants for Soviet Tanks and Armored Cars

In the building of bridges toward peaceful engagement nothing, of course, should be done which would threaten our national security.

WILLIAM BLACKIE, Chairman, Caterpillar Tractor Company

Production facilities for tanks and armored cars combine features required in automobile and truck production with those required for locomotive and tractor production. As a result, existing tractor, locomotive, and automotive plants can be—and have been—used to produce tanks, although mass production of tanks requires major equipment changes and new machine installations.

Such civilian-military plant conversions for tank and armored-car production have been successfully undertaken in automobile and locomotive plants in many countries. In the United States the Ford Motor Company, Cadillac, and Chrysler have mass-produced tanks. In Italy the Fiat Company and in France the Renault Company, Citroen, and other automobile manufacturers have produced tanks. In England the Vauxhall Motor Company was a tank producer in World War II. Among locomotive manufacturers both Baldwin Locomotive and American Locomotive in the United States have produced tanks, as have locomotive producers in other countries. Tractor plants have also been successfully converted to tank production—for example, Massey Harris in the United States and all the major Caterpillar tractor plants in the Soviet Union.

A tractor plant is well suited to tank and self-propelled gun production. The tractor plants at Stalingrad, Kharkov, and Chelyabinsk, erected with almost complete American assistance and equipment, and the Kirov plant in Leningrad, reconstructed by Ford, were used from the start to produce Soviet tanks, armored cars, and self-propelled guns. The enthusiasm with which this tank and armored-vehicle program was pursued, and the diversion of the best Russian engineers and material priorities to military purposes, have been responsible for at least part of the current Soviet problem of lagging tractor production and periodic famines.

Since 1931, up to a half of the productive capacity of these "tractor" plants has been used for tank and armored-car production.[1]

In both the State Department and the German Oberkommando files, there are reports confirming the *planned* adaptability of Soviet general-equipment plants for war use—that is, confirming that they were originally planned for war use. For example, "The heavy industry plants are fitted with special attachments and equipment held in reserve which in a few hours will convert the plants into munitions factories."[2]

Tank assembly, like the production of automobiles, trucks, and tractors, is normally straight-line with components fed into the main assembly operation from subassembly lines. The components required for tanks are usually peculiar to such weapons. Tank power-plants and tank power-trains are not normally

[1] While, for example, the Soviet PT-76 tank used in 1972 in Vietnam came from the American-built Stalingrad plant (now called Volgograd), the exact percentage of the plant's capacity used for tank production is unknown. Release of U.S. government files would provide the information.

[2] Horace N. Filbert, "The Russian Industrialization Program" (unpublished manuscript in the Hoover Institution at Stanford University), p. 3.

used in commercial-type vehicles in the West. However, in the Soviet Union commercial engines have been used in tank installations by combining two power plants in one tank, for example the SU-76 self-propelled gun with two standard Dodge automobile engines.[3]

Machinery and machine tools for tank production are similar to those used in the production of heavy equipment, with some additional special-purpose tools. Transfer machines required for automotive-type engines, large boring mills, large planers, radial drills, and heavy welding equipment are also utilized.

Consequently, any automobile, truck, locomotive, or tractor production plant with straight-line assembly operations can be converted to the mass production of tanks by the addition of certain specialized equipment and by utilizing components and subassemblies made elsewhere for the specific tank vehicle to be assembled.

Soviet tractor plants before World War II were established in the early 1930s with major U.S. technical and equipment assistance. The Stalingrad tractor plant was completely built in the United States, shipped to Stalingrad, and then installed in prefabricated steel buildings also purchased in the United States. This unit, together with the Kharkov and Chelyabinsk plants and the rebuilt Kirov plant in Leningrad, comprised the Soviet tractor industry at that time, and a considerable part of the Soviet tank industry as well. During the war, equipment from Kharkov was evacuated and installed behind the Urals to form the Altai tractor plant, which opened in 1943.

Three postwar tractor plants were in operation by 1950, and thereafter there was no further construction. The Vladimir plant opened in 1944, the Lipetsk plant in 1947, the Minsk plant and the Kharkov assembly plant in 1950. This was the basic structure of the Soviet tractor industry in the 1960s. In brief, additions to tractor capacity and therefore to tank-assembly capacity between 1917 and the late 1960s can be identified in two phases:

[3] Aberdeen Proving Grounds Series, *Tank Data I* (Old Greenwich, Conn.: WE Inc., n.d.), p. 143.

Phase 1, Pre–World War II:
  Leningrad (rebuilt 1929), Stalingrad (1930), Kharkov (1931), Chelyabinsk (1933); U.S. equipment and design with U.S. tractors.

Phase 2, Post–World War II:
  Altai (1943), Vladimir (1944), Lipetsk (1947), Minsk (1950), Kharkov tractor-assembly plant (1950); U.S. and German equipment, with U.S. (and one German) models.

These plants produced a limited range of tractors with a heavy emphasis on crawler (caterpillar-tread) models rather than the rubber-tired tractors more commonly used in the United States. The 1959 USDA technical delegation estimated that 50 percent of the current output was in crawler models, as constrasted to only 4 percent in the United States. The military implications of this product mix will be made obvious by a glance at Table 6.1.

TABLE 6.1

SELECTED SOVIET TANK MODELS PRODUCED IN TRACTOR PLANTS

Tank Model Number	Tractor-Tank Plant:	Where Tanks Were used:
T-26 (8-ton) A, B, C versions	Ordzhonikidze (Kharkov)	Spanish Civil War Manchuria Finland
T-37 (3-ton)	Stalingrad Chelyabinsk	Russo-Finnish War World War II
T-32 (34-ton)	Kirov works (Leningrad)	Russo-Finnish War World War II
BT (12-ton)	Chelyabinsk	Spanish Civil War Russo-Finnish War
BT-28 (16-ton)	Chelyabinsk	Russo-Finnish War
PT-76	Volgograd (Stalingrad)	Indo-Pakistan War Vietnam

The American-built Stalingrad "Tractor" Plant

In March 1929 a delegation of thirteen Soviet engineers arrived in the United States and in cooperation with several American companies outlined a plan for a plant to produce 50,000 Caterpillar-type tractors a year.[4] "The entire designing of the Stalingrad . . . tractor plant . . . was carried out in the United States."[5]

The Stalingrad Tractor Plant, the largest in Europe, was a packaged factory built in the United States, dismantled, shipped to the USSR, and re-erected at Stalingrad under the supervision of American engineers. All its equipment was manufactured in the United States by some eighty firms; it went into production with the Harvester 15/30 model and the T-37 3-ton tank.

The Stalingrad Tractor Plant was the first of three massive plants for the production of tractors in peace and tanks in war. It was built in every sense of the word in the United States and was reassembled in Stalingrad by 570 Americans and 50 Germans. The plant was delivered in component parts, installed in a building supplied by McClintock & Marshall, and erected under the supervision of John Calder of the Austin Company. *Za Industrializatsiiu* pointed out that "it is very important to note that the work of the American specialists . . . was not that of consulting but of actually superintending the entire construction and the various operations involved."[6]

Each item of construction and equipment was the responsibility of a major U.S. firm: the design of plant was by Albert Kahn, Inc.; the design of the forge shop was by R. Smith, Inc.; the design of the foundry was by Frank C. Chase, Inc.

Equipment for the cold-stamping department came from Niagara and Bliss, equipment for the heat-treating shops was

[4] Amtorg, *Economic Review of the Soviet Union,* 5:7 (Apr. 1, 1930), 135. "While preliminary work on the site of the Stalingrad Tractor Plant had been conducted for some time, the actual work on the construction of the principal departments started only in June when the plans arrived from the United States."

[5] *Ibid.,* 4:19 (Oct. 1, 1929), 336.

[6] July 5, 1930.

by Rockwell, equipment for the power station by Seper and Westinghouse.

Equipment for chain-belting in the conveyor system was by Chain Belt Co., and the supply of buildings by McClintock & Marshall.

The Stalingrad Tractor Plant, therefore, was American in concept, design, construction, equipment, and operation. It could just as easily have been located outside Chicago producing Harvester tractors, except for the placards claiming "socialist progress" and its massive tank quota.

It is worthwhile to recall that the contemporary Soviet press was quite open about this U.S. assistance. For example, an article in *Za Industrializatsiiu* drew three conclusions: first, that the preparation of the plans for the Stalingrad plant by American engineers with "participation" by Soviet engineers made completion of the plant possible within a "very short time"; second, that work and training by Soviet engineers in the United States resulted in a "considerable improvement in engineering processes" and the application of American standards; and third, that work in the United States gave the Soviets a firsthand opportunity to study American tractor plants and verify data on the operation of American machine tools.

As early as 1931 the Chain Belt Company representative, who was installing a conveyor system at Stalingrad, reported that the newly opened tractor plant was making "small tanks." In 1932 A. A. Wishnewsky, an American whose work took him into many Soviet factories, reported that the principal emphasis in all these new tractor plants was on the production of munitions and military supplies. In all factories, he stated, at least one department was closed, and he would from time to time run across "parts and materials for military production." This was particularly true of Tractorostroy (*sic*), where emphasis was placed on the production of tanks rather than tractors. "In his opinion, at least for the time being, the development of tractor production there has been designed to lead up the production of tanks for military purposes."

Such early reports were confirmed a few years later by German intelligence, which reported that in 1937–38 the Stalingrad Tractor Plant was producing a small 3-ton armored car, a self-propelled gun, and the T-37 tank, which was patterned on the British A-4 Ell.

Today Stalingrad (now Volgograd) produces the PT-76, an amphibious unit in the Soviet tank stock, which was used as recently as the spring of 1972 in the Communist attack on South Vietnam.

Light Tanks from the American-built Kharkov "Tractor" Plant

The Kharkov "tractor" plant was identical to the Stalingrad plant. Although the original intention was to build Kharkov as an all-Soviet undertaking, American engineers were called in at a very early point. Leon A. Swajian, a well-known engineer in the United States, became chief construction engineer and was subsequently awarded the Order of Lenin for his work. Swajian commented that no other construction job in his experience had required so much work in a single year, and that in the United States such giant plants are not built all at once, but a few departments at a time, by subcontract. The same American supervising engineers and similar U.S. construction equipment and methods were used. Thus, Swajian explained:

> Ford's River Rouge plant was more than a dozen years in building. When I took charge [at River Rouge] it was already partly built; I worked there six or seven years and when I left construction was still in progress. But in the U.S.S.R. with government financing and no other plants from which to buy spare parts, with the plant dependent on itself—down to the smallest operation on the basic raw material—the whole plant must be built at once. And very swiftly too, if it is not to tie up capital too long. The Kharkov

job was pushed to completion more swiftly than any
job I have ever had to do with.[7]

As at the Stalingrad and Chelyabinsk tractor plants, the
equipment was almost all foreign—either American or German
patterned after American makes. No equipment at the Kharkov
plant was Soviet-made. The forge shop contained $403,000
worth of American forging machines and dies, and the heat-
treating equipment and automatic furnace-temperature controls
were supplied by Leeds and Northrup of Philadelphia. A report
in late 1932 from the Kharkov Tractor Plant by Ingram D.
Calhoun, an engineer for the Oilgear Company of Milwaukee,
stated that Kharkov was turning out eight to ten tanks a day
and tanks took precedence over tractor production. Operators
were being trained "night and day . . . they can fool the tourists
but not the foreign engineers," Calhoun added.[8]

By 1938 Kharkov was producing self-propelled guns, armored
cars, and the T-26 tank, which was patterned after the British
Vickers-Armstrong 6-tonner.

The Chelyabinsk "Tractor" Plant

The Chelyabinsk plant was started in 1930, without foreign
technical assistance, as another duplicate of the Stalingrad
Tractor Plant. One year later, in March 1931, a letter to the
Soviet press signed by thirty-five Chelyabinsk Tractor Plant
engineers and economists charged that the project was "on the
verge of total collapse."

American engineers, including John Calder, the expert
troubleshooter, were then called in to take over construction of
the plant and initial operating responsibility. A pilot plant was
established and operated by John Thane and an American
assistant, both of whom were former employees of the Cater-

[7] Amtorg, *op. cit.*, 6:18 (Sept. 15, 1931), p. 413.
[8] U.S. State Dept. Decimal File, 861.5017—Living Conditions/576,
Dec. 28, 1932.

pillar Company. The chief consulting engineer from 1931 to 1933 was Edward J. Terry. The Stalinets S-60 tractor produced was an exact copy of the Caterpillar 1925–31 model. Ex-Caterpillar engineers supervised operations. In May 1933 practically all the machine tools and production equipment in the plant were American, British, or German.

By 1937 the plant employed about 25,000 workers. The only tractor produced between 1933 and 1937 was the Stalinets (Caterpillar) S-60, a 50-horsepower (drawbar) model of the crawler type. About 6,460 were produced in 1937, a long way from the planned 50,000 per year. In 1937 the production model was changed to the Stalinets S-65, which was a Caterpillar-60 with slightly increased horsepower and a diesel engine. A total of just over 3,000 were produced, including another model with a gas generator.

The Chelyabinsk Tractor Plant was also producing tanks of the BT series, which was patterned on the American Christie. Monthly output in 1938 consisted of thirty-two of the 12-tonners and 100 of the BT-38, a 16-tonner.

Thus, not only were all three of the new American-built tractor plants producing tanks throughout the 1930s, but they were by far the most important industrial units producing this type of weapon. Today, these plants still can, and do, produce tanks.

During World War II the German automotive industry moved eastward into the area later to be occupied by the Soviet Union. The second-largest auto manufacturer in Germany, Auto-Union, A.G., with six prewar plants dating back to 1932, was already located in the Chemnitz and Zwickau areas. It is noteworthy that Auto-Union and Opel, also partly located in the Soviet Zone, were more self-contained than other German vehicle manufacturers and met most of their own requirements for components and accessories. Although Auto-Union was the only German automobile producer to produce automobiles during the war, the firm did make a sizable percentage of Germany's tanks and army vehicles, and in 1944 it was the only producer of HL-230 engines for Tiger and Panther tanks.

The Siegmar works near Chemnitz, which also manufactured

tank engines, was in operation at the end of the war. It is note-worthy that the 1½-ton Steyr truck, produced at the rate of 750 per month at the Horch plant of Auto-Union, was specially designed for winter conditions in Russia.

When the Russians occupied Saxony in 1945, one of their first measures was to completely dismantle the Auto-Union plants and other factories and remove them to the Soviet Union. These key plants had complete facilities for producing 750 tank engines per month as well as a truck specially designed for Russian conditions.

The Development of Soviet Tank Design to 1945

Soviet tanks before World War II derived from American, British, and, to a lesser extent, French and Italian designs. Little German design influence can be traced in the period before 1939, except through the German tank center at Kazan in the USSR. During the 1920s and 1930s the Soviets acquired prototypes from all tank-producing countries and based their own development of tanks upon these foreign models. The Soviet tank stock in 1932 is shown in Table 6.2 (p. 111).

From this stock of Western models, together with technical-assistance agreements with foreign firms and the continuing purchase of foreign prototypes, the Soviets developed a formidable tank force for World War II.

The Carden-Lloyd (the predecessor of the British Bren-gun carrier of World War II) was a 1.69-ton machine-gun carrier first produced by Vickers-Armstrong Ltd. in 1929. The Mark-VI model sold to the Soviets had a Ford Model-T 4-cylinder 22.5-horsepower water-cooled engine and a Ford planetary transmission. This became the Soviet T-27 light reconnaissance tank produced at the Bolshevik plant in Leningrad.

The Ordzhonikidze Tractor Plant at Kharkov started work on the T-26, based on the British Vickers-Armstrong 6-tonner at about the same time. There were three versions—A, B, and C—of which B and C became the standard Soviet models produced until 1941. Similarly, the Soviet T-37 and T-38 amphibious vehicles were based on the Carden-Lloyd Amphibian, known as the Model-A4 E 11 in the British Army.

Walter Christie, a well-known American inventor with numerous automotive and tank inventions to his credit, developed the Christie tank—the basis of World War II American tanks. Numerous versions of Christie tanks and armored vehicles were produced in the late 1920s and 1930s. Two chassis of the Christie M-1931 model medium tank (MB) were purchased by the Soviet Union in 1932 from the U.S. Wheel Track Layer Corporation. After further development work this became not only the Soviet T-32 (the basic Soviet tank of World War II) but also several other development models in the USSR: first the BT (12 tons), followed by the BT-5 and the BT-28 produced at Chelyabinsk. They were standard equipment until 1941.

TABLE 6.2

SOVIET TANK STOCK (1932)

Tank (Model and Quantity)	Western Source
20 Carden-Lloyd Mark-VI	Vickers-Armstrong Ltd. (U.K.)
1 Fiat Type-3000	Fiat (Italy)
20 Renault	Renault (France)
16 "Russian-Renaults"	Made in France, modified in USSR
70 light tanks	Vickers 6-ton, Alternate-A (U.K.)
40 Vickers Mark-11	Vickers-Armstrong Ltd. (U.K.)
2 Christie M-1931	U.S. Wheel Track Layer Corp. (U.S.A.)
8 Medium Mark-A	Vickers-Armstrong Ltd. (U.K.)

Sources: R. E. Jones et al., *The Fighting Tanks Since 1916* (Washington, D.C.: National Service Publishing Co., 1933), p. 173.

R. M. Ogorkiewicz, "Soviet Tanks," in B. H. Liddell Hart, ed., *The Red Army* (New York: Harcourt, Brace and Co., 1956).

The Soviet T-34 and the American M-3, both based on the Christie, had the same 12-cylinder aero engine, a V-type Liberty of 338 horsepower. Ogorkiewicz comments on the Christie model series as follows:

> The power-weight ratio was actually higher than could be efficiently used, but the Russians copied it all and confined their development largely to armament, which increased from a 37-millimeter gun on the original models of 1931, to 45-millimeter guns on BT-5 of 1935, and eventually to short 76.2-millimeter guns on some of the final models of the series.

Both the Soviet T-28 medium 29-ton tank and the T-35 45-ton heavy tank resembled British models—the A-6 medium tank and the A-1 Vickers Independent, respectively. Imported French Renault designs also contributed to Russian tank knowledge. During the 1933 entente between France and the Soviet Union, the Renault Company delivered $11 million worth of "small fast tanks and artillery tractors" to the Soviet Union and supplied experts from the Schneider works and Panhard Levasseur, skilled in the armored-car and tank field.

The Soviet T-34 Medium Tank

The Soviet T-34 and the modified T-34/85 were first introduced in World War II and were used extensively against American troops in the Korean War. The model was later used in the Hungarian revolt when 25,000 Hungarians were killed and still is in reserve. The T-34 was an excellent design and a formidable weapon: it emphasizes the ability of the Soviets to design weapons while still dependent on the West for production facilities and basic technical advances.

In 1931 the Russians bought two Christie tanks from the U.S. Wheel Track Layer Corporation in the United States. The Russians copied these, built Christie tanks, and then incorporated the Christie suspension system into the T-34. The first Russian Christies had the same engines as the U.S. Christie—a Liberty 12-cylinder V-type of 338 horsepower with forced-water cooling. In the 1920s the Chase National Bank of New York (now Chase Manhattan) was actively engaged in attempting to arrange export of large quantities of these Liberty engines to the Soviet Union at the price of $2,000 each. Chase was thwarted by U.S. military regulations.

In any event, the T-34 incorporated the Christie suspension from the United States but generally used a 500-horsepower V-type diesel developed from the German B.M.W. diesel engine. The T-34/85 was the T-34 with significantly increased firepower. Ball bearings on the T-34 and T-34/85 were Swedish.

During World War II production of the T-34 was concentrated in tractor and automobile plants built by American firms (see Table 6.3).

TABLE 6.3

OUTPUT OF T-34 AND T-34/85 TANKS (JANUARY 1944)

Nishniy Tagil (Works No. 183)	700
Kirov Works at Chelyabinsk	200
Gorki, No. 112	260
Osmk Works No. 174	180
Uralmash (at Sverdlovsk)	190
	(previous July output)

The welding work on the T-34 was immensely crude, but as *The Welding Engineer* (Dec. 1952) pointed out: "The T-34 was designed with one idea in mind—to provide firepower. Any humanitarian considerations, like protection of the crew, are purely secondary."

In the 1930s the original T-34 models were built from several million tons of armor-plate imported from the United States. In July 1934 Henry Disston & Sons, Inc., requested War Department permission to accede to a Soviet request, "in training their technicians to make tank armorplate of the same quality as they now make for this Government" (Russia 400.114, War Office).

The T-34 was followed by the improved T-44 and then by the T-54, with the basic T-44 chassis and using Christie-system torsion-bar suspension. This was the standard Soviet tank until recently; it was used in the Hungarian revolt in 1956 and in South Vietnam in 1972. It is still the major tank for most Warsaw Pact countries.

Soviet Tank Engines

The Red Army has always used diesel engines in its medium and heavy tanks. This tank-engine series is the V-2 and V-12 water-cooled, rated at 550 brake horsepower (bhp) at 2,150 revolutions per minute (rpm). According to Ogorkiewicz, the original Russian water-cooled V-12 engine was a successful diesel adaptation of contemporary aero-engine designs. Used on all Soviet medium and heavy tanks up to World War II it was a large 2,860 cubic-inch engine, based on a German B.M.W. aircraft design, and developed about 500 bhp.[9] The Soviet emphasis on diesels has continued since World War II, while other Soviet armored vehicles have used automobile gasoline engines. The T-70 light tank uses two GAZ-202 70-horsepower engines from the Ford-Gorki plant. The SU-76 self-propelled gun also uses two engines of the same Ford type geared together.

Soviet Light Tanks

The American-built tractor plants at Stalingrad, Kharkov, and Chelyabinsk were the major tank producers of the Soviet Union up to World War II. Monthly tank output for 1938 (a year for which complete figures are available) is shown in Table 6.4; the overall annual tank output of American-built tractor plants for the same year is shown in Table 6.5 (p. 116).

[9] R. M. Ogorkiewicz, "Soviet Tanks," in B. H. Liddell Hart, ed., *The Red Army* (New York: Harcourt, Brace & Co., 1956), p. 301.

TABLE 6.4

Model	Monthly Output	Plant
BT-12	38	Chelyabinsk
BT-3	85	Kharkov
	60	Stalingrad
T-26	90	Kharkov
T-37 3-ton amphibian	90	Stalingrad
BT-28	100	Chelyabinsk

Armored Personnel Carriers

There are four groups of Soviet armored personnel carriers, all of basic U.S. design and all produced with U.S. equipment and technology.

During World War II the United States shipped M-3 A1 scout cars and M-3 half-tracks to the USSR. The Soviet BTR-40 is an almost exact copy of the U.S. M-3A1 scout car shipped under Lend-Lease. It is constructed on a GAZ-63 truck chassis built at the Ford-Gorki plant. The original version carried a driver and nine personnel. In 1962 the design was further modified for reconnaissance use.

In 1954 the BTR-40 was supplemented by the BTR-152, an armored personnel carrier. This is a 6 x 6 vehicle built onto a ZIL-151 or ZIL-157 truck chassis; most parts are interchangeable with the ZIL-151 and ZIL-157 cargo trucks, the two standard cargo trucks of the Red Army. The ZIL plant, Zavod imeni Likhachev, was rebuilt by the Brandt Company, the Budd Company and the Hamilton Foundry in the early 1930s.

The third group of personnel carriers comprises the BTR-50 introduced in 1961 as an improvement of the BTR-152. The chassis is the PT-76 tank chassis (see p. 107 for origins). The fourth group of armored personnel carriers is the BTR-60, which was introduced in the early 1960s; it is based upon the BTR-152, with a chassis similar to the MAZ or Ural tractors.

TABLE 6.5

OVERALL ANNUAL PRODUCTION OF TANKS IN U.S.-BUILT
TRACTOR PLANTS (1938)

Percentage of Total Produced in Each Plant	Construction of Plant by:	Origin of Tank Model	Origin of Tank Engine
Chelyabinsk: 28.9 percent	U.S. firms (1933)	Christie (U.S.A.) Carden-Lloyd (U.K.) Vickers (U.K.)	Liberty V-12 cycle, 338-horsepower (later Hispano-Suiza 350-horsepower)
Stalingrad: 32.8 percent	U.S. firms (1930)	Carden-Lloyd Vickers-Armstrong	U.K.
Kharkov: 38.3 percent	U.S. firms (1931)	Vickers-Armstrong	U.K.

After World War II, then, we continue to find Soviet dependence on Western technologies and production facilities. It is normal Soviet practice to design equipment as well as plants for conversion to military use; for example, the KD-12 logging tractor has been designed for conversion to military applications as an artillery tow. In self-propelled guns we find that the SU-76 has two Gorki (Ford) GAZ-202 engines. The PT-76, used by India in the attack on Pakistan in 1971 and by the North Vietnamese in their attack on South Vietnam in 1972, has a Christie-system torsion-bar suspension, and is also the chassis for the FROG-2, FROG-3, and FROG-4 missile systems and the BTR-50 armored personnel carrier. It is still produced at the American-built Volgograd plant.

In other words, an examination of the production history of individual Soviet tank models and related weapons shows them to be of American origin. The production facilities and input materials are also of Western origin, more often than not American.

CHAPTER SEVEN
American Assistance for Soviet Military Vehicles

If we do not develop our automobile industry we are threatened with the heaviest losses, if not defeats, in a future war.
PRAVDA, July 20, 1927

The Soviets officially stated their intention to use foreign automobile technology for their military vehicles as early as 1927. V. V. Ossinsky, a top planner, wrote a series of articles for *Pravda* in which the following forthright warning appeared:

> If in a future war we use the Russian peasant cart against the American or European automobile, the result to say the least will be disproportionately heavy losses, the inevitable consequences of technical weakness. This is certainly not industrialized defense.[1]

The Soviet military and civilian vehicle-manufacturing industry, as subsequently developed, produces a limited range of utilitarian trucks and automobiles in a few large plants designed, built by, and entirely equipped with Western, primarily American, technical assistance and machinery. These motor

[1] See *Pravda,* July 20, 21, and 22, 1927.

118

vehicle plants manufacture most of their own components and ship these to assembly plants elsewhere in the Soviet Union.

There is a high degree of integration between Russian military and civilian vehicle models. Military and civilian vehicles have many interchangeable parts and Soviet policy is for maximum unification of military and civilian designs to assist model changeover in case of war and to facilitate current production. This unification of military and civilian automobile design has been described by the Soviet economist A. N. Lagovskiy:

> The fewer design changes between the old and the new type of product, the easier and more rapidly the enterprise will shift to new production. If, for example, chassis, motors, and other parts of a motor vehicle of a civilian model are used for a military motor vehicle, of course the shift to the mass production of the military motor vehicle will occur considerably faster and more easily than if the design of all the main parts were different.

Lagovskiy also notes that current "civilian" tractors and motor vehicles can be used directly as military vehicles without major conversion. Soviet tractors (direct copies of Caterpillar models) were used as artillery tractors in World War II and Korea. General G. I. Pokrovski makes a similar argument with reference to the U.S. 106-millimeter recoilless weapon mounted on a Willys jeep and comments that "even relatively powerful recoilless artillery systems can, at the present time, be mounted on a light automobile without reducing the number of men accommodated."[2]

Almost all—possibly 95 percent—of Soviet military vehicles are produced in very large plants originally designed by American engineers in the 1930s. Their construction was supervised by American engineers and today they use American equip-

[2] G. I. Pokrovski, *Science and Technology in Contemporary War* (New York: Frederick A. Praeger, 1959), p. 122.

ment or European versions of American designs. A small percentage of Soviet vehicles are produced in plants built with German equipment and technical assistance.

Lend-Lease subsequently made another significant contribution to the Russian vehicle stock and provided the basic designs for postwar production. Vehicles supplied under Lend-Lease included 43,728 jeeps and 3,510 jeep-amphibians, 25,564 ¾-ton trucks, 218,664 1½-ton trucks, 182,938 2½-ton trucks, 586 2½-ton amphibians, and 814 5-ton trucks. In addition, 2,784 special-purpose trucks, 792 Mack 10-ton cargo trucks, 1,938 tractor trailers, and 1,000 spare engines were sent to Russia.

At the end of World War II the U.S. government appointed an interagency committee to consider the future of the German automobile industry, particularly in regard to its war-making potential. This committee concluded that *any* motor vehicle industry in *any* country is an important factor in that country's war potential and supported its case by listing 300 military products manufactured in motor vehicle plants,* as well as "war shipments" by the U.S. motor vehicle industry (see Table 7.1).

Note that more than half these tanks, almost all the armored and half-track vehicles, and one-third of the guns over 33-millimeter were manufactured in "peaceful" auto plants.

In the light of these findings, the committee unanimously made the following recommendations:

1. Any vehicle industry is a major force for war.
2. German automotive manufacturing should therefore be prohibited because it was a war industry.
3. Numerous military products can be made by the automobile industry, including aerial torpedoes, aircraft cannon, aircraft control instruments, aircraft engines,

---

* The committee's report is entitled *Study by Interagency Committee on the Treatment of the German Automotive Industry from the Standpoint of National Security* (Washington, D.C.: Foreign Economic Administration, July 14, 1945), Report T.I.D.C. No. 12.

TABLE 7.1

WAR SHIPMENTS BY U.S. AUTOMOTIVE INDUSTRY AND BY ALL METAL-PRODUCTS INDUSTRIES
EXCLUSIVE OF GOVERNMENT-OPERATED AND NEW PLANTS (FIRST QUARTER 1944)

| Item | Value in Dollars | | Percent from Automotive Industry |
	(Automotive Industry)	(All Metal-Products Industries)	
Ammunition, 20 mm. and above	$ 87,046,000	$ 369,748,000	23.0
Ammunition, under 20 mm.	14,538,000	55,951,000	26.0
Bombs, depth charges, mines, and torpedoes	36,591,000	147,988,000	24.0
Guns and mounts, 20 mm. and above	77,231,000	256,455,000	30.0
Machine guns, under 20 mm.	8,727,000	66,456,000	13.0
Small arms, under 20 mm.	12,863,000	82,134,000	1.1 _6.5%_
Fire control equipment	1,668,000	153,834,000	1.1
Combat tanks and parts	199,397,000	371,152,000	53.0
Armored scout, half-track vehicles, parts	208,729,000	235,673,000	88.0
Aircraft and parts	315,750,000	1,821,376,000	17.0
Aircraft engines and parts	351,624,000	865,304,000	40.0
Aircraft propellers and parts	3,891,000	64,173,000	6.0 _16%_
Aircraft accessories	51,357,000	160,510,000	32.0
Aircraft instruments	16,183,000	156,844,000	10.0
Airplane landing mats	1,650,000	14,848,000	11.0
Auxiliary vessels	2,145,000	235,066,000	0.9
Navigation instruments	3,670,000	33,553,000	10.9
Ship equipment and parts, N.E.V.	10,156,000	139,185,000	7.3
Motor vehicles (except combat)	408,009,000		
Motor vehicle parts (except combat)	330,757,000		
Motor buses	4,321,000		
Motorized fire apparatus	1,100,000		
Portable fire extinguishers and stirrup pumps	3,480,000		
Diesel engines and accessories	8,745,000		
Internal combustion engines and accessories	22,005,000	8,116,471,000	13.6
Marine engines (except steam)	31,403,000		
Cranes, hoists, winches, and derricks	4,432,000		
Tractors, wheel-type	10,755,000		
Radio and radar equipment	8,002,000		
Motors and generators	9,122,000		
Industrial trucks and tractors	1,155,000		
All others	257,325,000		
Total Shipments	$2,502,827,000	$13,346,721,000	

Source: Foreign Economic Administrator.

aircraft engine parts, aircraft ignition testers, aircraft machine guns, aircraft propeller subassemblies, aircraft propellers, aircraft servicing and testing equipment, aircraft struts, airframes, and so on. A total of 300 items of military equipment was listed.

A comparison of the recommendations of this committee in 1946 with subsequent administrative recommendations and policies concerning the export of automobile-manufacturing plants to the Soviet Union should demonstrate consistency. If automobile-manufacturing capacity had "warlike" potential for Germany and the United States in 1946, then it also has "warlike" potential in the Soviet Union today. But the recommendations in the cases of Germany and the Soviet Union are totally divergent. Some explanation should be offered for this divergence, particularly since some of the same Washington bureaucrats (for example, Charles R. Weaver of the Department of Commerce) participated in making both sets of decisions.

The Soviet Military Truck Industry

As might be expected from the above information, Soviet civilian and military trucks are produced in the same plants and have extensive interchangeability of parts and components. For example, the ZIL-131 is the main 3½-ton 6 x 6 Soviet military truck used in Vietnam. It is produced also in a civilian 4 x 2 version as the ZIL-130. Over 60 percent of the parts of the ZIL-131 military truck are common to the ZIL-130 civilian truck. All Soviet truck technology and a large part of Soviet truck-manufacturing equipment has come from the West, mainly from the United States. While some elementary transfer-lines and individual machines for vehicle production are made in the Soviet Union, these are copies of Western machines and therefore are always obsolete in design.

Many major American companies have been prominent in building up the Soviet truck industry. The Ford Motor Company, the A. J. Brandt Company, the Austin Company, General Electric, and others supplied the technical assistance, design work, and equipment for the original giant plants. For example, General Electric stated (in the company publication *Monogram* of November 1943):

> When the Soviet Union built its mass production automobile and truck plants in Moscow and Gorki, where the ZIL and GAZ cars and trucks take shape on moving conveyors, General Electric, in addition to supplying hundreds of motors and controls for various high speed and special machine tools, also supplied especially designed electric apparatus to aid the mass production of vital parts.... For the mass production of drive shafts and rear axle housings for the GAZ cars and trucks General Electric designed and built special high speed arc welding machines to suit the exact requirements set down by the Soviet Engineering Commission.

The Soviet military-civilian truck industry comprises two main groups of plants. The first group uses models, technical assistance, and parts and components from the Ford-built Gorki automobile plant (GAZ is the model designation). The second group of production plants uses models, parts, and components from the A. J. Brandt–rebuilt ZIL plant in Moscow (Zavod imeni Likhachev, formerly the AMO and later the Stalin plant).* Consequently this plant was called the BBH-ZIL plant after the three companies involved in its reconstruction and expansion in the 1930s: A. J. Brandt, Budd, and Hamilton Foundry.

---

* There is a fundamental difference between the Ford and Brandt contracts. Brandt has had only one contract in the USSR, to rebuild the old AMO plant in 1930. AMO in 1930 had a production of only 30,000 trucks per year, compared to the Gorki plant, which was designed from scratch by Ford for an output of 140,000 vehicles per year. Ford, of course, is still intensely interested in Russian business. Brandt is not and has not been since 1930.

The Ford-Gorki group of assembly plants includes the plants at Ulyanovsk (model designation UAZ), Odessa (model designation OAZ), and Pavlovo (model designation PAZ). The BBH-ZIL group includes the truck plants at Mytischiy (MMZ model designation), Miass (or URAL Zis), Dnepropetrovsk (model designation DAZ), Kutaisi (KAZ model), and Lvov (LAZ model). Besides these main groups there are also five independent plants. The Minsk truck plant (MAZ) was built with German assistance. The Hercules-Yaroslavl truck plant (YaAz) was built by the Hercules Motor Company. The MZMA plant in Moscow, which manufactures small automobiles, was also built by Ford Motor Company. In the late 1960s the so-called Fiat-Togliatti auto plant was opened. Three-quarters of its equipment came from the United States. In 1972 the U.S. government issued $1 billion in licenses to export equipment and technical assistance for the Kama truck plant. Planned as the largest truck plant in the world, it will cover 36 square miles and will produce more heavy trucks than the output of all U.S. heavy truck manufacturers combined.

This comprises the complete Soviet vehicle manufacturing industry—all built with Western, primarily American, technical assistance and technology. Military models are produced in these plants utilizing the same components as the civilian models. The two main vehicle production centers, Gorki and ZIL, manufacture more than two-thirds of all Soviet civilian vehicles (excluding the new Togliatti and Kama plants) and almost all current military vehicles. For a listing of the military models produced by each of these groups of plants, see Table 7.2.

As these two plant groups produce all Soviet military vehicles, except for some specialized production at Minsk, the history of these central plants will be examined in detail.

Henry Ford and the Gorki "Automobile" Plant

In May 1929 the Soviets signed an agreement with the Ford Motor Company of Detroit. According to its terms the Soviets agreed to purchase $13 million worth of automobiles and parts

TABLE 7.2
PLANT GROUP AND MILITARY VEHICLES PRODUCED

Ford-Gorki Group (including: Gorki, Ulyanovsk, Odessa, Pavlovo)	BBH-ZIL Group (including: im Likhachev, Mytishchiy, URAL* Zis, Dnepropetrovsk, Kutaisi, Lvov)
Ford-Gorki GAZ-69: SHMEL missile carrier	BBH-ZIL-131: 3½-ton truck
Ford-Gorki GAZ-54: tow for the ZPU-4 antiaircraft gun	BBH-ZIL-111: radar-computer truck
	BBH-ZIL-111: tow for 122-mm. howitzer
Ford-Gorki GAZ-46: Soviet jeep	URAL* BM-24 rocket-launcher
Ford-Gorki GAZ-69A: command car	URAL* prime mover for 100-mm. antiaircraft gun
Ford-Gorki GAZ 69: army patrol vehicle	URAL*-M66 130-mm cannon tow
Ford-Gorki GAZ-47: amphibian vehicle	BBH-ZIL-151: 2½-ton 6 x 6
Ford-Gorki GAZ-66: cross-country 4 x 4	BBH-ZIL-157: 2½-ton 6 x 6
Ford-Gorki GAZ-69: airborne tow vehicle for 57-mm. antitank gun and 14.5-mm. double-barrelled antiaircraft gun	BBH-ZIL-141 or ZIL-157: chassis for BTR-152 armored personnel carrier
	BBH-ZIL-157: TPP bridge-equipment vehicle
	BBH-ZIL-157: chassis for most Soviet rocket-launchers

* Built at URAL (Chelyabinsk) from parts and components from the BBH-ZIL plant in Moscow.

before 1933 and Ford agreed to render technical assistance until 1938 to construct an integrated automobile-manufacturing plant at Nizhni-Novgorod. Actual construction of this plant was completed in 1933 by the Austin Company for production of the Ford Model-A passenger car and light truck. Today this plant is known as Gorki. With its original equipment now supplemented by imports and domestic copies of imported equipment, it produces the GAZ range of automobiles, trucks, and military vehicles. All Soviet vehicles with the model prefix GAZ (*Gorki Avtomobilnyi Zavod*) are from Gorki, and models with prefixes UAZ, OdAZ, and PAZ are made from Gorki components. In 1930 Gorki produced the Ford Model-A (known as

GAZ-A) and the Ford light truck (called GAZ-AA), and both these Ford models were immediately adopted for military use. By the late 1930s production at Gorki was 80,000–90,000 "Russian Ford" vehicles per year.

The engine production facilities at Gorki were designed under another technical-assistance agreement with the Brown Lipe Gear Company for gear-cutting technology and with the Timken-Detroit Axle Company for rear and front axles.

Furthermore, U.S. equipment has been shipped in substantial quantities to Gorki and its subsidiary plants since the 1930s—indeed some shipments were made from the United States in 1968 during the Vietnamese War. However, U.S. government censorship restricts public knowledge of the exact nature of this equipment and its precise end uses.

As soon as Ford's engineers left Gorki in 1930 to return to the United States, the Soviets began production of military vehicles. The Soviet BA armored car of the 1930s was the GAZ-A (Ford Model-A) chassis, intended for passenger cars but converted to an armored car with the addition of a DT machine gun. The BA was followed by the BA-10—the Ford Model-A truck chassis with a mount containing either a 37-millimeter gun or a 12.7-millimeter heavy machine gun. These Ford armored cars were produced until the end of the 1940s. A Red Army staff car was also based on the Ford Model-A in the prewar period.

During World War II Gorki produced the GAZ-60—a hybrid half-track personnel carrier that combined the GAZ-63 truck body with a German suspension. After the war Gorki converted to the BTR-40 armored personnel carrier based on a GAZ-63 chassis. In the late 1940s the plant switched to production of an amphibious carrier—the GAZ-46. This was a standard GAZ-69 chassis on which was mounted a U.S. quarter-ton amphibious body.

In the mid-1950s Gorki produced the GAZ-47 armored amphibious cargo carrier with space for nine men. Its engine was the GAZ-61, a 74-horsepower Ford-type 6-cylinder in-line gasoline engine—the basic Gorki engine. In the 1960s production continued with the improved version of the GAZ-47 armored cargo carrier, using a GAZ-53 V-8-type engine developing 115 horsepower.

In brief, the Ford-Gorki plant has a long, continuous history of production of armored cars and wheeled vehicles for Soviet army use.

In addition to armored cars, the Ford-Gorki factory also manufactures a range of truck-mounted weapons. This series began in the early thirties with a 76.2-millimeter field howitzer mounted on the Ford-GAZ Model-A truck. Two similar weapons from Gorki before World War II were a twin 25-millimeter antiaircraft machine gun and a quad 7.62-millimeter Maxim antiaircraft machine gun—also mounted on the Ford-GAZ truck chassis.

During World War II Gorki produced several rocket-launchers mounted on trucks. First the 12-rail, 300-millimeter launcher; then, from 1944 onwards, the M-8, M-13, and M-31 rocket-launchers mounted on GAZ-63 trucks. (The GAZ-63 is an obvious direct copy of the U.S. Army's 2½-ton truck.) Also during World War II Gorki produced the GAZ-203, 85-horsepower engine for the SU-76 self-propelled gun produced at Uralmashzavod. (Uralmash was designed and equipped by American and German companies.)

After World War II production of rocket-launchers continued with the BM-31, which had twelve 300-millimeter tubes mounted on a GAZ-63 truck chassis. In the late 1950s another model was produced with twelve 140-millimeter tubes on a GAZ-63 truck chassis. In the 1960s yet another model with eight 140-millimeter tubes was produced on a GAZ-63 chassis.

Finally, in 1964 Gorki produced the first Soviet wire-guided-missile antitank system. This consisted of four rocket-launchers mounted on a GAZ-69 chassis. These weapons turned up in Israel in the late 1960s. The GAZ-69 chassis produced at Gorki is also widely used in the Soviet Army as a command vehicle and scout car. Soviet airborne troops use it as a tow for the 57-millimeter antitank gun and the 14.5-millimeter double-barrelled antiaircraft gun. Other Gorki vehicles used by the

Soviet military include the GAZ-69 truck, used for towing the 107-millimeter recoilless rifle (RP-107), the GAZ-46, or Soviet jeep, and the GAZ-54, a 1½-ton military cargo truck.

In brief, the Gorki plant, built by the Ford Motor Company and the Austin Company and equipped by numerous other U.S. companies under the policy of "peaceful trade," is today—and always has been—a major producer of Soviet army vehicles and weapons carriers.

Military Vehicles from the
A. J. Brandt-Budd-Hamilton-ZIL Plant

In addition to the Ford agreement, a technical-assistance agreement was made in 1929 with the Arthur J. Brandt Company, also of Detroit, for the reorganization and expansion of the tsarist AMO truck plant, previously equipped in 1917 with new U.S. equipment. Design work for this expansion was handled in Brandt's Detroit office and plant and American engineers were sent to Russia. The AMO plant was again expanded in 1936 by the Budd Company and Hamilton Foundry and its name was changed to ZIS (now ZIL). During World War II the original equipment was removed to establish the URALS plant and the ZIS plant was re-established with Lend-Lease equipment. In 1948–49 some of this equipment—for example, crankshaft lathes—was copied by the Soviets.

In the late 1950s it was reported that "Likhachjov [*sic*] does its own design and redesign and in general follows American principles in design and manufacture." The same source suggested that Soviet engineers were quite frank about copying, and that their designs lagged about three to five years behind those current in the United States. The plant's production techniques were described as "American with Russian overtones." The plant had developed the "American Tocco process" for brazing and many American machines were in use, particularly in the forging shops.

The first armored vehicle produced at AMO was an adaptation of the civilian ZIL-6 truck produced after the Brandt re-organization in 1930. This vehicle was converted into a mount for several self-propelled weapons, including the single 76.2-millimeter antiaircraft gun and the 76.2-millimeter antitank gun. The truck itself was equipped with a protective steel shield.

In World War II the ZIL-6 was adapted for the 85-millimeter antitank and antiaircraft guns, quadruple 7.62 Maxims, and several self-propelled rocket-launchers, including the M-8 36-rail, 80-millimeter, and the Katyusha model M-13/A 16-rail, 130-millimeter rocket-launcher. In the immediate postwar period the ZIL-150 truck chassis was used as a mount for the model M-13 rocket-launcher and the ZIL-151 truck was used as a mount for the M-31 rocket-launcher. In addition, the ZIL-151 truck was used as a prime mover for the 82-millimeter gun.

In 1953 the ZIL-151 truck was adapted for several other weapons, including the BM-24, 240-millimeter, 12-tube rocket-launcher; the RM-131-millimeter, 32-tube rocket-launcher; the BM-14, 140-millimeter, 16-tube rocket-launcher, and the 200-millimeter, 4-tube rocket-launcher.

A decade later the ZIL-157 truck became the mount for the GOA-SA-2 antiaircraft missile. In 1963 the same truck became a prime mover for another rocket system, as did the ZIL-135.

The ZIL plant has also produced unarmored cargo and troop vehicles for the Soviet Army. In 1932 the ZIL-33 was developed. This was an unarmored half-track used as a troop carrier. In 1936 the ZIL-6 was developed as a half-track and during World War II the ZIL-42 was developed as a 2½-ton tracked weapons carrier. In the postwar period the ZIL-151 truck chassis was adapted for the BTR-152 armored troop carrier. In the 1950s the ZIL-485 was developed. This was a replica of the American DUKW mounted on a ZIL-151 truck, and it was followed by an improved DUKW mounted on a ZIL-157 truck.

From 1954 onwards new versions of the BTR-152 were added, based on the ZIL-157 truck. Later in the 1960s a new BTR-60 (8 x 8) amphibious personnel carrier was developed with a ZIL-375 gasoline engine.

Other ZIL vehicles are also used for military purposes. For example, the ZIL-111 is used as a radar and computer truck for antiaircraft systems and as a tow for the M-38 short 122-millimeter howitzer. The ZIL-111 is copied from Studebaker 6 x 6 trucks supplied under Lend-Lease.

There is a great deal of interchangeability between the military and civilian versions of the ZIL family of vehicles. For example, an article in *Ordnance* states:

> In the 1940s the ZIL-151, a 2½-ton 6 x 6 was the work horse of the Soviet Army. It was replaced in the 1950's by the ZIL-157, an apparent product improved version. In the 1960's however this vehicle class requirement was met by the ZIL-131 a 3½-ton 6 x 6 vehicle, essentially a military design. It is of interest to note that a civilian version was marketed as the ZIL-130 in a 4 x 2 configuration. Over 60 percent of the components in the military version are common to the civilian vehicle.

Thus the ZIL plant, originally designed and rebuilt under the supervision of the A. J. Brandt Company of Detroit in 1930 and equipped by other American companies, was again expanded by Budd and Hamilton Foundry in 1936. Rebuilt with Lend-Lease equipment, ZIL has had a long and continuous history of producing Soviet military cargo trucks and weapons carriers.

On April 19, 1972, the U.S. Navy photographed a Russian freighter bound for Haiphong with a full load of military cargo, including a deck load of ZIL-130 cargo trucks and ZIL-555 dump trucks (*Human Events,* May 13, 1972). Thus the "peaceful trade" of the 1930s, the 1940s, the 1950s, and the 1960s comes home in the form of the means to kill Americans in Vietnam.

The original 1930 equipment was removed from ZIL in 1944 and replaced by Lend-Lease equipment, which in turn was supplemented by other imports in the 1950s and 1960s. The

Urals plant at Miass (known as Urals ZIS or ZIL) was built in 1944 and largely tooled with equipment evacuated from the Moscow ZIL plant. The Urals plant started production with the Urals-5 light truck, utilizing an engine with the specifications of the 1920 Fordson (original Ford Motor Company equipment supplied in the late 1920s was being used, supplemented by Lend-Lease equipment). The Urals plant today produces weapons models: for example, a prime mover for guns, including the long-range 130-millimeter cannon, and two versions—tracked and wheeled—of a 12-ton prime mover.

American Equipment for the Volgograd Plant

Although the military output of Gorki and ZIL is well known to U.S. intelligence and therefore to successive administrations, American aid for construction of even larger military truck plants was approved in the 1960s and 1970s.

The Volgograd automobile plant, built between 1968 and 1971, has a capacity of 600,000 vehicles per year, three times more than the Ford-built Gorki plant, which up to 1968 was the largest auto plant in the USSR.

Although Volgograd is described in Western literature as the "Togliatti plant" and the "Fiat-Soviet auto plant," and does indeed produce a version of the Fiat-124 sedan, the core of the technology is American. Three-quarters of the equipment, including the key transfer lines and automatics, came from the United States. It is truly extraordinary that a plant with known military potential could have been equipped from the United States in the middle of the Vietnamese War, a war in which our enemies received 80 percent of their supplies from the Soviet Union.

The construction contract, awarded to Fiat S.p.A. included an engineering fee of $65 million. The agreement between Fiat and the Soviet government included:

The supply of drawing and engineering data for two automobile models, substantially similar to the Fiat types of current production, but with the modifications required by the particular climatic and road conditions of the country; the supply of a complete manufacturing plant project, with the definition of the machine tools, toolings, control apparatus, etc; the supply of the necessary know-how, personnel training, plant start-up assistance, and other similar services.

All key machine tools and transfer lines came from the United States. While the tooling and fixtures were designed by Fiat, over $50 million worth of the key special equipment came from U.S. suppliers. This included:

1. Foundry machines and heat-treating equipment, mainly flask and core molding machines to produce cast iron and aluminum parts and continuous heat-treating furnaces.
2. Transfer lines for engine parts, including four lines for pistons, lathes, and grinding machines for engine crankshafts, and boring and honing machines for cylinder linings and shaft housings.
3. Transfer lines and machines for other components, including transfer lines for machining of differential carriers and housing, automatic lathes, machine tools for production of gears, transmission sliding sleeves, splined shafts, and hubs.
4. Machines for body parts, including body panel presses, sheet straighteners, parts for painting installations, and upholstery processing equipment.
5. Materials-handling, maintenance, and inspection equipment consisting of overhead twin-rail Webb-type conveyers, assembly and storage lines, special tool sharpeners for automatic machines, and inspection devices.

Of course, some of this equipment was on the U.S. Export Control and CoCom lists as strategic, but this proved no setback to the Johnson Administration: the restrictions were arbitrarily abandoned. Leading U.S. machine-tool firms participated in supplying the equipment: TRW, Inc., of Cleveland supplied steering linkages; U.S. Industries, Inc., supplied a "major portion" of the presses; Gleason Works of Rochester, New York (well known as a Gorki supplier) supplied gear-cutting and heat-treating equipment; New Britain Machine Company supplied automatic lathes. Other equipment was supplied by U.S. subsidiary companies in Europe and some came directly from European firms (for example, Hawker-Siddeley Dynamics of the United Kingdom supplied six industrial robots). In all, approximately 75 percent of the production equipment came from the United States and some 25 percent from Italy and other countries in Europe, including U.S. subsidiary companies.

In 1930, when Henry Ford undertook to build the Gorki plant, contemporary Western press releases extolled the peaceful nature of the Ford automobile, even though *Pravda* had openly stated that the Ford automobile was wanted for military purposes (see page 118). Notwithstanding the naive Western press releases, Gorki military vehicles were later used to help kill Americans in Korea and Vietnam.

In 1968 Dean Rusk and Walt Rostow once again extolled the peaceful nature of the automobile, this time in reference to the Volgograd plant. Unfortunately for the credibility of Dean Rusk and Walt Rostow, there exists a proven military vehicle with an engine of the same capacity as the one produced at the Volgograd plant. Moreover, we have the Gorki and ZIL experience. Further, the U.S. government's own committees have stated in writing and at detailed length that *any* motor vehicle plant has war potential. Even further, both Rusk and Rostow made explicit statements to Congress denying that Volgograd had military potential.

It must be noted that these Executive Branch statements were made in the face of clear and known evidence to the contrary. In other words, the statements must be considered as deliberate falsehoods to mislead Congress and the American public.

134

The War Potential of the Kama Truck Plant

Up to 1968 American construction of Soviet truck plants was presented as "peaceful trade." In the late 1960s Soviet planners decided to build what is going to be the largest truck factory in the world. This plant, situated on the Kama River, will have an annual output of 100,000 multi-axle 10-ton trucks, trailers, and off-the-road vehicles. It was evident from the outset, given the absence of adequate Soviet technology in the automotive industry, that the design, engineering work, and key equipment for such a facility would have to come from the United States.

In 1972, under President Nixon, the pretense of "peaceful trade" was abandoned and the Department of Commerce admitted (*Human Events,* Dec. 1971) that the Kama plant will have military potential. Not only that, but according to a department spokesman, military capability was taken into account when the export licenses were issued.

So far, Export-Import Bank direct loans for Kama amount to $86.5 million, and Chase Manhattan Bank of New York anticipates it will grant loans up to $192 million. In March 1973, contracts had been granted to Swindell-Dressler Co. for the Kama foundry ($14 million), and to Combustion Engineering Inc. for molding machines ($30 million). Other companies involved are Ingersoll Milling Machine Co., Rockford, Ill.; E. W. Bliss Co., Salem, Ohio; Warner & Swasey Co., Cleveland; LaSalle Machine Tool Inc., Warren, Michigan; and Wickes Machine Tool of Saginaw, Michigan.

The Soviets have no indigenous truck-manufacturing technology. The Soviet trucks on the Ho Chi Minh trail are from Western-built plants and Kama is projected to build 100,000 multi-axle heavy trucks per year—more than the output of all U.S. heavy-truck manufacturers combined. The historical evidence is strong and clear. The United States has built for the Soviets a capability for military trucks and wheeled, armored, and weapons-carrying vehicles. This construction job has taken forty years and was undertaken with full knowledge of the military potential of any vehicles production industry. Further, this knowledge has been censored and not given to either Congress or the American public.

Finally, the evidence suggests that successive administrations have made misleading and untruthful statements when challenged on the export of equipment with military potential to the USSR. Moreover, in 1972 President Nixon's administration was sufficiently self-confident to admit that current exports to the Soviets did indeed have military potential, although the precise technical nature of these exports was still being kept from Congress and the public.

CHAPTER EIGHT
Peaceful Explosives, Ammunition, and Guns

The idea of "gun control" in a free society is an absurdity. The ONLY reason for the disarming of the populace is the control of the populace, . . . those "humanitarians" who express their concern for the unfortunate victims of the coercive use of firearms by criminals have no concept of "liberty" other than something granted for the "common good" as THEY see it . . . The responsibility of liberty cannot be faced by these men—the very concept of "responsibility" is repugnant to them, witness the fact that these are invariably the same men who blame "society" for the acts of criminals. Their theme is common guilt. Their purpose is common slavery.

LIBERTARIAN HANDBOOK, 1972, p. 97

It is fascinating to observe how, more often than not, the most vocal proponents of trade with totalitarian countries are also the most vocal proponents of gun control. Let's see how "peaceful trade" has helped to build up the Soviets' (uncontrolled) weapons stock.

How the Soviets Make Nitrocellulose

Propellant powders for use in ammunition, rockets, and other projectiles require specific chemicals and organic materials and the associated manufacturing facilities. These materials comprise purified cellulose, which is manufactured from cotton, wood pulp, or other cellulose by-products; concentrated nitric and sulfuric acids; ethyl alcohol; and double-based nitroglycerine for use in rockets. High explosives also require ammonia and ammonium nitrate. These are the basic materials used in propellants and explosives manufacture and in each case we can trace present Soviet technology and capacity back to a Western—usually American—source (see Table 8.1).

TABLE 8.1
SOVIET ACQUISITION OF CHEMICAL TECHNOLOGIES FOR EXPLOSIVES MANUFACTURE

Technology	Western Process and Firm	Soviet Plant
Nitrogen fixation	Nitrogen Engineering Corp (U.S.A.)	Berezniki (1929–32)
	Nitrogen Engineering Corp (U.S.A.)	Bobriki (1929–32)
	Casale Ammonia S.A. (Italy)	Dzerdjinski (1927)
	Fauser (Italy)	Gorlovka (1930)
Nitric acid	Du Pont Company (U.S.A.)	Five plants (one erected before 1930 plus 1/350,000 tons p.a.)
Sulfuric acid	Bersol (Russo-German Company)	Samara
	Hugo Petersen (Germany)	
	Lurgie Gesellschaft für Chemie und Hüttenwesen m.b.H. (Germany)	

Sources: 1. V. I. Ipatieff, *Life of a Chemist*, Stanford, 1946.
2. U.S. State Dept. Archives.
3. German Foreign Ministry Archives.

In mid-1930 an agreement was concluded between the Soviets and the Hercules Powder Company of Wilmington, Delaware, for technical assistance in the production of nitrocellulose and cotton linters for explosives manufacture. Under the agreement Hercules Powder was required to "communicate the secrets of production and indicate all the production methods of bleaching common as well as oily cotton linter, first and second cut of any viscosity." This had to be done in Soviet plants, and for this purpose Hercules sent engineers to the USSR and received three Soviet engineers annually into its own plants for periods ranging from three to six months. For nitrocellulose manufacture Hercules Powder Company agreed to:

> prepare a complete design of a nitrocellulose plant for the production of 5,000 tons yearly, arranged so as to enable the Vsekhimprom to double production in the future. The design shall be according to the method used in the plants of the Hercules Powder Co. and shall include all the mechanical appliances of production and all the technical improvements of the present time.[1]

The complete design includes a description of the technological process, a description of the equipment, and the dimensions of the buildings, in addition to working drawing of the apparatus and buildings which would enable Soviet construction organizations to erect buildings for the production of nitrocellulose.

Zaeringer, in his *Soviet Space Technology* (pages 11–12), points out that Soviet rockets use "Russian cordite" containing 56.5 percent nitrocellulose, which is similar to British and American propellants. So, says Zaeringer, "United States and USSR propellant compositions were close by experimental coincidence and similar technology."

Nitrocellulose is also the most commonly used ammunition propellant. Witness the following propellants in Russian ammunition:

> Revolver, 7.62-mm. (M-1895)—nitrocellulose flake
> Submachine gun, 7.62-mm. (tracer and API)—nitrocellulose flake
> Rifle and machine gun, 7.62-mm. (models after M-1908)—cylindrical nitrocellulose.
> Heavy machine gun, 12.7 mm. (models after M-1930)—tubular nitrocellulose

---

[1] U.S. State Dept. Decimal File, 861.659/Nitrocellulose.

Antitank rifle, 14.5 mm. (models after M-1932)—tubu-
lar nitrocellulose

A brief glance at the list of Russian weapons in use in Korea
and Vietnam (p. 146) will readily make apparent the link between our export of explosives technology and the weapons
used against us in Korea and Vietnam.

One of the great achievements of American technology in the
1920s was the development of the technique of handling the
very great pressures and temperatures necessary for the production of synthetic ammonia. This achievement introduced a new
low-cost method of manufacturing nitric acid—an essential raw
material in the manufacture of explosives. There was only a
small production of nitric acid in tsarist Russia, while in 1920,
eight small plants produced barely 360 tons per year. In 1927
more than two-thirds of U.S. nitric acid was being used for
explosives, and today nitric acid is, for example, the oxidizer in
the operational Soviet T-7A rocket. Nitric acid can be manufactured either in special plants or in fertilizer plants converted
for its manufacture. The North Vietnamese nitrate fertilizer
plant was long ago converted to manufacture of nitric acid for
explosives.

Synthetic nitrogen technology came to the Soviet Union in
part from the Nitrogen Engineering Corp. A company letter
in the State Department files states:

> Since the Soviet Government was already copying
> equipment patented by NITROGEN and adopting
> various processes worked out by NITROGEN and
> since, in view of the peculiar nature of Soviet patent
> laws, no effective steps could be taken to prevent them
> from so doing, I [Colonel Pope] assented to a provision
> in this contract which gave the Soviet Government the
> right to employ the processes of NITROGEN and to
> use its patents for a period of five years.

By 1934 the Soviets had become obligated to Nitrogen Engineering Corp. to the extent of $1 million for this technology. By the late 1930s the Nitrogen Engineering–designed complex at Berezniki employed 25,000 workers and manufactured thermite, powder, and nitroglycerin.

In the early 1930s, the Soviets began negotiating with Du Pont for the purchase of the firm's ammonia oxidation and nitric acid technologies. Du Pont had expended over $27 million developing these processes. In requesting advice from the State Department, Du Pont argued that the process was neither secret nor covered by patents, that the end-use of nitric acid is the manufacture of fertilizer, that if Du Pont did not supply the process it could be bought elsewhere, and that several plants had already been erected in the USSR by Casale and Nitrogen Engineering of New York.

The letter from Du Pont to Henry L. Stimson of the State Department with reference to the proposed contract (dated April 20, 1929) states in part, "It is true of course that nitric acid is used in the manufacture of munitions." Du Pont then claimed, "It is impossible to distinguish between chemicals used for strictly commercial purposes and chemicals used for strictly munitions purposes." And as justification for its proposal, the firm said, "We submit that the contemplated contract will in no way give assistance for the manufacture of munitions which cannot easily be acquired elsewhere by the Soviets."

Further, the company argued, there was nothing exclusive about the Du Pont process. The copy of the agreement in the State Department files indicates that the Soviet Union:

> [wishes] to use in Russia the Du Pont process for the oxidation of ammonia and [Du Pont] to place at its disposal sufficient data with respect to the design, construction and general information as to permit the satisfactory operation of such plants ... the Company shall serve the Russian Corporation in an advisory capacity and furnish upon request services of engineers and chemists so as to accomplish the purpose of the contract.

The agreement further stipulated that the Soviets might use the Du Pont processes for the oxidation of ammonia to manufacture 50–65 percent nitric acid and that Du Pont agreed "to place at the disposal of Chemstroi sufficient data, information and facts with respect to the design, construction and operation of such plants as will enable Chemstroi to design, construct and operate ammonia oxidation plants."

Later in 1932, negotiations were concluded between Du Pont and the Soviets for construction of a gigantic nitric acid plant with a capacity of 1,000 tons per day. This approximates 350,000 tons annually. Twenty-five years later, in 1957, the largest Du Pont–process nitric acid plant in the United States, at Hopewell, had an annual capacity of 425,000 tons. Under its earlier contract Du Pont was also obliged to supply technical assistance to the USSR for a period of five years. The firm inquired of the State Department whether this plant of "excessively large capacity" would meet with objections from the U.S. government: "While we have no knowledge of the purpose of the proposed plant, yet the excessively large capacity contemplated leads us to believe that the purpose may be a military one."[2]

The State Department position is summarized in a memorandum of April 6, 1932, which reviewed export of military materials to the Soviet Union and concluded that the department would have no objection to construction of such a large nitric acid plant.[3]

In the late 1950s and 1960s, the Soviets lagged in all areas of chemical production outside the basic chemical technology absorbed in the 1930s and 1940s. This lag had major military implications and between 1958 and 1967 inspired a massive purchasing campaign in the West. In the three years 1959–61 alone, the Soviet Union purchased at least fifty complete chemi-

[2] U.S. State Dept. Decimal File, 861.659, Du Pont de Nemours & Co/5, Du Pont to Secretary of State Stimson, Feb. 19, 1932.

[3] U.S. State Dept. Decimal File, 861.659, Du Pont de Nemours & Co/1–11.

cal plants or equipment for such plants from non-Soviet sources. Indeed, the American trade journal *Chemical Week* commented, with perhaps more accuracy than we then realized, that the Soviet Union "behaves as if it had no chemical industry at all." Not only was Soviet industry producing little beyond basic heavy chemicals but, of greater consequence, it did not have the technical means of achieving substantial technical modernization and expansion in a product range essential for a modern military state.

Western firms, then, supplied designs and specifications, process technology, engineering capability, equipment, and startup and training programs. These contracts were package deals that provided more than the typical Western "turn-key" contract. Such contracts are unusual in the West (except perhaps in underdeveloped areas lacking elementary skills and facilities) but were very attractive and highly profitable to Western firms.

Many of the chemical plants built in the 1960 program had direct military applications. In 1964 a British company—Power Gas Corporation, Ltd.—built a $14 million plant for the manufacture of acetic acid in the USSR. Hygrotherm Engineering Ltd. of London contracted to supply an automatic heating and cooling plant (with heat generators, circulating pumps, and control equipment) and other equipment for use in the manufacture of synthetic resins. In 1960 a plant was supplied for the production of synthetic glycerin, which is used in explosives manufacture. Other plants were for the production of ethyl urea (one plant, 1,000 tons per year), synthetic fatty acids (one plant, 5,000 tons per year), sodium tripolyphosphate (one plant), carbon black (one plant), and germanium (two plants). All these products have military end-uses.

Sulfuric acid, the most important of inorganic acids and industrial chemicals, is required in large quantities for explosives manufacture. Production of sulfuric acid in Russia increased from 121,000 tons in 1913 to just under 3,000,000 tons in 1953, 4,804,000 tons in 1958, and 8,518,000 tons in 1965.

The Soviets have always utilized basic Western processes for the manufacture of their supply of sulfuric acid and have duplicated the equipment for these processes in their own machine-building plants. A recent Russian paper on sulfuric-acid manufacture indicates that in the mid-1960s, 63 percent of sulfuric-acid production was carried out according to a standardized version of a Western process. The remainder was produced by a "Soviet process" (utilizing fluidized bed roaster, electric precipator, towers, and contact apparatus) similar to the contact processes in use in the West. In 1965 Nordac Ltd. of the United Kingdom sold a sulfuric-acid concentration plant with a capacity of 24 tons per day of 78 percent sulfuric acid to update Soviet sulfuric acid technology.

Up to 1960, Russian output of fertilizers was mostly in the form of low-quality straight fertilizers. There was no production of the concentrated and mixed fertilizers that are used in the West. Fertilizer plants are easily converted to explosives plants. Part of the fertilizer expansion program of the 1960s was the purchase from the Joy Manufacturing Company of Pittsburgh of $10 million worth of equipment for potash mining. Congressman Lipscomb protested the issue of a license for this sale (*Congressional Record,* Aug. 28, 1963). While Lipscomb pointed out that potash can be used for manufacture of explosives, Forrest D. Hockersmith, of the Office of Export Control in the Department of Commerce, replied, "Our decision to license was heavily weighed by the fact that potassium fertilizer can best be characterized as 'peaceful goods' " (Aug. 21, 1963). Hockersmith did not, of course, deny that potash had an explosives end-use.

A series of ten fertilizer plants for the Soviets was arranged by the Occidental Petroleum Corporation (Armand Hammer's company) and built by Woodall-Duckham Construction Company, Ltd., and Newton Chambers & Company, Ltd., of the United Kingdom. Other fertilizer plants were built by Mitsui of Japan and Montecatini of Italy. Ammonium nitrate, an ingredient in fertilizer manufacture, also has an alternate use in explosives manufacture. It is used for example in 60/40 Amatol in the explosive warheads of the T-7A rockets.

A highly significant factor has gone unnoticed in the discussion of "peaceful trade." Fertilizer plants can produce explosives. The conversion procedure is known and straightforward. The only nitrate fertilizer plant in North Vietnam had been producing explosives for years—until knocked out of action by U.S. bombers. Whether fertilizer plants are used for explosives depends, of course, on *intent*. But if Soviet intent is hostile, then the "fertilizer plant construction program" can equally well be termed the "explosives plant construction program."

Origins of Soviet Machine Guns

During the 1920s the Soviets undertook a secret aircraft machine-gun development program. This program yielded the Shkas class of aircraft machine guns, first produced in 1933, and followed by the standard version (KM-35) after 1935. The gun was capable of firing 1,800 rounds per minute and was believed by the Soviets to be the best in existence. Chinn, in his *The Machine Gun* (Washington, D.C., 1952), states that "the Shkas is an innovation based on the features of the Maxim (ejection and buffer), the Szakats (rotating feed) and the Berthier (piston actuated, propped breech, locking)." All these systems originated in the West. The Shvak, a very light and extremely compact automatic aircraft gun, with a range comparable to that of the U.S. M-3 cannon, was based on the operating principles of the French Berthier. This came about because during the 1933 French-Soviet "entente," the French sent machine-gun experts to the Soviet Union and their work developed the Shvak class.

The Shkas aircraft machine gun was replaced in 1940 with the 12.7-millimeter Beresin, copied from a captured Finnish Lahti 20-millimeter machine cannon. The VYa 23-millimeter aircraft cannon was a scaled-up version of the Finnish Beresin.

According to Chinn, "the Russians demonstrated great skill in adapting at low cost the best of time-proved principles to their particular needs." Their weapons were characterized by extreme simplicity of design and rough exterior finish but some Soviet weapons were probably the best in their class in World War II.

The Maxim, a famous Western gun, underwent various modifications by Soviet designers: the Maxim-Tokarev, the Maxim-Koleshnikov, and the Maxim-Esivnin. The Maxim Model-1910 became the basis of almost half of the Soviet's 1944 machine-gun production, as is shown below:

Soviet Machine Gun Production (1944)

Maxim machine gun	270,000
Degtyarev infantry machine gun	120,000
Degtyarev tank machine gun	40,000
Degtyarev Shpagin heavy machine gun	50,000
	(for anti-
	aircraft use)
Goryunov machine gun	10,000
Shkas aircraft gun	40,000
Beresin aircraft gun	60,000
Total:	590,000

The Soviets did introduce some innovations. The Goryunov (SG-43) machine gun was hailed as an entirely new weapon, but although some of its features were new to Russian weaponry, it used principles and patents originated earlier by designers in other countries. For example, the operating principle of the Goryunov gun was patented but never used by John M. Browning. The gun also had a Mauser-type extractor and ejector. Most Soviet machine guns developed in the post–World War II period have a modified Kjellman-Friberg operating system.

Soviet machine gun development through the late 1960s can be summarized as follows:[4]

[4] G. M. Chinn, *The Machine Gun* (Washington: U.S. Department of the Navy, Bureau of Ordnance, 1952), Vol. II, Part VII.

Weapon	*Based On*
Maxim-Tokarev	
Maxim-Koleshnikov	Maxim Model-1910
Maxim-Esivnin	
SG-43 (Goryunov)	Browning Patent No. 544657
	Mauser-type extractor, ejector
Degtyarev	Mauser locking; Vickers feed
	Maxim ejection and buffer,
	Szakats (rotating feed)
Shkas aircraft gun	Berthier (piston actuated
	propped breach, locking)
Shvak aircraft cannon	Berthier action
Beresin aircraft gun	Finnish Lahti 20-mm.
V-Ya aircraft cannon	Scaled-up version of the Lahti

Soviet Weapons Used against Americans in Vietnam

Weapons used against the United States and its allies in Vietnam were largely of Soviet manufacture or origin, utilizing the traditional propellants discussed earlier in this chapter.

The following is a list of the more important types of Soviet weapons used against the United States in South Vietnam:

Rocket-Launchers
Soviet 122-mm. rocket-launcher
Soviet 140-mm. launcher and rocket
Soviet 140-mm. rocket-launcher BM-14
Soviet 140-mm. rocket-launcher M-1965
Soviet 140-mm. rocket-launcher BMD-20
Soviet 240-mm. round rocket-launcher on AT-S
tractor

Antitank and artillery weapons
Soviet 14.5-mm. AT rifle PTRS-41
Soviet M-1943 57-mm. antitank gun
Soviet 76-mm. field gun M-1943

Soviet 85-mm. field gun D-44
Soviet 122-mm. howitzer D-30
Soviet 122-mm. howitzer M-1938 (M-30)
Soviet 130-mm. field gun M-46
Soviet 152-mm. howitzer M-1937 (M-20)
Soviet 70-mm. support gun SU-76

Antiaircraft guns
Soviet 15.5-mm. AA machine gun ZPU-2
Soviet 14.5-mm. AA machine gun ZPU-4
Soviet 23-mm. AA gun ZU-23
Soviet 57-mm. self-propelled AA gun ZPU-57-a
Soviet 57-mm. AA gun S-60
Soviet 85-mm. AA gun KS-12
Soviet 100-mm. AA gun KS-19

Moreover, there are numerous Czech weapons manufactured by Skoda in Vietnam, including the Czech 130-millimeter rocket-launcher (R17-130-32), the 45-millimeter launcher (P-27), and the Czech 17.7-millimeter antiaircraft machine gun (M38/46).[5] For details of U.S. assistance to Skoda while the Vietnamese war was in progress, see pages 88–89.

In brief, we can trace the origin of the propellants of the Soviet ammunition used in Vietnam (and all Soviet ventures before Vietnam) to America. Further, we find that the American companies involved—Du Pont, Hercules Powder, and Nitrogen Engineering—were aware of the military applications of their exports at the time the contracts were signed. Even if valid, the argument used by these companies—that the Soviets could obtain the technology elsewhere—was not based on principle. When it comes to mens' lives, principle alone should reign. In practice, American businessmen and the Washington policymakers have rigidly excluded from the discussion any factors that might militate against sales of technology or equipment. We have paid the price.

[5] Granville N. Rideout, *The Chi-Com Series* (Boston: Yankee Publishing Co., 1971).

CHAPTER NINE
Helping the Russians at Sea

Q: Does the Soviet Navy worry you?
A: The Soviet Navy is dramatically more powerful than it was 10
   years ago. You can trace, almost to the moment the point at
   which the Soviets began their tremendous construction
   program...
            ADMIRAL ELMO R. ZUMWALT, JR., Chief of Naval Operations,
            in U.S. NEWS & WORLD REPORT, Sept. 13, 1971

Admiral Zumwalt, Chief of Naval Operations, recently expressed deep concern over the massive Soviet Navy and merchant marine construction program. The admiral's concern is
real enough—there has been a dramatic increase in Soviet naval
power in the last decade. On the other hand, almost no one
has expressed concern for the verifiable fact that *we* in the
West provided the technical and economic means for this
dramatic Soviet buildup. This chapter will outline our contribution to the dramatic performance of the Russians at sea.

Soviet Facilities for Construction of Naval and Merchant Vessels

Ship and submarine construction requires sheet steel, steel
plate, and steel sections in numerous specifications. Armor-
plate is produced by rolling high-alloy steel, which is then heat-

treated to develop its ballistic properties. Multiple layers of such plates can be used for armor protection. Therefore, assistance to the Soviet iron and steel industry—which is significant and continuing—is also assistance to Soviet ship-construction programs.

A U.S. government agency report has asserted that "any shipyard capable of building a merchant ship hull is equally capable of building a combatant ship of the same length." The report also states that merchant ships can be designed for conversion into naval ships, and that in any event the facilities required to build a steel merchant ship are exactly the same as the facilities required to build a steel warship. The main differences are the armament and the varying specifications for engines and other equipment. Almost 70 percent of the present Soviet merchant fleet has been built outside the Soviet Union. This has released Soviet shipyards and materials for Soviet naval construction. All diesel engines in Soviet merchant ships use a technology originating outside the Soviet Union.

The Soviets provided 80 percent of the supplies for the North during the war in Vietnam. Most of these supplies were transported by merchant ship. The ocean-going capacity required to supply the North Vietnamese on this scale and so keep them in the war was dependent upon ships previously built outside the USSR. Technology of U.S. origin has been a prominent feature in this foreign supply of ships for Soviet strategic use. While the supply of such maritime technology was formally forbidden by Congress, grossly inefficient administration of the export control laws allowed the Soviets to acquire a massive military transportation capacity.

Role of the United States and Its Allies in Building the Soviet Navy before World War II

Only one Soviet battleship was built before World War II—the *Tretii International* ("Third International"), laid down on July 15, 1939 in the Leningrad yards. This was a 35,000-ton

battleship. The guns, turrets, armor, and boilers were purchased in the United States and Germany, and the ship was
completed in the late 1940s. Other prewar Soviet battleships—
the *Marat, Kommuna,* and *Oktyabrskaya Revolutsia*—were re-
conditioned and refitted ex-tsarist vessels. Attempts to build
three battleships of the Italian *Vittorio Veneto* class came to
nothing.

Three aircraft carriers were under construction at the end of
the 1930s. The *Stalin* (formerly the tsarist *Admiral Kornilov*)
was a 9,000-ton ship built in 1914, redesigned in 1929, and
completed in 1939 as an aircraft carrier. Two other carriers of
12,000 tons each were built "on the basis of American blue-
prints"—the *Krasnoye Znamye* and the *Voroshilov,* laid down
at Leningrad in 1939 and 1940.

Several World War II Soviet cruisers were refitted tsarist-era
vessels, including the *Krasni Kavkaz* (formerly the *Admiral
Lazarov,* built in 1916 at Nikolaev), the *Profintern* (formerly
the *Svetlana,* built in 1915 at Reval [now Tallinn] and refitted
in 1937), and the *Chevonagy Ukraina* (formerly the *Admiral
Nakhimov,* built in 1915). The first Soviet attempt at cruiser
construction was the *Kirov* class of 8,000 tons. Three ships were
laid down in 1934–35 with Tosi engines manufactured in Italy
and the ships were built according to Italian plans at Putilovets
(the *Kirov* and *Maxim Gorki*) and at Nikolaev (the *Kuibyshev*)
under the technical direction of Ansaldo, an Italian firm.

There were three categories of Soviet destroyers before World
War II. First, there were fourteen tsarist vessels—four in the
Petrovski-class (built in 1917–18), nine in the *Uritski*-class
(built in 1914–15), and one ex-*Novik* (built in 1911). Second,
some new classes of destroyers were built under the Soviets to
French and Italian designs. Between 1935 and 1939, fifteen
destroyers of 2,900 tons each, based on French drawings, were
built as the *Leningrad*-class: six in the Leningrad yards, eight
on the Black Sea, and one at Vladivostok. The first units, supervised by French engineers, were quite similar to French vessels.

The third category encompassed the *Stemitelnie*-class, the
largest Soviet destroyer class of the 1930s. Between 1936 and
1939, thirty-five of these 1,800-ton ships were built under

Italian supervision, mainly in Leningrad and the Black Sea yards, utilizing an Italian Odero-Terni-Orlando design and some British machinery. Their engines were Tosi (Italy) 50,000-shaft-horsepower geared turbines. In addition, the *Tashkent,* another Odero-Terni-Orlando design, was built in Italy—the only Soviet surface warship built abroad in the 1930s.

In January 1939 the American firm of Gibbs and Cox, naval architects, was requested to design two destroyers in addition to the 45,000-ton battleship already under design for the Soviet Union in the United States. In July of the same year General Electric and Westinghouse signified their intention to quote on the propulsive units for these destroyers.

From 1939 to 1941 the Soviets received German military assistance. The Nazis sent the partly finished cruiser *Lützow,* laid down at Bremen in 1937, and in May 1941 the latest available report was that the "construction of the cruiser 'L' in Leningrad was proceeding according to plan." In the Leningrad yards German technicians took over construction and repair of several large Soviet ships. This cooperation lasted for eighteen months, from late 1939 until May 1941.

All told, in 1941 the Soviet fleet comprised 3 battleships, 8 cruisers, 85 destroyers and torpedo boats, 24 minelayers, 75 minesweepers, 300 motor torpedo boats and gunboats, and 250 submarines. Most of these were built in the West or to Western designs.

Lend-lease added 491 ships to this total: 46 110-foot submarine chasers and 59 65-foot submarine chasers, 221 torpedo boats (24 of them from the United Kingdom), 77 minesweepers, 28 frigates, 52 small landing craft, 2 large landing craft from the United Kingdom, and 6 cargo barges. In addition to these combat vessels, Lend-Lease provided numerous merchant ships and marine engines.

In terms of tonnage, Lend-Lease probably doubled the size of the Soviet Navy. Only a small number of these naval ships have been returned, although the Lend-Lease master agreement required the return of all vessels.

Since World War II, assistance to the Soviet naval construction program has taken two forms—export of shipbuilding equipment and shipyard cranes from European countries, and to a lesser extent from the United States, and use of plans and designs obtained from the United States and NATO through espionage. For example, the sophisticated equipment of the U.S.S. *Pueblo,* transferred by the North Koreans to the USSR, was about fifteen years ahead of anything the Soviets had in the late 1960s. In other words, the *Pueblo* capture took the Soviets in one leap from postwar German and Lend-Lease technical developments to the most modern of U.S. technology.

Submarine Construction, 1920–1972

Extensive tsarist submarine work was adapted by the Soviets at the end of the 1920s and a few tsarist-model submarines were still operating in 1940.

Soviet domestic construction began in 1928 with the L and M classes. The L-class was based on the British *L-55,* which sank off Kronstadt and was raised by the Soviets; twenty-three of the L-class and one L-Special were built to this model by 1938. The M-class, a small 200-ton coastal submarine of limited performance, was made possible only by the introduction of electric welding under the terms of the General Electric technical-assistance contract.

All subsequent Soviet submarine development has been heavily influenced by German U-boat designs and more recently by U.S. designs. In 1926 a German naval mission under Admiral Spindler visited the USSR and provided the plans of the most successful German submarines, details of operational experience, and the services of German submarine experts. The Russians obtained sets of U-boat plans, the most important of which were those of the B-III type, one of the most successful designs for a conventional submarine ever produced. As the type-VII the B-III was the backbone of the German U-boat fleet in World War II. A variant of the design was built in Russia— first known as the N-class—nicknamed *Nemka* ("German girl")—and later as the S-class. The *Chuka*-class was based on German B-III plans; the S-class (enlarged *Chuka*) is the German type-VII U-boat.

Italian influence came in two submarine classes. The eight vessels in the *Garibaldi*-class were of Adriatico design and the seventeen *Pravda*-class submarines were a development from the *Garibaldi*. Two submarines were bought from Vickers-Armstrong in the United Kingdom in 1936, and the Soviet V-class comprised Vickers-Armstrong submarines built in the United Kingdom in 1944 and transferred to the USSR under Lend-Lease.

The United States sold submarine equipment to the Soviet Union in the first five or six years of the 1930s. A proposal was received by the Electric Boat Company of Groton, Connecticut, in January 1930 for the construction of submarines and submarine ordnance equipment for shipment to the USSR. In a letter to the Secretary of State, Electric Boat argued that there was "no objection" to the construction of submarines for such "friendly foreign powers," and further said that this was in the interest of the Navy as it kept domestic shipbuilders at work. The State Department, though admitting there was no legal restriction on shipments of munitions to the Soviet Union, said it viewed "with disfavor" the construction of periscopes, submarines, and ordnance equipment for shipment to the Russians.

There was also a flow of American technology under the Sperry Gyroscope technical-assistance contract for marine instruments, and many Soviet engineers were trained by the company in the United States, although attempts in 1937–38 to buy fire-control equipment were thwarted by Navy Department officers. By 1937 Electric Boat was negotiating with the Soviets for construction of submarines, this time with the blessing of the State Department.

The massive postwar expansion of the Soviet submarine fleet has depended upon the designs and technical and construction resources of Germany and the United States. After World War II the Soviets carefully studied German submarines and operational techniques. Using equipment and material received under Lend-Lease, and transferring complete shipyards and great quantities of submarine-building equipment from Germany, a large submarine construction program was undertaken—a program still in progress.

In 1972 the Soviet W-class attack submarine accounted for about half of the Soviet submarine fleet. The W-class is a direct copy of the successful German type-XXI U-boat. The vessel has a 1,621-ton displacement and is capable of traveling 11,000 miles without refueling. Although the Germans built 120 type-XXI boats by early 1945, few went to sea. Almost all of these completed submarines fell into Soviet hands. Thus a substantial portion, perhaps one-quarter, of the Soviet submarine force was built in Germany to German construction standards. A modification of type-XXI became the Soviet Z-class, slightly larger, with greater range. The most modern Soviet diesel-powered submarine, the F-class, was also developed from these advanced German designs.

Early Soviet nuclear-powered submarines are similar to the U.S.S. *Nautilus* in configuration. The Soviet Y ("Yankee")-class is copied from the U.S.S. *Polaris* ballistic missile submarine, with plans obtained through the massive Soviet espionage program in Great Britain. Submersibles for deep-sea work have been purchased in the West, the most recent sale being the Hyco *Pisces-IV* sold in 1972. Missile-carrying submarines are fitted with GOLEM-class missiles. GOLEM I and GOLEM II are direct descendents of the German V-2 while GOLEM III is a two-stage solid-fuel equivalent of the Lockheed Polaris.

The Strategic Merchant Marine of 1972

The Soviet merchant marine is an essential segment of the Soviet armed forces and in Soviet strategic plans it has the the prime function of carrying weapons and military supplies for Soviet ventures overseas—Korea, Vietnam, and Cuba being the most prominent of these.

There are two extraordinary facts about the gigantic and strategic Soviet merchant marine:

First: over two-thirds (68 percent to be exact) of its ship tonnage has been built outside the Soviet Union. The remaining 32 percent was built in Soviet yards and to a great extent with shipbuilding equipment from the West, particularly Finland and the NATO allies, Great Britain and Germany.

Second: four-fifths (79.3 percent to be exact) of the main marine diesel engines used to propel the vessels of the Soviet merchant marine were built in the West. In other words, only one-fifth of the main diesel engines were built in the USSR. Moreover, even this startling statistic does not reflect the full nature of Soviet dependence on foreign marine diesel technology because *all of the main engines manufactured in the USSR are built to foreign designs.* The full scope of the dependence of Soviet marine-diesel technology on foreign assistance is shown in Table 9.1.

The manufacture of marine diesels in the Soviet Union has received considerable foreign technical assistance. Technical-assistance agreements were made with both M.A.N. and Sulzer in the 1920s, and the Soviet Union has continued since that time to receive M.A.N. (Maschinenfabrik Augsburg-Nürnberg) and Sulzer technology. In addition, it negotiated new assistance agreements with Burmeister & Wain of Denmark and Skoda of Czechoslovakia in the fifties and sixties.

An important agreement was signed in early 1959 in Copenhagen by Niels Munck, managing director of Burmeister & Wain, and Mikoyan, who visited the company on his way back

TABLE 9.1
ORIGIN OF DIESEL ENGINES* OF SOVIET MERCHANT SHIPS

Size of Merchant Ship (Gross Registered Tonnage)	Engines of Foreign Design and Construction (percent)	Engines Soviet-built under Foreign License (percent)
15,000 and over	100	0
10,000–14,999	87.9	12.1
5,000–9,999	56.9	43.1

* This includes diesel-electric units but not steam turbines. The chart is based on gross registered tonnage, not rated capacity of the engines, therefore it is an approximate measure only.

to Moscow from a visit to the United States. The Danish company also has a licensing agreement with the Polish engine-manufacturers Stocznia Gdanska, and most of that organization's annual production of 350,000 bhp of B & W designs goes to the Soviet Union.

Under the 1956 scientific and technical cooperation agreement between the USSR and Czechoslovakia, the Skoda works send technical documentation and technical assistance to the USSR on the latest marine diesel designs. Skoda is also a major direct supplier of diesel engines to the USSR.

The available evidence strongly indicates that all Russky Disel (Leningrad) marine engines are made under the technical-assistance agreement with Skoda of Czechoslovakia, while all diesels at Bryansk are certainly built under the B & W agreement. Under the COMECON (Council for Mutual Economic Assistance of East European Countries) specialization agreements, Czechoslovakia undertakes development and production of large marine diesels while the Soviet Union is not listed for that responsibility—nor indeed for development or production of marine diesels of any size. The 1956 scientific and technical cooperation agreement required Czechoslovakia to send the USSR technical documentation for the manufacture of the latest designs in diesel engines. Further, Czechoslovakia is not only the fourth largest producer of diesel engines in the world—far larger than the USSR—but it also exports 80 percent of all its diesels, and the USSR is by far the largest buyer.

The most important diesel design in tonnage terms is from Skoda of Czechoslovakia. Engines built according to this design contribute a total of 630,000 horsepower to the Soviet merchant fleet. The next design in terms of contribution to aggregate horsepower is that of Bukau-Wolf, contributing 423,900 horsepower; this is numerically the most common unit. Other prominent designs are M.A.N. of Germany with 264,000 horsepower and Burmeister & Wain (the 11,000-horsepower unit), which contributes some 242,000 horsepower to the total.

All modern large diesels of more than 11,000 horsepower used in the Soviet Union are built to a single foreign design—

Burmeister & Wain of Copenhagen, Denmark. Denmark is a NATO ally of the United States. The export of this Danish technology could have been stopped by the State Department under the Battle Act and CoCom arrangement. All Burmeister & Wain diesels are designed with a U.S. Univac computer. Burmeister & Wain engines propelled the Soviet ships that were active in the Cuban Missile Crisis in 1962 and in the supply of North Vietnam from 1966 to date.

The State Department could also have intervened indirectly to restrict export of military technology by Eastern European Communist governments—for example, Skoda armaments—to the USSR and this was the very claim made by State to Congress in order to bring about trade liberalization. In 1966 Dean Rusk submitted legislation to Congress for "most favored nation" treatment for East European Communist countries. This would, said Dean Rusk, "give the United States an important political tool in Eastern Europe."[1] But the East European Communist countries went right on supplying North Vietnam and providing technical assistance for the Soviets, and the State Department maintained a steadfast blind eye to the military end-uses of this technical assistance to the Soviet Union. Indeed, State approved an important technical-assistance agreement made by Simmons, an American firm, with Skoda—which at the very time was supplying armaments to North Vietnam.

How the Soviets Have Used Their Western-built Merchant Marine

In the 1920s the Soviets used their merchant fleet to deport fellow Russians to slave labor camps. Three U.S.-built ships the *Svirstroi,* the *Volkhovstroi,* and the *Shatourstroi* were used by the NKVD to transport political prisoners. According to Dallin only about 1 or 2 percent of such political prisoners ever returned home from Siberia. These ships were used as transports

[1] *New York Times,* May 13, 1966.

from Black Sea ports to the Far East, from whence prisoners were transported overland to the Siberian forced labor camps.[2] The Dutch-built ship *Djurma* was also used to transport political prisoners to Siberia—and on one trip all 12,000 prisoners died en route.[3]

More recently, Western-built ships have been used to foment armed rebellions around the world. For example, the *Ristna* carried arms to rebels in Ghana in 1967.[4] This ship has West German engines built by M.A.N., and once again the State Department could have enforced the Battle Act and halted export of the engines under the CoCom agreements. More significant, however, is the use of Western technology in Soviet vessels supplying Cuba and North Vietnam.

State Department Approval for the Soviet Vessels That Carried Missiles to Cuba

The *Poltava*-class of Soviet merchant vessels, which is equipped with special hatches for the purpose, was used to carry missiles to Cuba in 1962. The main engines for the first two vessels in this class were manufactured by Burmeister & Wain in Copenhagen. Engines for the remaining eighteen ships in the class came from the Bryansk plant in the Soviet Union. Both the Danish and the Bryansk engines were built to the same specification: 740-millimeter cylinder diameter and 1,600-millimeter piston stroke. The Danish engines have six cylinders while the Soviet engines have seven cylinders; in all other respects they are identical Burmeister & Wain–design engines. In 1959 the Danish company made a technical-assistance agreement with the Soviets for manufacture of large marine diesels, not manu-

---

[2] A. Dallin and B. Nicolaevsky, *Forced Labor in Soviet Russia* (London: Hollin and Carter, 1947), p. 125; V. Kravchenko, *I Chose Justice* (New York: Scribner's, 1950), p. 290.

[3] Dallin and Nicolaevsky, *op. cit.,* p. 128.

[4] *Current Digest of the Soviet Press,* vol. 19, Mar. 29, 1967.

factured in the USSR at that time, and the U.S. State Department, through CoCom, approved the export of this technology as nonstrategic. As any member of CoCom has veto power, objection by State Department representatives would have effectively blocked the agreement.

The *Poltava*-class ships were used to carry Soviet missiles to Cuba in 1962. The first *Poltava* engines were manufactured in Denmark in 1959 and the ships entered service in 1962, only a few months before they were used for transporting missiles to Cuba. In other words, the first operational use of these diesel engines—approved by State as nonstrategic—was in a challenge to the United States which brought us to the brink of nuclear war. The *Poltava*-class ships have extra long hatches: eight of 13.6 meters length and 6.2 meters width: ideal for loading medium-range missiles.

After near nuclear conflict between the United States and the Soviet Union the Soviets removed their missiles—as deck cargo on other merchant ships. The *Labinsk* was one of the ships used. The *Labinsk* is a 9,820-ton freighter built in 1960 in Poland on Soviet account and has Italian engines, made by Fiat in Italy (8,000 bhp, eight cylinders, 750-mm. cylinder diameter, 1,320-mm. piston stroke). This is the same Fiat Company that later in the sixties provided technical assistance for the largest automobile plant in the USSR.

In 1962 the U.S. Navy photographed Russian merchant ships unloading missile supplies at the Cuban port of Mariel—then, and now, a Russian naval base in Cuba. These ships included the *Dvinogorsk,* an 8,000-ton freighter built in Poland on Soviet account with Dutch engines (7,800 bhp Sulzer diesels made by N. V. Werkspoor of Amsterdam). Holland is a NATO ally and again the export of such engines to the USSR is illegal and could have been halted by the State Department.

When we look closely at the transportation technology used to bring about the most dangerous international crisis in the last decade, we find that the U.S. State Department not only had the knowledge and the capability to stop the transfer but was required by law to ensure that the technology was not passed to the Soviets. In other words, there would have been no Cuban Missile Crisis in 1962 if the State Department had followed congressional instructions and carried out the job it is paid to do.

"Soviet" Merchant Ships on the Haiphong Supply Run

In 1967, while the Johnson Administration was campaigning for yet more "peaceful trade" with the Soviet Union, Soviet ships previously supplied by our allies as "peaceful trade" were carrying weapons to Haiphong to kill Americans (see Table 9.2).

TABLE 9.2
ANALYSIS OF SOME SOVIET SHIPS USED ON HAIPHONG RUN

Soviet Registration No.	Year of Construction	Name and GRT of Ship	Place of Construction	
			Engines	Hull
M26121	1960	Kura (4,084 tons)	West Germany	West Germany
M25151	1962	Simferopol (9,344 tons)	Poland	Switzerland
M11647	1936	Arlika (2,900 tons)	United Kingdom	United Kingdom
M17082	1962	Sinegorsk (3,330 tons)	Finland	Sweden
M3017	1961	Ingur (4,084 tons)	West Germany	West Germany
M26893	1952	Inman (3,455 tons)	East Germany	West Germany

In addition to the ships listed in Table 9.2, the *Kuibyshev*, a 6,000-ton freighter built in the United States, was unloading at Haiphong in August 1966 when American planes attacked. So was the *Sovetsk*, built in Poland with Swiss engines, and the *Ustilug*, a 4,400-ton freighter with West German M.A.N. engines.[5] A Soviet ship involved in an altercation with U.S. de-

[5] *Los Angeles Times,* May 7, 1967; *San Francisco Chronicle,* Aug. 6, 1966.

stroyers in 1966 was the *Ingur,* a 4,000-ton freighter built in West Germany in 1961 with a M.A.N. specification engine.

For further details of the Haiphong-run case, see Table 9.3.

As Table 9.3 shows, if the State Department had done an effective job according to the laws passed by Congress, thirty-seven of the ninety-six ships would *not* have been in Soviet hands—and would not have been able to take weapons and supplies to Haiphong.

Specifically, the State Department could have stopped the export of marine-diesel technology to the Soviets under the

TABLE 9.3

ENGINES OF SOVIET SHIPS ON HAIPHONG RUN AND ABILITY OF UNITED STATES TO STOP EXPORT UNDER BATTLE ACT AND COCOM*

Origin of Diesel Engines	Number of Engines Manufactured		Could Export Have Been Stopped?
	In USSR	*Outside USSR*	
Manufactured in USSR to Soviet Design			— —
Manufactured in USSR under license and to foreign design:			
Skoda (at Russky Diesel)	5		— No
Burmeister & Wain (at Bryansk)			8 Yes
Manufactured outside USSR to foreign design:	8		
Skoda (Czechoslovakia)		5	— No
M.A.N. (West Germany)		11	11 Yes
Fiat S.A. (Italy)		2	2 Yes
Burmeister & Wain (in Denmark and elsewhere under license)		8	8 Yes
Sulzer (Switzerland)		13	— No
Lang (Hungry)		4	— No
Görlitz (East Germany)		10	— No
United States (Lend-Lease)		7	7† Yes (?)
United States (not Lend-Lease)		1	— No
Krupp (Germany)		1	1 Yes
Total: Diesel engines	13	62	37 Yes

* See Appendix C.
† Lend-Lease—should be returned under the Master agreement.

TABLE 9.3 continued

Steam Turbines and Reciprocating Steam Engines	Number of Engines Manufactured		Could Export Have Been Stopped?
	In USSR	Outside USSR	
Manufactured in USSR to Soviet design	0		
Manufactured in USSR to foreign design	1 (possibly)		
Manufactured outside USSR:			
Canada		1	
United States		3	
United Kingdom		1	
Switzerland (Sulzer)		3	
Total: Steam turbines	1	8	
Grand Total: Diesel engines	75	Not identified	12
Steam turbines	9	Identified	84
	84		96*

* See Appendix C for names of these vessels.

Battle Act. The ships listed in Table 9.4 were used by the Soviets to supply Hanoi and have engines manufactured under the Burmeister & Wain technical-assistance agreement of 1959, that is, eight years after the Battle Act was passed by Congress.

Could the Soviets have used other ships? Turn to page 155. Over two-thirds of Soviet merchant ships and more than four-fifths of the marine diesels in Soviet merchant ships were *not* built in the USSR. The Soviets would certainly not have attempted foreign adventures with a merchant marine substantially smaller than the one they have now in operation. In other words, we have always had the absolute means to stop the Soviet tide of aggression—if that was our objective.

The provision of fast, large ships for Soviet supply of the North Vietnamese indicates where export control has failed. Segments of the Soviet merchant marine were examined to determine the relationship between Western origins and the maximum speed of Soviet ships. It was anticipated that because of the NATO limitations on the speed of merchant ships supplied to the USSR (reflected in the export control laws) that the average speed of NATO-supplied ships would be considerably less than ships supplied either by Eastern European countries to the USSR or built within the USSR itself. The results of an analysis of forty-two Soviet ships on the Haiphong supply run are as follows:

> Merchant ships with engines manufactured in the Free World, average speed 14.62 knots.
> Merchant ships with engines manufactured in Eastern Europe, average speed 13.25 knots.
> Merchant ships with engines manufactured in Soviet Union, average speed 12.23 knots.
> (All forty-two ships were built after 1951, the year the Battle Act was implemented.)

TABLE 9.4

HAIPHONG-RUN SHIPS WITH ENGINES MADE UNDER BURMEISTER & WAIN TECHNICAL-ASSISTANCE AGREEMENT OF 1959

Soviet Ship	Soviet Register No.	Year	Tonnage and Type	Engine Model No. (Burmeister & Wain)
Belgorod Dnestrovskiy	4776	1965	11,011 cargo	B & W774 VT2BF 160
Berezovka	5450	1967	10,996 cargo	B & W674 V12BF 160
Bryanskiy Rabochiy	569	1964	11,089 cargo	B & W774 V12BF 160
Partizanskaya Slava	5492	1967	10,881 cargo	B & W674 V12BF 160
Pavlovsk	2127	1964	11,089 cargo	B & W774 VT2BF 160
Perekop	2172	1963	11,089 cargo	B & W774 VT2BF 160
Polotsk*	2232	1963	9,500 cargo	B & W774 VT2BF 160
Pridneprovsk	2268	1964	11,089 tanker	B & W774 VT2BF 160

* Lloyd's indicates built at Bryansk; Soviet Register indicates built in Denmark.

Source: U.S. Naval Institute Proceedings, January 1970.

The most obvious point to be made is that the average speed of Western-supplied ships used by the Soviets on the Haiphong run was 2.4 knots (i.e., about 20 percent) above that of Soviet domestic-built ships on the run. This includes only those ships built after 1951 (i.e., after implementation of the Battle Act and its limitation of speed and tonnage on ships supplied to the USSR).

The illegal administration of the Battle Act also applies to weight limitations—the faster, larger Soviet ships are from the West and the slower, smaller ships are from domestic Soviet shipyards.

Under the CoCom machinery each nation participating in the embargo of strategic materials submits its own views on the shipment of specific items. There is also a unanimity rule. In other words, no item may be shipped to the USSR unless all participating nations agree. Objections by any nation would halt shipment. Douglas Dillon, former Under Secretary of State, has pointed out, "I can recall no instance in which a country shipped a strategic item to the Soviet bloc against the disapproving vote of a participating member of CoCom."

It must therefore be presumed that the United States delegates approved the export of ships of high average speed, as well as marine diesel engines and the Burmeister & Wain technical-assistance agreement of 1959 for Soviet manufacturers of marine diesels, all of which were later used against the United States by the Soviets in supplying North Vietnam.

It is clear from this evidence alone that successive administrations have been long on words but short on action to stop the Soviets from carrying out their world ambitions. Further, successive administrations have committed American soldiers to foreign wars without the resolve to win and obviously in the knowledge that American technical assistance was being provided to both sides in these wars.

Under CoCom arrangements in the Battle Act, the State Department can enter an objection to CoCom concerning any technological exports to the Soviet Union. No CoCom member can make such exports over the objection of any other member of CoCom. In other words, if the State Department had wanted to implement the intent of Congress, it had the ability to stop the transfer of marine engines and marine engine technology to the USSR. It did not do so. The result was that thirty-seven out of the ninety-six Soviet ships on the Haiphong run had Western-built engines, manufactured after 1951, which could have been restricted by the State Department.

Even further, other Soviet ships have marine diesels originating in Czechoslovakia (Skoda), Hungary (Lang), and East Germany (Görlitzer), countries for which State has demanded most favored nation status and trade as a "political weapon." If there is indeed a polycentralist trend, then why was the State Department unable to stop the flow of military technology to the Soviet Union? It had the political weapon (trade) it asked for to do the job.

In brief: the State Department had the means to stop the transfer of marine-diesel technology. The department was required to do so under the law. It did not do so. These ships carried the weapons and supplies to North Vietnam to kill Americans and their allies. The blame in this tragic case is squarely at the door of the State Department.

We may therefore derive two conclusions:

1. The Soviet Union could not have supplied North Vietnam without assistance from the United States and its Western allies. This assistance takes the form of technology transferred through the vehicle of trade.
2. The State Department had the absolute means to stop this transfer through its veto power in CoCom. It did not do so.

The position is more serious than even these conclusions would suggest, because the State Department has excellent—and expensive—intelligence facilities. The department was therefore aware of item (1) above. It is also aware of its powers in CoCom. Yet a departmental spokesman went before Congress to make the following statement:

> If there were no trade at all between West and East, the Soviet Union would still be perfectly competent to supply North Vietnam with its requirements, many times over. I think the proposition that our restrictions or any restrictions on trade with Eastern Europe can defer or affect in any significant way the ability to supply North Vietnam is simply wrong.

This bland assertion, without evidence, of course, was made to the Senate by Philip H. Trezise, present Assistant Secretary for Economic Affairs in the department. Trezise has been described by Senator Mondale as "one of the most remarkable men that this Committee could hear from." That is certainly an accurate statement.

The most charitable conclusion we can draw about State Department officials like Dean Rusk, Edward Martin, Philip Trezise, Charles Yost, and the host of others involved in these CoCom decisions is that they are mystics. Mystics incapable of assessing evidence and arriving at logical conclusions in the national interest. These officials have substituted fantasy for reality. Emotion for logic. Altruism for rational self-interest. When challenged they are evasive and untruthful.

These are the men to whom America has entrusted the administration of its foreign affairs. When Admiral Zumwalt says the Soviet Navy is dramatically more powerful, he is correct. We have to do more than raise the alarm, we must fire as incompetent the officials who have brought about this dramatic and tragic situation.

CHAPTER TEN
From the "Ilya Mourometz" to the Supersonic "Konkordskiy"

The aircraft industry was lagging well behind the West owing to constant political interference, political purges, and the general low level of technical efficiency. Consequently, at the end of World War II the Soviets had not produced a single jet engine or guided missile.

GENERAL G. A. TOKAEV, Red Army

British and French aeronautical engineers have their own name for the new Russian Tu-144 supersonic plane. They call it the "Konkordskiy." A comparative glance at the configurations of the Anglo-French Concorde and the Russian Tu-144 will—even without supporting evidence—readily explain the nickname.

Yet tsarist Russia produced and successfully flew the world's first four-engined bomber, a quarter of a century before the United States developed one. This early bomber had a wing span of over 100 feet, or only 21 inches less than that of the World War II Boeing B-17 Flying Fortress. In 1913 in St. Petersburg, Igor Sikorsky (who later founded the Sikorsky Aircraft Company in America) designed the "Russki-Vityazyi." Weighing 5 tons with a load of seven passengers, this four-engined plane established a contemporary endurance record of

1 hour and 54 minutes aloft. By 1917 a fleet of seventy-five IM ("Ilya Mourometz") four-engined bombers, based on the original 1913 model, were in service—several decades before the American four-engined bomber fleets of World War II.

Obviously there was nothing wrong with indigenous Russian aeronautical talent half a century ago. While Russians have a natural affinity and geographic impulse towards aeronautics, the Soviets have only kept up with the West by prolific "borrowing" and heavy importation of technology and manufacturing equipment. Russian dependence on Western aeronautical design and production equipment and techniques goes back to the early 1920s.

At that time, soon after the Bolshevik Revolution, the Russian aircraft industry depended heavily on foreign aircraft and engine imports. There was considerable Soviet design activity, but this work was not converted into usable aircraft technology. Consequently, in the early 1930s the Soviet stock of military planes was almost completely foreign: 260 fighters comprising 160 De Havilland Type 9a (from Great Britain) and 100 Heinkel HD-43 fighters (from Germany); 80 Avro 504-K training biplanes (from Great Britain) and some Moraine-Saulnier monoplanes (from France); 52 R-3 biplanes (Russian TsAGI design); 20 R-6 reconnaissance planes (Russian TsAGI design); 242 I-4 Jupiter-engine planes (from Great Britain); 80 Ju-30 and ANT-6 (Junkers design); 20 ANT-6 bomber seaplanes (Russian design); 18 Avro-504L seaplanes (from Great Britain); 40 Savoia S-62 scouting flying boats (from Italy); 150 Heinkel HD-55 scouting flying boats (from Germany); 46 MR-5 (Savoia S-62 license) flying boats (from Italy); 12 TBI (Russian TsAGI design); and 43 Ju-30 naval bombers (from Germany).

From about 1932 onward, and particularly after 1936, there was extensive acquisition of Western aeronautical advances, which were then integrated with the developments of the 1920s. Fortuitously for the Soviet Union, this much-needed acquisition coincided with a period of increased competition among

Western aircraft manufacturers. In many cases, military aircraft were designed in the West on Soviet account and the heavy, slow, underpowered designs of the early 1930s were replaced by efficient Western designs.

By 1937 the Soviet government was convinced that the American method of building aircraft was the best for Russian conditions, as the American system of manufacture could more easily be adapted to mass production than any of the European systems. The United States thus became the main source of Soviet aircraft technology, particularly as the builder of new Soviet aircraft plants. Between 1932 and 1940 more than twenty American companies supplied either aircraft, accessories, or technical assistance for complete planes and aircraft-manufacturing plants. Technical-assistance agreements were made for Vultee attack bombers, the Consolidated Catalina, the Martin Ocean flying boat and Martin bombers, Republic and Sikorsky amphibians, Seversky amphibians and heavy bombers, Douglas DC-2 and DC-3 transports, the Douglas flying boat, and other aircraft. Kilmarx has well summarized this acquisition:

> The objectives of the Soviet Union were more straightforward than its methods. By monitoring aeronautical progress and taking advantage of commercial practices and lax security standards in the West, the Russians sought to acquire advanced equipment, designs, and processes on a selective basis. Emphasis was placed on the legitimate procurement of aircraft, engines (including superchargers), propellers, navigational equipment, and armament; specifications and performance data; design, production and test information and methods; machine tools; jigs and dies; semi-fabricates and critical raw materials. Licenses were obtained to manufacture certain modern military aircraft and engines in the U.S.S.R. At the same time, a number of Soviet scientists and engineers were educated at the

best technical institutes in the West. Soviet techniques also included assigning purchasing missions abroad, placing inspectors and trainees in foreign factories, and contracting for the services of foreign engineers, technicians and consultants in Soviet plants.[1]

The First Commercial Plane Able to Fly the Atlantic Nonstop

By 1937 the Soviet Union possessed the world's first commercial plane able to fly the Atlantic Ocean nonstop, with a payload of 7,500 pounds. Known as the Martin Ocean Transport, Model-156, with four 1,000-horsepower Wright Cyclone engines, it was built by the Glenn L. Martin Company of Baltimore. Model-156 cost the Soviet Union $1 million. Although capable of being flown directly to the Soviet Union, it was flown only to New York, then was dismantled and shipped to the USSR by boat.

Also in 1937 the Martin Company agreed to design a Soviet bomber. Loy Henderson, the U.S. chargé in Moscow reported:

> . . . since January 1, 1937, the Embassy granted visas to fourteen Soviet engineers and specialists who are proceeding to Baltimore to the Glenn L. Martin factory. This information would appear to be significant in view of the statements that the Martin Company is to design and develop a new type of large plane for the Soviet air force instead of selling somewhat obsolete models which may have been released for export by the American military authorities . . .[2]

[1] R. A. Kilmarx, *A History of Soviet Air Power* (New York: Praeger, 1962).

[2] U.S. State Dept. Decimal File, 711.00111—Armament Control/1384, Nov. 4, 1938.

Bombers and Amphibians from Seversky Aircraft Corporation

In May 1937 the *New York Times* reported a $780,000 Soviet contract with Seversky Aircraft Corporation involving construction of, and manufacturing rights for, Seversky amphibians, which then held the amphibian world speed record of 230.4 miles per hour. Under a technical-assistance agreement, Seversky Aircraft provided assistance for manufacture of these planes in the Soviet Union at the rate of ten per day.

Alexander P. de Seversky, president of the company, then informed the State Department that the Soviets had contracted to purchase from the company a large number of bombing planes of a new type to be designed by him. After being informed that a license would be granted if the planes involved no military secrets, Seversky suggested that the War and Navy Departments might object to its exportation "merely" on the ground that the new bomber would be superior to any bombing plane then in existence. Seversky indicated that he intended to address his request for an export license to the State Department, "in hope that the Department might expedite action in this."[3]

The Consolidated Aircraft Company (Catalina), Douglas, and Vultee

The first domestic flying boats under the Soviets were constructed at Leningrad and Taganrog. In 1932 Plant No. 23 in Leningrad produced 18 Avro 504-L seaplanes and 40 Savoia S-62 scouting flying boats, the latter under a license from the Società Idrovolanti Alta Italia of Milan—an outstanding designer of high-performance flying boats. Also in 1932, Taganrog Plant No. 31 produced 196 flying boats: 150 scouting HD-55s

[3] U.S. State Dept. Decimal File.

and 46 MR-5s, both built under license from Heinkel. The Soviets also acquired a license from the Macchi Company of Italy to produce the MBR series of Russian flying boats.

Then in 1937 came an agreement with the Consolidated Aircraft Company of San Diego for technical assistance for Catalina flying boats under supervision of Etienne Dormoy. With the Catalina flying boat we once again see the extraordinary ability of the Soviets to acquire anything they set their hearts on. The very *first* commercial Consolidated PBY ("Catalina") off the assembly line in San Diego was sold to the American Museum of Natural History—which promptly transferred it to the Soviets.[4] This is not the first time the American Museum of Natural History turns up in the Soviet files. In 1919 a shipload of Soviet propaganda was seized—en route to the United States and addressed to the American Museum of Natural History.[5]

Also in 1937–38 the Vultee Aircraft Division of Aviation Manufacturing Corporation of Downey, California, built a fighter aircraft plant for the Soviets in Moscow.

Equally as important, the Soviets acquired rights to build the famous Douglas DC-3, probably the most successful transport plane in the history of aviation. Donald Douglas produced his first DC-3 in March 1935 and within one year the Soviets decided this was to be the basic transport plane for the USSR. A technical-assistance agreement with the Douglas Aircraft Company was signed on July 15, 1936 for three years. Within thirty days of contract signature, Douglas delivered the blueprint materials required to fulfill the assistance contract.

In October 1937 the Soviet aircraft industry placed a $1.15 million order with Douglas for additional parts, tools, assemblies, and materials. The order included one complete DC-3 in subassembly and another in "first-stage" production. In addition, aluminum extrusions were ordered for another fifty aircraft, together with two complete sets of raw materials and twenty-five sets of finishing materials ranging from ash trays to

[4] *Aircraft Year Book, 1938,* p. 275.
[5] U.S. State Dept. Decimal File, 316–25–684.

zippers. Construction facilities, ordered at the same time, included one complete set of 6,485 templates, a set of 350 lead and zinc drop hammer dies, three sets of hydraulic mechanisms, all the necessary wood and plaster patterns, drill and assembly fixtures, a complete set of drophammer stamps, hydraulic-press parts, two crowning machines, and a set of 125 special tools. Later, another six complete transports were purchased, but it was not until 1940, four years after the agreement, that the Soviets got any domestic DC-3s (renamed the PS-84 or the LI-2) off a Soviet assembly line.

For input materials for military aircraft operation and construction the Soviets also depended on American construction assistance and technology. Even after the extensive American construction of refineries in the early 1930s the Soviet Union continued to be dependent on American technology for cracking petroleum into light gasoline fractions. Lend-Lease equipment deliveries brought the output of aviation gasoline from a mere 110,000 metric tons per year in 1941 to 1.67 million metric tons in 1944, despite the fact that several Lend-Lease cracking units were not delivered until after the end of the war. The Standard Oil Company of New York supplied the Soviet Union with technical information, plant designs, and a pilot manufacturing plant for sulfuric acid alkylation for production of 100-octane gasoline, and "voltolization" of fatty oils for production of aviation lubricating oils.

Efficient and specialized tools were developed by American aircraft-manufacturers and their equipment suppliers and these in turn were purchased by the Soviets. For example, in 1938 the Lake Erie Engineering Corporation received a Soviet order for six hydraulic presses for forming metal aircraft sections. In the same year, Birdsboro Steel Foundry and Machine Company of Birdsboro, Pennsylvania, filled a half-million-dollar order for hydraulic presses for aircraft manufacture. Similarly, in 1938 the Wallace Supplies Manufacturing Company of Chicago, Illinois, sold seven bending machines "specially designed to bend tubing for aircraft and parts of motors" for $34,000. Most, if not all, Soviet aircraft accessories were straight copies of foreign products. When biplanes were used, "the streamline wires [were] of English pattern, landing wheels of Palmer type, bomb-releases . . . of their own design, and the duralumin machine-gun rings . . . of French pattern. Aircraft fuel pumps were the French A.M. type and mobile starters were the Hucks type."

At the request of the State Department and the Buckeye Pattern Works of Dayton, Ohio, the Secretary of War granted "release of Records of Tests made of certain aluminum exhaust stacks at the Aviation Depot at Wright Field, Dayton, Ohio, for benefit of the Russian Soviet Government." No military objections were made to the production of Wright aeronautical engines in Russia, and to an application by Sperry Gryoscope to sell bombsights. Nor was objection made to export of Type D-1 and D-2 oil bypass relief valves in 1935 by the Fulton Sylphon Company of Knoxville. The Stupino plant also manufactured U.S. Hamilton 2-blade and 3-blade variable-pitch propellers for military aircraft.

The United Engineering and Foundry Company contracts of January 1938 exemplify the advanced nature of the aircraft materials technology supplied by Western firms to the Soviet Union. Indeed, some of these projects strained the research and development abilities of the most advanced Western firms and were far beyond the capability of the Soviet Union at that time. The contracts do suggest, however, that the Soviet Union has had remarkable ability to recognize advanced military aircraft technology and enlist front-rank foreign firms in the acquisition process. The January 1938 United Engineering agreement involved the sale of $3 million worth of equipment and technical assistance for aluminum mills at Zaporozhe. These were 66-inch (1,680-mm.) hot and cold mills complete with auxiliary equipment—the most modern aluminum mills in the world. Jenkins, the United Engineering chief engineer in the USSR, said of the Zaporozhe mill that "not even the Aluminum Company of America has machinery as modern as it is." Both mills were "completely powered and controlled by General Electric apparatus."

The Stupino mill (Plant No. 150) near Moscow, by far the most important Soviet aluminum-development project, was also the subject of an agreement in May 1939 between Mashinoimport and United Engineering and Foundry for installation of hot and cold rolling mills. These were mills of extraordinary size to produce aluminum sheet for aircraft manufacture.

The Stupino installation comprised two sections: a hot mill and a cold mill. The hot mill had two units. One was a 2-high 66-inch hot rolling mill for rolling cast duralumin, including aircraft specification Type 17-S and 24-S ingots. The 66-inch mill came into regular operation about February 1, 1940 and the 112-inch mill a few weeks later. The cold mill contained two mills of similar size for cold working sheets produced in the hot mill. The 66-inch cold mill started about March 1940 and the 112-inch cold mill late in 1940. All finishing equipment was supplied and placed in operation by United Engineering for the Soviets. The complete contract was worth about $3.5 or $4 million to United Engineering. For this sum the Soviets acquired an installation capable of rolling 2,000-foot aluminum sheets for aircraft. United Engineering said of it, "Nothing of such a size has ever been produced before."

During World War II the Soviets produced 115,596 aircraft from these materials and items of equipment while Lend-Lease delivered to the USSR only an additional 14,018. However, the Russian-produced aircraft were mainly obsolete prewar types and many were one-engine wood and canvas models with inferior engines. The full utilization of U.S. equipment came after World War II. Domestic production was assisted by a high degree of production specialization in a few plants with almost all foreign equipment. The only Soviet dive bomber, the Stormovik (IL-2), was in production at three plants; each plant produced about the same number of IL-2s but no other aircraft. Fighter production was concentrated on the YAK-3, the YAK-2 and YAK-6 being advanced trainer versions. The YAK was produced in six widely scattered plants producing only YAK aircraft at a rate of between 65 and 400 per month.

Two-engined bomber production included the PK-2 (based

on the French Potez) at two plants, and the IL-4 at three plants, of which only Komsomolsk (which Henry Wallace said was like the Boeing Seattle plant because it had all U.S. equipment) produced other aircraft. The LI-2 (Douglas DC-3) transport was produced only at Tashkent, and the PO-2 (or De Havilland Tiger Moth) was produced only at Kasan. Thus Soviet aircraft production was concentrated on a few types, each for a single flying function. Lend-Lease provided large quantities of advanced equipment for the development of the Soviet aircraft industry. Henry Wallace, after his visit to the important Komsomolsk aircraft plant, commented as follows:

> The aircraft factory in [Komsomolsk] where Stormovik bombers were built, owed both its existence and its production to the United States. All the machine tools and all the aluminum came from America. . . . It looks like the old Boeing plant at Seattle.

American and French Designs for Soviet Aircraft Engines

By acquiring rights to manufacture foreign engines under license and with Western technical assistance, the Soviets were able to acquire a sizable engine-producing capacity for high-quality engines at low cost. For example, in the 1930s, Plants No. 24 and 25 were built in Moscow. Plant No. 24 made Wright Cyclone engines under license and Plant No. 25 made parts for Wright engines. Table 10.1 summarizes Soviet production of aircraft engines in 1940. All Soviet engines were foreign models produced under license.

Before this production program was established, prototypes of every Western aircraft engine were purchased (or stolen). These acquisitions were minutely examined and copied, or composite "Soviet" designs were built incorporating the best features of several foreign engines. A report by Bruce Leighton of Curtiss-Wright describes one of these early Soviet models at the Engine Research Institute in 1931:

> They've taken Packard, Conqueror, Rolls-Royce, Kestral, Hispano-Suiza, Fiat, Isetta-Franchini—tested them all, analyzed them down to the minutest details, including microphotographs of piston rings, flow lines in crank shafts, etc., taken good features of all, added some ideas of their own (particularly regards valve cooling) and built-up [sic] an engine which we're going to hear more of or I miss my guess.

In 1944, in the entire world, there were about 130 basic types and 275 variations of aircraft engines, either in production or recently in production. Each of the three Soviet engine-types was an adaptation of a foreign engine built under a licensing agreement. The M-63 liquid-cooled 9-cylinder radial model was developed from the 1936 M-25, in turn developed

TABLE 10.1
SOVIET AIRCRAFT-ENGINE PRODUCTION (1940)

Plant	Model No. of Engines Manufactured	Western Licenser of Engine Manufactured	Monthly Production
Aircraft motor works No. 29 Baranov	M-85, followed by M-87B and M-88	Gnome et Rhône (France)	130
Aircraft motor works No. 24 Frunze and No. 25	M-25, then M-63 and M-64	Curtiss-Wright (U.S.A.)	250
Aircraft motor works No. 26 Aviatroi Pavlov	M-100, M-103, then M-105P and M-105R	Hispano-Suiza (France)	270
Aircraft motor works No. 10, Tula	M-17, then M-38	BMW (Germany)	Not known

Source: German OKW files.

from the Wright Cyclone, and used in the Soviet Consolidated Catalina patrol plane. The M-88 was a 14-cylinder air-cooled radial engine based on the French Gnome-Rhône 14-N, used in DB bombers, SU dive bombers, and PS transport planes. The third engine type was the M-105, a 12-cylinder liquid-cooled V-type of 1,100 horsepower based on the French Hispano-Suiza 12-Y engine, and used in the PE dive bombers, YAK fighters, and L-760 transport planes.

The Wright Cyclone Engine in the Soviet Union

In 1931 the Curtiss-Wright liquid-cooled engine was the only liquid-cooled American engine still in production. The U.S. Army initially supported development but, dissatisfied with the basic design, cut off funds in 1932. Development support for two other liquid-cooled engines, including the Curtiss-Wright H-2120, was continued by the U.S. Navy. Testing and development continued from 1933 to 1936, when the Navy withdrew support and reverted to air-cooled engines. The second U.S. Navy–supported Curtiss-Wright project was a 12-cylinder V-engine known as the V-1800. This was intended to replace the Curtiss-Wright Conqueror, and successfully completed its testing in 1934. Shortly after this test was completed, the Navy was forced by lack of funds to abandon most of its high-speed program and stopped support of the V-1800. The V-1800 engine was then licensed to the Soviet Union, which funded further research work to raise the engine rating to 900 horsepower from the U.S. Navy's test rating of 800 horsepower. This work was done at Aircraft Engine Plant No. 24 (Frunze) in Moscow, with parts manufactured at Plant No. 25. By 1938 these plants were producing about 250 Wright Cyclones (the Soviet M-25) per month. A plant for manufacturing Cyclone engines was also built at Perm—it was twice the size of the Wright plant in the United States.

The Pratt and Whitney Aircraft Engine in the Soviet Union

The Soviet M-26 was based on the Pratt & Whitney Hornet. In July 1939 the corporation licensed the Soviet Union for production of the Pratt & Whitney Twin Wasp 1830 and the Twin Hornet 2180 aircraft engines. No further information has been found at this time.

The Gnome-Rhône (France) Engine in the Soviet Union

The Gnome rotary, manufactured by the Sociéte des Moteurs Gnome et Rhône, was one of the finest early aircraft engines. After World War I the Gnome Company purchased the license of the British Bristol Jupiter-II and during the decade of the 1920s the Gnome-Rhône engineering department was dominated by English engineers from the Bristol Aeroplane Company. After producing the Bristol Jupiter engine for some years, the Gnome Company came up with an improved engine of its own design, using American lined cylinders. This cross-fertilization of ideas led to the exceptional Gnome rotary engines of the 1930s, which were then adopted by the Soviets.

The Gnome-Rhône 114 was built at the Kharkov engine-building plant (Plant No. 29) and the French engine became Soviet models M-85, M-87B, and M-88. About 1,500 M-88s a year were produced by 1940.

Similarly, the French Hispano-Suiza engine was produced in Moscow at an enormous plant twice the size of either the Pratt & Whitney or the Wright factories in the United States, themselves gigantic. This French Hispano-Suiza engine became the Soviet M-105 engine.

The German and British Contribution to the Postwar Soviet Air Force

In 1945 and 1946 the Russian aircraft industry concentrated on mastering the achievements of the German aircraft industry as it had been developed from 1941 to 1943. The years immediately after 1946 witnessed a remarkable expansion in the Soviet industry, based on this and on additional British technical assistance. Technical assistance from the West flowed in from the United Kingdom, particularly through transfer of the Rolls-Royce Nene, Derwent, and Tay jet engine technologies, and from Germany via the transfer of about two-thirds of the enormous German wartime aircraft industry to the Soviet Union.

The postwar aviation and space industries in the USSR have their roots in German World War II aircraft and rocket developments. In 1945 the Germans had a large and relatively undamaged aircraft and rocket manufacturing industry that had been dispersed under threat of Allied bombing toward the eastern regions of Germany—the area later occupied by the Soviets, or transferred to the Soviets on July 1, 1945. Over two-thirds of this productive capacity fell intact into Soviet hands and was removed to the USSR.

The major design units of the German aircraft industry, including most of the Junkers, Siebel, Heinkel, and Messerschmidt plants, were transported to Podberezhye, about 90 miles north of Moscow. Professor Walter Baade of Junkers continued development of the Ju-287K (as the EF-125) after moving to Podberezhye and followed this with the T-140 and T-150 bombers. These were jets capable of carrying an atomic bomb and, according to one report, they could outperform the U.S. B-47. There were eleven major Junkers aircraft plants in the Soviet Zone and six of these are known to have been completely removed to the USSR, among them the main Otto Mader works two miles east of Dessau (where Professor Baade had been located), and the Aschersleben, Bernburg, Leopoldshall, and Schonebeck plants. Aschersleben was a fuselage-building plant in process of changing over to the production of the jet He-162; its instrument storeroom, "virtually intact," was placed under military guard by the U.S. Army until the Soviets were able to take it over for removal to the Soviet Union. Bernburg was also intact.

In 1944, the outstanding German rocket-plane designer Sanger was working on the Sanger-Bredt project to develop a long-range rocket aircraft. Former Russian General G. A. Tokaev recalls that in 1947 he was summoned to a Moscow conference at which Stalin said, "Von Braun, Lippish, Sanger, Tank and all kinds of other experts are working for the Allies, we must concentrate very seriously on German specialists."

Voznesensky then completed a draft decree, and read it aloud to the conference:

> The Council of Ministers of the U.S.S.R. decrees that a Government Commission shall be formed for the purpose of directing and co-ordinating scientific research into aviation problems, with special relation to piloted rocket planes and the Sanger Project. The Commission shall be composed of the following:
> Colonel General Comrade Serov (President)
> Engineer Lieutenant Colonel Comrade
>   Tokaev (Deputy President)
> Academician Comrade Keldysh (Member)
> Professor Comrade Kishkin (Member)
> The Commission shall leave immediately for Germany, to undertake its preliminary work. A full report of its activities, and of the results it has attained, must be rendered to the Council of Ministers by August 1st.
> Marshal of the Soviet Union Comrade Sokolovsky is hereby directed to give the Commission every assistance.
>
> Moscow, the Kremlin, April 17th, 1947[6]

[6] G. Tokaev, *Stalin Means War* (London: Weidenfeld & Nicolson, 1951), p. 158.

182

"A thorough examination of the Sanger Project was invaluable," said Tokaev, because "of the experience such research would give our scientists in solving related problems and preparing a base for future activities. In other words, by mastering Sanger's theories our experts would be able to begin where he had left off."

Despite these high-level efforts, Professor Sanger was never captured by the Soviets, although the transfer involved almost all other German projects and technologies under development in 1945.

A troublesome gap in 1945 Soviet technology was modern fighter aircraft. Dr. Siegfried Gunther and Professor Benz, both developers of German fighter aircraft, were removed to the USSR. Gunther had been chief designer for Heinkel and a designer of jet fighters since the late 1930s, while Benz designed the German He-162 Volksjager jet fighter.

Among the Soviet acquisitions in Saxony was the Siebel works at Halle, where the experimental rocket-powered research aircraft DFS-346 (comparable to the U.S. Bell X-1 and X-2 and the Douglas X-3) was in final assembly. This work was continued at Halle on behalf of the Russians until October 1948, when it was moved to the OKB-2 combine at Podberezhye with technicians from the Junkers, Heinkel, and Siebel plants. Flight testing of versions built in the USSR was begun in early 1948 using a Lend-Lease North American Mitchell B-25 bomber and later a Boeing B-29 Superfortress as mother aircraft. The first test pilots were Germans, later replaced by Russian pilots.

The aircraft-manufacturing facilities removed from Germany contained some unique equipment. Two German Wotan presses of 15,000 tons were taken and at least four copies were made in the Soviet Union and other units developed from these presses. Aircraft-equipment-manufacturing plants included the former Nitsche plant at Leipzig, used in the USSR to manufacture curve potentiometers, and the Karl Zeiss plant, for position-finders, wind-tunnel parts, and various precision instruments. It is estimated that in 1954 this segment of the wartime

German aircraft industry supplied about 75 percent of Soviet radar equipment and precision instruments.

The Boeing B-29 Four-engined Bomber Becomes the Tu-4 and the Tu-70

During World War II the United States was unwilling to send four-engined heavy bombers to the Soviet Union under Lend-Lease. Although in April 1944 General John R. Deane recommended U.S. approval of Russian requests for heavy bombers, the War Department refused on the grounds that the Soviets could not train a bombing force prior to the spring of 1945 and that certain special equipment for such bombers was in short supply. The official State Department Lend-Lease report on war aid (see Bibliography) lists Russian acquisition of only one four-engined bomber (a B-24 that force-landed in Siberia), although the Soviets were in fact able to acquire four B-29s by retaining force-landed bombers in the Far East.

The Soviets then started work on the Tu-4 four-engined bomber and the Tu-70 civilian-transport version. In 1946 Amtorg attempted to purchase from the Boeing Aircraft Company a quantity of B-29 tires, wheels, and brake assemblies. In 1947 the Soviets produced the Tupolev Tu-70, which was immediately identified as a direct copy of the Boeing B-29. The similarity has been described in *Boeing Magazine:*

> The famed Boeing 117 airfoil on the Tu-70 is an exact replica of the Boeing B-29 wing. Along with the wing are the Superfortress nacelles: outline, cooling air intake, auxiliary air scoop, cowl flaps and inboard and outboard fairings. The cabin cooling air inlet in the wing leading edge between the body and the inboard nacelle is the same. The trailing edge extension on the flap between the inboard nacelle and the side of the fuselage are also identical, according to the evidence provided by the photographs.

On the landing gear, Boeing comments:

> The Tupolev Tu-70 uses the Twenty-nine's main landing-gear structure as well as its fairings and doors. The nose gear also appears to be that of the Superfortress, with the upper trunnion located closer to the body contour of the Tu-70 than on the Boeing bomber.

The tail surfaces of the Russian transport also came directly from the Boeing engineering department. On comparison it is apparent that the vertical tail and the dorsal outline as well as the leading edge of the rudder are the same on the two planes. The rudder of the Tu-70 appears to end at what would be the top of the tail-gunner's doghouse on the Superfortress. The shape of the stabilizer and the elevator is the same on the two planes, and the Tu-70 also uses the inverted camber of the B-29's tail.

The propellers of the Tupolev Tu-70 were original B-29 props, less cuffs. The hubs are characteristic of the Hamilton-Standard design. Boeing engineers also report that the drift-meter installation of the Russian transport looked like that of the Superfortress, as did the pitot head type and location match-up.

The Soviets did design a new fuselage, higher on the wing of the Tu-70 than the fuselage of the B-29, larger in diameter, and a little longer (119 feet as compared to 99 feet). The Tu-70 transport retains the bomber nose, including the bombardier's plate-glass window.

How did the Soviets advance from an inability to produce modern bombers in 1940 to an ability to produce a workman-like design requiring an extensive period of research and flight testing in 1947? Even if the finest designs were available, jigs and dies to put the plane into quantity production were also required. The 18-cylinder Wright engines for the B-29 had been extremely difficult to manufacture—even in the United States. Further, the Soviet's only experience in the production of four-engined bombers was the very unsuccessful Tupolev PE-8. We also know that in 1940 the Soviets had enormous difficulties putting the DC-3 twin-engined transport plane into production and repeatedly came back to the Douglas Aircraft Company for aluminum sections, parts, and technical advice.

Obviously, the record of a great deal of our assistance to the Soviets still lies buried in U.S. government files. One area worthy of research is the so-called "special programs" under Lend-Lease—unpublicized and still classified.

Aircraft Plant No. 1 at Kuibyshev

Aircraft Plant No. 1 at Kuibyshev, built by Lend-Lease during World War II, absorbed the equipment from the Junkers facility at Bernburg, which was transferred from Germany along with Junkers engineers, designers, foremen, and test pilots. The function of the plant was to utilize the emerging German jet technology to build the first Soviet jet fighters and bombers. The Soviet designers Tupolev and Gurevich began by visiting German aircraft factories to examine their prototypes and production methods. The Junkers Company organized an exhibition of secret German aircraft projects and arranged for tours of inspection. Equipment was then removed under the program of OKBs (Osoboye Konstruktorskoye Byuro): OKB No. 1 was at the Junkers plant in Dessau.

The bulk of the German engineers and scientists were moved to Russia by train on the night of October 22–23, 1946, in what was probably the largest mass movement of scientific brains in the history of the civilized (or the uncivilized) world. These engineers and scientists were divided into small groups of about fifteen persons, with about thirty Russian engineers attached to each German nucleus for study and work. Each project was handled by stages—the draft stage, the technical project stage, and finally the presentation stage. Whenever a project was almost complete it was canceled by the Soviets and the related drawings, papers, biographies, and technical material were turned over by the Germans. Duplicate work was undertaken by separate all-Russian groups some distance from the location of the original German pilot-groups. In addition German groups were put in competition with each other.

Most German designers and engineers in the aeroengine industry were sent to Kuibyshev Plant No. 1. They came mainly from the Junkers and BMW plants, no less than 800 engineers and technicians from these two companies alone. Among the members of the BMW contingent was Kurt Schell, former head of the BMW rocket laboratory, and engineers Winter, Kaul, Schenk, Tietze, Weiner, and Muller. The Junkers group led by Walter Baade was the most important. Dr. Baade, formerly chief engineer of Junkers with ten years experience in American aeronautical plants, was fully familiar with American methods of aircraft construction. With Dr. Baade was a group of engineers including Feundel, Haseloff, Wocke, Elli, Lilo, Rental, Hoch, Beer, Antoni, Reuss, Heising, and Hartmann.

The Junkers engine team in the Soviet Union was headed by Dr. Scheibe, who designed the Junkers P-1 turbine; he was assisted by engine designers Gerlach and Pohl, who at Dessau had been in charge of the engine testing department. Also in the Scheibe group were Steudel and Boettger and a large number of personnel from the Junkers turbojet department, including engineers, foremen, and skilled workers. Another prominent designer, Ernst Heinkel, worked in the Soviet Union at the Kalinin Experimental Station.

The Junkers plant itself was rebuilt at Kuibyshev, "almost exactly" as it had been in Leipzig.

Development of the First Soviet Jet Engine

German engineers were used to develop jet engines for the Soviets. First came reproductions of the Junkers-004 and the BMW-003 jet engines, which had been removed to the Soviet Union with their associated production equipment. The 004 became the Soviet RD-10, and the BMW-003 was produced as the Soviet RD-20 on a stop-gap basis until more advanced designs came along from British sources.

The first project given to the German design groups was a Soviet specification for a 3,000-horsepower jet engine, a development of the Junkers-012 turbojet, which had been in the design stage in Germany at the end of World War II. By 1947 the Junkers-012 had been developed as a 12-burner assembly, but operating inefficiencies halted development of this engine in 1948. The next project specification given to the German designers was for a 6,000-horsepower turboprop that could attain a speed of 560 miles per hour at sea level. This engine was developed from the Junkers-022 turboprop engine, with the same general design and characteristics as the 012. By 1949 the Brandner design teams had essentially met the Soviets' specification and immediately set to work on yet another project—a power plant with 12,000 horsepower in contrast to the 6,000 horsepower developed by the Junkers-022. Finally, the Type-K turboprop was developed by the Junkers-BMW team as a 14-stage compressor and 5-stage turbine engine, a logical evolution from the German engines under development during the latter stages of World War II. Type-K engines produced by the mid-1950s power the operational Soviet four-engined bomber (Tu-20 Bear) with four MK-12M turboprop engines of 12,000 horsepower capacity, and the civilian version, Tu-114 (the Rossiya).

The AM series (after Mikulin) developed from the work of a Junkers-BMW team in the USSR under engineer Brandner. The end result of this design, the AM-3, was seen in 1958 by an American engineer, whose comment was, "The engine is not an outstanding power plant, being of simple design of very large diameter and developing about 15,000 pounds thrust with 8 compression stages."

The AM series of turbojets is currently used in the Tu-104 Camel civilian version of the Tu-16 Badger bomber.

MiG Fighters with Rolls-Royce Turbojets

In 1946 the Soviets bought fifty-five Rolls-Royce centrifugal compressor-type turbojets—twenty-five Nenes and thirty Derwents. These Rolls-Royce engines, the most advanced in the world for the time, were well suited to Soviet production methods and introduced the Soviets to the use of a centrifugal turbojet. Up to 1947 Russian jets were all of the axial-flow type based on German designs. These Rolls-Royce turbines proved to be the best possible equipment for the MiG-15, which was designed by Siegfried Gunther and put into serial production under the name of the Soviet designers Mikoyan and Gurevich. Gunther was brought to Moscow and appointed chief designer in the construction office in Podberezhye.

Two versions of the Rolls-Royce engines were produced at Engine Plant No. 45 near Moscow from 1948 to the late 1950s. The plant was toured in 1956 by U.S. Air Force General Nathan Twining, who noted that it contained machine tools from the United States and Germany, and had 3,000 workers engaged in producing the Rolls-Royce Nene.

In 1951 the American counterpart to this Rolls-Royce engine was the Pratt & Whitney J-42 Turbo-wasp, based on the Nene but not then in quantity production. When the Korean War broke out in 1950, therefore, the Russians had thousands of improved Rolls-Royce Nene engines in service powering MiG-15s, whereas the U.S. Air Force had only a few hundred F-86A Sabres with comparable engines. Several engines from MiG-15s captured in Korea were evaluated by the United States Air Force. Reports were prepared by engineers of Pratt & Whitney Aircraft Division of United Aircraft Corporation, the Wright-Patterson Air Force Base, and Cornell Aeronautical Laboratory. We know from these analyses that by 1951 the Soviets had two versions of the original Rolls-Royce Nene in production quantities. The first version, the RD-45 that powered an early MiG-15, was a direct copy of the original Rolls-Royce Nene and delivered 5,000 pounds of thrust. The second version of the RD-45 delivered 6,000 pounds of static thrust at sea level and 6,750 pounds of thrust with water injection. The turbine blades in the Soviet RD-45 engines were made of a stainless steel alloy of the Nimonic-80 type, while the burner liner and swirl vanes were made of Nimonic-75. Parts of the Nene sold to Russia in 1948 were fabricated from Nimonic alloys—"Nimonic" being the registered trademark of Henry Wiggin and Company of Birmingham, England. Both Nimonic-75 and Nimonic-80 were developed by Mond Nickel about 1940, and the specifications had previously been published by the Ministry of Supply in the United Kingdom on the grounds that it was nonstrategic information.

The RD-45 (Nene) was produced in Moscow and also at Magadan from 1951 onwards, at Khabarovsk, at Ufa Plant No. 21, and at the Kiev Plant No. 43 from 1951 until sometime after 1958.

In 1967 the Soviet Strategic Air Force operated about 120 Tu-14 Bison bombers, 70 Tu-20 Bear bombers, and 1,000 Tu-16 Badger bombers. The Soviet Navy also operated these three types of aircraft.

From the information in Table 10.2 we can trace the operational jet engines of the 1960s from the Junkers and BMW prototypes taken from Germany at the end of World War II or

TABLE 10.2
WESTERN ORIGIN OF SOVIET MILITARY AIRCRAFT AND ENGINES

Aircraft Model	Date in Service	Engine Utilized	Origin of Engine
MiG-9 fighter	1946–47	RD-20	BMW 003
MiG-15 fighter	1947–1960s	RD-45	Rolls-Royce Nene
MiG-17 fighter	1954 to date	VK-2JA	Rolls-Royce Nene
MiG-19 fighter	1955 to date	VK-5 or (M-205)	Rolls-Royce Tay and Derwent
Tu-70 (Boeing B-29)	1950	4 piston-type engines	Wright 18-cylinder
Tu-16 Badger bomber	1954 to date	AM-3M turbojets	Junkers-BMW team
Tu-104 airliner version of Badger bomber	1957 to date	AM-3M turbojets	Junkers-BMW team
Tu-20 Bear bomber	1955 to date	NK-12M turbo-props	Junkers-BMW team
Tu-114 airliner version of Bear bomber Rossiya	1957 to date	NK-12M turbo-props	Junkers-BMW team

from those sold by the Rolls-Royce Company as "peaceful trade" in 1946. Both groups of prototypes were developed by German engineers transferred to Russia as forced labor, with equipment and instruments imported as "peaceful trade." When the K-series and the AM-series turbojets were well along the development road the Germans were returned home. The Soviets have had no difficulty since in making design improvements to the original German and British concepts and technologies. These are the engines that power operational Soviet military aircraft.

The Supersonic Tu-144 (Alias "Konkordskiy")

The configurations of the Russian supersonic Tu-144 and the Anglo-French supersonic Concorde are strikingly similar. Given the history of Soviet technical dependence on the West we can pose the question: Did the Soviets use the design of the Anglo-French Concorde for the Russian Tu-144?

Design work for Concorde began a decade before the British and French signed the Concorde agreement in 1962. Wind-tunnel testing, which yielded the data for the shape of the plane, began in the early 1950s. The Soviets had many other pressing problems in the early 1950s that were more important than research on a supersonic delta plane. However, the Tu-144 has a design concept very close to that of the Concorde. Both have modified double-delta wings, fixed geometry and low-aspect ratio for minimum drag. Fins and rudders are similar; neither aircraft has tailplanes. The major external differences are relatively slight variations in landing gear and engine position. In other words, superficially the Tu-144 is quite unlike anything the Soviets have designed previously, it is a significant jump in the technological horizon (but not as much as the aborted titanium U.S. supersonic plane) and should have required many years of testing and design work.

Dr. William Strang, technical director of British Aircraft Corporation's commercial aircraft division, has stated, "I think it likely that they did have some knowledge of the work we were doing which led to the general shape definition" (*London Times,* Sept. 27, 1971).

In September 1971 the British government expelled 105 Russian "diplomats" from England on charges of spying, and specifically military and industrial spying. According to the *London Times,* this espionage included "information on electronics, transformers, semi-conductors, computer circuitry, and technical details of the Concorde and Olympus 593 engine" (Sept. 25, 1971).

Finally, Doyle, a reformed member of the British Communist party, confessed to accepting £5,000 from the Soviets for information on Concorde, "including manuals, sketches and small pieces of equipment." Security was so lax at the plant that Doyle and his Soviet friends once considered smuggling out a 16-foot missile disguised as a telegraph pole. This was no real problem as Doyle had keys to all secret departments and security was nonexistent, but he balked at having to answer to his chief for a missing missile. Concorde was one thing, a missile was something else.

British and French engineers may have some justification for renaming Tu-144 the "Konkordskiy."

CHAPTER ELEVEN
Space, Missiles, and Military Instrumentation

The Russians were never ahead in space . . . the Soviet Union's
backwardness in space research is perfectly natural and inevi-
table, because the Soviet Union is a backward country and in
particular is a technologically backward country.

LEONID VLADIMIROV, Russian engineer and
former editor of ZNANIE-SILA, Moscow

Signal rockets were used by the Russian Army as early as 1717.
Russian theoretical development of rockets, beginning in 1903,
stems from the work of K. E. Tsiolkovskii, who investigated
atmospheric resistance, rocket motion, and similar problems.
This work was continued in the Soviet Union during the twen-
ties and thirties but in 1928 pioneer Tsiolkovskii suggested that
the value of his contribution had been in theoretical calculations, while nothing had been achieved in practical rocket
engineering. Then in 1936, V. F. Glushke designed and built a
prototype rocket engine, the ORM-65; this rocket used nitric
acid and kerosene as a propellant. After this the Soviets developed the ZhRD R-3395, an aircraft jato rocket using nitric
acid and aniline as a propellant (during the early 1930s Du
Pont had provided technical assistance and equipment for the
construction of large nitric acid plants). During World War II,
Soviet rockets used "Russian cordite," which was 56.5 percent
nitrocellulose. The nitrocellulose was manufactured under a

technical-assistance agreement made in 1930 with the Hercules Powder Company of the United States. Finally, under Lend-Lease, 3,000 rocket-launchers and large quantities of propellants were shipped from the United States to the USSR.

German Assistance for the Soviet Missile and Space Program

A major boost to Soviet ambitions in rocketry came from Germany at the end of World War II. The facilities transferred to the USSR included the testing stations of Blizna and Peenemunde, which were captured intact and removed to the USSR; the extensive production facilities for the V-1 and V-2 at Nordhausen and Prague; the records of reliability tests on some 6,900 German V-2s; and 6,000 German technicians (but not the top theoretical men), most of whom were not released until the late 1950s.

The German weapons program was in an advanced state of development in 1945. About 32,050 of the V-1 "flying bomb" weapons had been produced in the Volkswagen plant at Fallersleben and in the underground Central Works at Nordhausen. In addition, 6,900 V-2 rockets had been produced—6,400 at the underground Middelwerke at Nordhausen and 500 at Peenemunde. Rocket fuel facilities had been developed in the Soviet Zone: liquid oxygen plants at Schmeidebach in Thuringia and at Nordhausen, and a hydrogen peroxide plant at Peenemunde.

The Germans undertook two and one-half years of experimental work and statistical flight and reliability evaluation on the V-2 before the end of the war. There were 264 developmental launchings from Peenemunde alone.

Mittelwerke at Nordhausen was visited in June 1945 by U.S. Strategic Bombing Survey teams who reported that the enormous underground plant could manufacture V-1s and V-2s as well as Junkers-87 bombers. V-2 rockets were manufactured in twenty-seven underground tunnels. The plant was well equipped with machine tools and with "a very well set up assembly line for the rocket power unit." Its output at the end of the war was about 400 V-2s per month, and its potential output was projected at 900–1,000 per month.

When the Soviets occupied part of the American Zone in July 1945 under arrangement with General (later President) Eisenhower, the Nordhausen plant was removed completely to the USSR.

The United States and Britain were not successful in gaining access to German rocket-testing sites in Poland. The Sanders Mission reached the Blizna test station, after considerable delays in Moscow, only to find that its equipment had been removed "in such a methodical way as to suggest strongly to the mission's leader that the evacuation was made with a view to the equipment being reerected elsewhere." The Sanders Mission accumulated 1.5 tons of rocket parts; unfortunately, when the mission reached home it was found that the rocket parts had been intercepted by the Soviets. The rocket specimens so carefully crated in Blizna for shipment to London and the United States were last seen in Moscow. The crates arrived at the Air Ministry in London, but contained several tons of "old and highly familiar aircraft parts when they were opened." The rocket specimens collected at Blizna themselves had vanished.

Many German rocket technicians went or were taken to the Soviet Union. The most senior was Helmut Groettrup, who had been an aide to the director of electronics at Peenemunde. Two hundred other former Peenemunde technicians are reported to have been transferred. Among those were Waldemar Wolf, chief of ballistics for Krupp; engineer Peter Lertes; and Hans Hock, an Austrian specialist in computers. Most of these persons went in the October 22–23 round-up of ninety-two trainloads comprising 6,000 German specialists and 20,000 members of their families. Askania technicians, specialists in rocket-tracking devices, and electronics people from Lorenz, Siemens, and Telefunken were among the deportees, as were experts from the Walter Raketentriebwerke in Prague.

Asher Lee sums up the transfer of German rocket and missile technology:

The whole range of Luftwaffe and German Army radio-guided missiles and equipment fell into Russian hands. There were the two Henschel radar-guided bombs, the Hs-293 and the larger FX-1400 ... the U.S.S.R. also acquired samples of German antiaircraft radio-guided missiles like the X-4, the Hs-298 air-to-air projectile with a range of about a mile and a half, the Rheintochter which was fitted with a radar proximity fuse, and the very promising Schmetterling which even in 1945 had an operational ceiling of over 45,000 feet and a planned radius of action of about twenty miles. It could be ground- or air-launched and was one of the most advanced of the German small-calibre radio-guided defensive rockets; of these various projectiles the Henschel-293 bomb and the defensive Schmetterling and Hs-298 [the V-3] are undergoing development at Omsk and Irkutsk ... [and later at] factories near Riga, Leningrad, Kiev, Khaborovsk, Voronezh, and elsewhere.

Other plants produced improved radars based on the Wurzberg system; the airborne Lichenstein and Naxos systems were reported in large-scale production in the 1950s.

The Soviets froze rocket design in the late 1950s on developments based on German ideas. The German technical specialists were then sent home. The Soviets landed a rocket on the moon in 1959. In the early 1970s they were still landing rockets on the moon, but no men.

From the German V-2 to *Sputnik* and *Lunik*

From the German V-2 rockets, the associated German production facilities, and the all-important German reliability tests stem the contemporary Soviet ICBM and space rockets.

In the 1960s there were four types of large liquid rockets in the Soviet Union: the Soviet version of the V-2, the R-10 (a

77,000-pound thrust scale-up of the German V-2), the R-14 (a scaled-up V-2 with 220,000-pound thrust), and a modification known as R-14A (based on the R-14). The R-14 was designed and developed by a joint German-Russian team, until the Germans were sent home in the late 1950s.

The Soviets do not (or did not until recently) use single boosters—they use clusters of rockets strapped onto a central core. The strap-ons are the scaled-up and modified German V-2. Thus, for example, *Sputnik I* and *Sputnik II* had a first stage of two R-14A units, a second stage of two R-14A units, and a third stage of a single R-10 (the German V-2 produced in the Soviet Union). *Lunik* was a similar cluster of six rocket units. The *Vostok* and *Polyot* series are clusters of six units. The planetary rockets, *Cosmos* series and *Soyuz* family are seven-unit clusters. An excellent photograph of one of these cluster vehicles is to be found in Leonid Vladimirov's book, *The Russian Space Bluff*.[1]

In the mid-sixties, any foolhardy person who insisted that the United States would be first on the moon because the Russians were technologically backward, was dismissed as a dimwitted neanderthal. But at least two skilled observers with firsthand access to the Soviet program made a detailed case, one in 1958 and one in 1969. Lloyd Mallan wrote *Russia and the Big Red Lie* in 1958, after an almost unrestricted 14,000-mile trip through Russia to visit thirty-eight Soviet scientists. He took 6,000 photographs. It was Mallan who first drew attention to the Soviet practice of illustrating space-program press releases with photographs from the American trade and scientific press. The Remington Rand Univac computer was used in the fifties to illustrate an article in *Red Star* on the Soviet computer program—the captions were translated into Russian. In 1969, *Tass* issued a photograph for use in American newspapers purporting to show a Russian space station at a time when one Soviet space ship was in orbit and another en route. The *Tass* photograph was reproduced from *Scientific American* (Feb.

[1] (London: Tom Stacey, Ltd., 1971), p. 88.

1962) and was identical to an advertisement by Sperry Gyro-scope Company of Great Neck, New York. Sperry commented, "Apparently it is the same as the ad we ran."[2]

In 1972 we did not hear so much about the Soviet space program, for its job had been done. Charged with providing the propaganda cover for Soviet technical backwardness, the program achieved its objective superbly. The United States got sucked into a multi-multibillion-dollar extravaganza, using funds from American taxpayers propagandized into thinking there was some kind of race in progress. The only race was between the United States and its shadow. Today, without further Western help, the Soviet Union can make no dramatic advances. But help will be forthcoming from the United States in the form of "cooperative" space ventures.

Why Did the Soviets Embark on a Space Program?

From an economic viewpoint, a Soviet space program makes no sense at all: such a program only makes sense from a geopolitical viewpoint.

In 1957, the year of *Sputnik,* the Soviet Union had fewer telephones than Japan (3.3 million in the USSR versus 3.7 million in Japan). On a per-hundred population basis, the Soviet Union could provide only 3.58 telephones compared to 49.8 in the United States. Even Spain provided 9.6 telephones per 100 of population, or three times more than the Soviet Union.

In automobiles, the Soviet Union was even less affluent. In 1964 the Soviet Union had a stock of 919,000 automobiles, all produced in Western-built plants, only slightly more than Argentina (800,000) and far less than Japan (1.6 million) and the United States (71.9 million).

Even today the Soviet Union is so backward in automobile technology that it has to go to Italy and the United States for a

<hr>

[2] *Santa Ana Register,* Oct. 25, 1969.

new automobile plant and to the United States for the new Kama heavy truck plant.

Although *we* in the West might see this technical backwardness as a natural reason for *not* going into space, the Soviets saw it as a compelling reason to embark on a space program.

A "technical extravaganza" was necessary to demonstrate Soviet "technical superiority" to the world and maintain the myth of self-generated Soviet military might.

The Soviet economic problem in the mid-1950s was acute. The Soviet economy had shown good rates of growth but this was due to the impetus given by Lend-Lease equipment and by war reparations. There were no signs of technical viability; in fact, numerous industries were decades out of date with no indigenous progress on the horizon. The only solution was a massive program of acquiring complete plants and up-to-date technology in the West. Beginning in the late 1950s and continuing through the 1960s, this program had to be disguised because of the obvious military implications and one facet of the disguise was the space program. The usual stock of reasons for backwardness had run dry (the Civil War, the Revolution, intervention, warmongering capitalists)—even the damage done by the Nazis could only be spread so far. So two new elements made their appearance:

1. A space program—to get the Western world looking upwards and outwards, literally away from the Soviet Union and its internal problems.
2. Concurrent articles and press releases in the West on Soviet technical "achievements," spotted particularly in Western trade journals and the more naive newspapers, such as the *New York Times*.

Around the same time, the West (or rather the United States and Germany) resurrected Edwin Gay's 1918 proposal to mellow the Bolsheviks, and this proposal now became "bridges for peace" to provide a rational explanation for the massive transfers of Western technology that were required to fulfill Soviet programs. The United States appears, in historical perspective, to have been almost desperate in its attempts to help the Soviets in space. Of course, if the Soviets did not succeed in space, there could be no "competing" American space program and many politicians, bureaucrats, and politically oriented scientists were determined—for their own good reasons—that there had to be a major American space effort.

U.S.-Soviet "Cooperation" in Space

In the ten years between December 1959 and December 1969, the United States made eighteen approaches to the USSR for space "cooperation."

In December 1959, NASA Administrator R. Keith Glennan offered assistance in tracking Soviet manned flights. On March 7, 1962, President Kennedy proposed an exchange of information from tracking and data-acquisition stations, and on September 20, 1963, President Kennedy proposed joint exploration of the moon, an offer later repeated by President Johnson. On December 8, 1964, the administration proposed an exchange of teams to visit deep-space tracking and data-acquisition facilities. On May 3, 1965, NASA suggested joint communications tests via the Soviet *Molniya I*. On August 25, 1965, NASA asked the Soviet Academy of Sciences to send a representative to the *Gemini VI* launch, and on November 16, NASA inquired about joint *Molniya I* communications tests. Four U.S. offers were made in 1966; in January NASA inquired about Venus probes; on March 24 and May 23 Administrator James Webb suggested that the Soviets propose subjects for discussion; and in September Ambassador Arthur Goldberg again raised the question of tracking coverage by the United States for Soviet missiles.

The only agreement for information exchange came in June 1962. It had only mediocre success. An agreement to exchange meteorological information was made but "to date [1972] the Soviet data have not been operationally useful to us." No exchange of data on magnetic-field mapping took place between

1962 and 1969, and arrangements for exchange of ground-based data "have not been completely successful either." Cooperative communications using the U.S. passive satellite *Echo II* were completed in February 1964: "The Soviets received communications only, declining to transmit." In space biology and medicine, a U.S. team spent two years putting together materials, while the Soviet side has failed to respond.

A direct Washington-Moscow bilateral circuit for the exchange of meteorological information went into effect in September 1964. The United States has transmitted to Moscow cloud analyses for half the world and selected cloud photographs, but from the Soviet side,

> there have been numerous interruptions in the transmission for data, at one time for a period of four months. Because of insufficient coverage by Soviet satellites, the Soviet data have been limited, or marginal quality and received after the period of maximum usefulness.

In 1972 plans were in progress for joint docking operations by American and Soviet space vehicles by the mid-1970s. Interestingly, docking is a precise operation requiring exact compatibility of equipment. Presumably the Soviets are using U.S. designs.

In sum, the Soviets have received considerably more from "cooperation" in space than they have delivered to the United States.

The ABM Treaty

The Soviet-American ABM treaty of 1972 is another case where the United States apparently cannot resist giving the lion's share to the Soviets. The treaty limits each nation to two ABM sites, one in its capital city (i.e., Moscow and Washington) and one at any other location within the United States or the Soviet Union.

On the surface this appears to be rigid equality. A little reflection suggests that the American side could not have given away more if it had tried. The treaty exchanges defense of a heap of waste paper and empty buildings—because that is what Washington would amount to in the event of nuclear attack—for defense of the most important military-industrial complex in the USSR. An atom bomb dropped on Washington would not inhibit the U.S. defense effort in the slightest—government personnel would have been evacuated and Washington has no industry. On the other hand, an atom bomb on Moscow would effectively remove the key center of Soviet defenses. Under SALT Moscow is given an ABM system.

The Ford-built MZMA plant is in Moscow. It is the largest producer of automobiles and the second-largest producer of trucks in the Soviet Union. The ZIL plant, producer of military trucks (see p. 128) is in Moscow. Out of nineteen plants in the Soviet Union making computers and mechanical apparatus for calculation, twelve are in Moscow (the largest computer plant, however, is in Kiev). Large aircraft and electronics plants are located to the south of Moscow, including the Fili complex. Moscow is the most important single element of the Soviet military-industrial complex.[3]

In other words, in the event of war, if there is one obvious target for the United States in Russia it is Moscow—the other targets *relatively* do not amount to a hill of beans. Moreover, if there is one target in America the Soviets would *not* go for, it is Washington, D.C.

Our government mystics have exchanged protection of nothing in the United States for protection of the main element of the Soviet military-industrial complex.

And the Senate approved.

Military Instrumentation

In August 1971 the U.S. Department of Defense paid $2 million to Hamilton Watch Company for precision watchmaking equipment. Watchmaking equipment is used in fabricating

[3] See *Soviet Trade Directory* (London: Flegon Press, 1964).

bomb and artillery-shell fuses, aircraft timing gear, pinions, and similar military components.

Most Soviet watch-manufacturing equipment has been supplied from the United States and Switzerland; in some cases the Soviets use copies of these foreign machines.

In 1929 the old Miemza concession factory, formerly a tsarist plant, received the complete equipment of the Ansonia Clock Company of New York, purchased for $500,000. This became the Second State Watch Factory in Moscow, brought into production by American and German engineers, and quickly adapted to military products.

In 1930 the complete Deuber-Hampton Company plant at Canton, Ohio, was transferred to the Soviet Union, and brought into production by forty American technicians. Up to 1930 all watch components used in the Soviet Union had been imported from the United States and Switzerland. This new U.S.-origin manufacturing capability made possible the production of fuses and precision gears for military purposes; during World War II it was supplemented by Lend-Lease supplies and machinery.

After World War II Soviet advances in military instrumentation were based essentially on U.S. and British devices, although the German contribution was heavy in the 1950s. About 65 percent of the production facilities removed from Germany were for the manufacture of power and lighting equipment, telephone, telegraph, and communications equipment, and cable and wire. The remainder consisted of German plants to manufacture radio tubes and radios, and military electronics facilities for such items as secret teleprinters and antiaircraft equipment.

Many wartime military electronic developments were made at the Reichpost Forschungsinstitut (whose director later went to the USSR) and these developments were absorbed by the Soviets, including television, infrared devices, radar, electrical coatings, acoustical fuses, and similar equipment. But although 80 percent of the German electrical and military electronics industries was removed, the Soviets did not acquire modern computer or control-instrumentation technologies from Germany.

The computer is the heart of modern military instrumentation. The components, tubes, diodes, and transistor technologies for early computers came from Germany (the reparations removals) and postwar purchases of electrical equipment. Western designs had—and have—a great deal of influence, however, and most Soviet equipment today is copied from American and British models. A review by a "top German scientist," based on interviews of German electronics engineers returning from the USSR in the late 1950s, concluded that the engineers were returned because the Soviets had nothing more to learn from them. The Soviets were said to "always have working models of the latest U.S. equipment," and were at that time testing the latest U.S. Tacan navigation system. The Decca Tracking system was acquired from Britain through espionage (the Lonsdale case). The U.S. Loran system was copied in the Soviet Union as the Luga system.

Lloyd Mallan, in his *Russia and the Big Red Lie,* reports other cases of direct utilization of American instruments. For example, the Remington-Rand Univac computer was used to illustrate an article in *Red Star* on Soviet computers with captions translated into Russian. Soviet computers had such primitive characteristics as cooling by air blowing over tubes, while calculations for the trajectory of *Lunik* were done by use of a hand calculator made in Germany. The equipment at a Soviet tracking station was an aerial camera that could be purchased at a war surplus store in the United States for $80. There was a General Electric radio telescope at the Byurakan Observatory; Mallan saw Soviet copies of the U.S. Navy space suit and the nose-cone spring release from the Viking rocket. German rocket-launchers were used and there were copies of the C-123, Convair, and B-29. Numerous B-29 parts were used on the Tu-104, which had no servo-mechanisms and thus required brute force to fly; there were no radarscopes on the IL-18. This backwardness in electronics was still apparent in the 1960s. The American trade journal *Electronics* (Nov. 25, 1960, p. 43) illustrated Soviet space components and their U.S. counterparts, and noted the bulky and obsolescent nature of Soviet components—

without printed circuits and using conventional World War II military-type cables and plugs for space work. The journal cites an example of an ionization detector and amplifier used in the 1961 U.S. moon shot in one package 6 inches long and the comparable Soviet instruments in *Sputnik III*—two packages about 2 feet long.

In 1968 a Sidewinder missile was stolen from the German Air Force and NATO Zell Air Base in Bavaria and shipped to the USSR. Warrant Officer Wolf Knoppe, a West German Air Force pilot, and Joseph Linowsky, a mechanic, shipped the 9.5-foot missile to the Soviets by commercial airliner. The wholesale expulsion of Soviet espionage agents from the United Kingdom in 1971 was triggered by Soviet acquisition of the British electronic counter (EC) device capable of blacking out ground radar detection systems. A-bombers with such devices have been able to penetrate American defenses without detection. The Soviets now have the British EC system.

In brief, where the Soviets are operating modern systems, either civilian or military, the origins can be traced to the West. For example, in 1966 a Standard 7/8 instrument-landing system comprising localizer, glide slope, and beacon, valued at $280,000, was installed at the Sheremetyevo Airport in Moscow—the international airport—by Standard Cables & Telephone, Ltd., at that time a subsidiary of International Telephone and Telegraph Corporation (ITT) of New York. As a result, the pilot on the first Soviet flight to the United States was able to make a rather interesting claim:

> Captain Boris Yegorov said that the efficiency of traffic flow around Moscow was a good deal better than it was around New York, which has been suffering exasperating traffic delays. In Moscow, everything is on time, said the captain after his own flight had to circle New York for an hour and 35 minutes and had come within 10 minutes of having to turn back to Montreal.[4]

[4] *San Jose Mercury,* Aug. 28, 1968.

In 1967 Le Materiel Telephonique S.A. of Paris, France, another subsidiary of ITT, was awarded a contract to equip an all-purpose telephone information center in Moscow. The system was large, employing 500 operators, and used advanced microfilm techniques.

U.S. Assistance for Soviet Military Computers

All modern technology, including modern military technology, depends on the use of computers. To make any progress in weapons systems the Soviets have to utilize modern high-speed computers. These computers and the necessary computer technology have come from the West and still come from the West, almost exclusively from the United States.

This conclusion parallels that of Professor Judy at the University of Toronto, who states that "virtually all" Soviet computer technology is of Western origin. Judy provides no examples of Soviet-origin computer technology, nor has the present writer been able to discover any computers of Soviet origin.[5]

Soviet computer production is notably weak. At the end of the 1950s the United States had about 5,000 computers in use, while the Soviet Union had only about 120. These Soviet computers, as reported by well-qualified observers, were technically well behind those of the West and barely out of the first-generation stage even as late as the 1960s. This logically follows from the Soviet requirement to copy Western advances.

Today, in 1973, the Soviets have about 6,000 first- and second-generation computers. The United States has over 70,000 computers, of which three-quarters are third-generation or integrated circuits, and the balance second-generation.

The only Soviet computer in continuous production in the 1960s was the URAL-I. It was followed by the URAL-II and

[5] Stanislaw Wasowski, *East-West Trade and the Technology Gap* (New York: Praeger, 1970).

URAL-IV modifications of the original model. The URAL-I has an average speed of 100 operations per second, compared to 2,500 operations per second on U.S. World War II machines and 15,000 operations per second for large U.S. machines of the 1950s. Occupying 40 square meters of floor space, URAL-I contains 800 tubes and 3,000 germanium diodes; its storage units include a magnetic drum of 1,024 cells and a magnetic tape of up to 40,000 cells—considerably less than U.S. machines of the 1960s. URAL-II and URAL-IV incorporate slightly improved characteristics. The URAL series is based on U.S. technology.

In the late fifties the Soviets produced about thirty to forty BESM-type computers for research and development work on atomic energy and rockets and missiles. The original version of the BESM had 7,000 tubes; the later version had 3,000 tubes and germanium diodes. In general, the BESM type has most of the features typical of early U.S. computers.

Production methods for both the URAL and the BESM machines were also the same as American methods. On the other hand, Soviet computers were operationally far less efficient. The STRELA, for instance, was reported to have only a ten-minute mean free time between errors, while U.S. machines in the fifties normally operated eight hours without error.

Software has also been copied from U.S. equipment. An American computer expert, Willis H. Ware, has commented:

> We were shown about 40 card punches. About half of these were 90-column machines and the other half 80-column machines; all were generally similar to United States designs . . . We also saw a 500-card per minute sorter which closely resembled a corresponding American product. It has electromechanical sensing of the holes and a set of switches for suppressing specific row selections as in American sorters.

Until recently, direct import of computers from the United States was heavily restricted by export control regulations. In 1965 only $5,000 worth of electronic computers and parts were directly shipped from the United States to the Soviet Union, and only $2,000 worth in 1966. In 1967 computer exports increased to $1,079,000 and this higher rate of export of U.S. electronic computers to the USSR has been maintained since that time. The precise amount and nature of IBM computer sales to the Soviet Union since World War II is censored, but it is known that after World War II IBM sales to the Communist world came "almost entirely from [IBM's] Western European plants," partly because of U.S. export control restrictions and partly because U.S. equipment operates on 60 cycles whereas Russian and European equipment operates on 50 cycles.

American computer sales may be traced from 1959 with sale of a Model-802 National-Elliott sold by Elliott Automation, Ltd., of the United Kingdom. (Elliott Automation is a subsidiary of General Electric in the United States.) Towards the end of the sixties Soviet purchases of computers were stepped up, and by late 1969 it was estimated that Western computer sales to all of Communist Europe, including the USSR, were running at $40 million annually, in great part from European subsidiaries of American companies. In 1964–65 Elliott Automation delivered five Model-503 computers to the USSR, including one for installation in the Moscow Academy of Sciences. The Elliott-503 ranged in price up to $1 million, depending on size, and has a 131,000-word core capacity. By the end of 1969 General Electric–Elliott automation sales to Communist countries were four times greater than in 1968 and the market accounted for no less than one-third of General Electric–Elliott's computer exports. Other General Electric machines, for example a Model-400 made in France by Compagnie des Machines Bull, were also sold to the USSR.

Olivetti–General Electric of Milan, Italy, has also been a major supplier of GE computers to the USSR. In 1967 the Olivetti firm delivered $2.4 million worth of data-processing equipment systems to the USSR in addition to Model-400 and Model-115 machines.

In sum, General Electric from 1959 to 1970 sold to the Soviet Union through its European subsidiaries a range of its medium-capacity computers, including the fastest of the 400-series.

Of perhaps even greater significance are sales by English Electric, which include third-generation microcircuit computers utilizing Radio Corporation of America technology. In 1967 English Electric sold to the USSR its System Four machine with microcircuits; this machine incorporates RCA patents and is similar to the RCA Spectra-70 series.

The largest single supplier of computers to the USSR has been International Computers and Tabulation, Ltd., of the United Kingdom, which also licenses RCA technology, and has supplied at least twenty-seven of the thirty-three large computers presently in Russia. In November 1969, for example, five of the firm's 1900-series computers (valued at $12 million) went to the USSR. These large high-speed units with integrated circuits are, without question, considerably in advance of anything the Soviets are able to manufacture, even by copying previously imported technology. Such machines are certainly capable of solving military and space problems. Indeed, a computer cannot distinguish between civilian and military problems. There is no way at all that a Western firm or government can prevent the Soviets using computers for military work. Even armed GIs stationed at the site could be fooled. Given the complete lack of indigenous Soviet computer technology (and Dr. Judy of the University of Toronto agrees with the author's conclusions on this point), the Soviets have to use either imported computers or imported technology for weapons-design work.

The only alternative would be the abacus, a device thousands of years old, and that is not feasible for the lengthy, complex calculations needed for modern weapons technology, atomic energy, and space work, although Mallan reports that hand calculators were used in the Soviet space program. (These are also copies or imported.) In sum, Soviet military computers are either imported American "civilian" computers or copies of imported American computers redesigned for specific military purposes.

In 1971 the Soviets announced the new RJAD series of computers, a direct copy of the IBM-360 series.

Also in 1971 came the ultimate insult. The Soviets indicated that if International Computers Ltd. of Great Britain were allowed to sell two big, fast, highly sophisticated 1906A computers, American scientists would be allowed to participate in further research at the Serpukhov Institute of High Energy Physics. The key equipment at Serpukhov, including the bubble chamber, came from the West. Indeed, without the assistance of Weisskopf of the U.S. Atomic Energy Commission, there would be no linear accelerator at all at Serpukhov.

The Soviets gave "ironclad" guarantees not to use these new British (RCA) 1906A computers for military research. Personal intervention by President Nixon brought about a relaxation of U.S. opposition to the British sale,[6] but he has not yet indicated how he proposes to prevent the Soviets from using the 1906As for military purposes.

Some members of Congress are not impressed by Soviet protestations of good intent. Congressman Chet Holifield, in reply to the Russian promise not to misuse the advanced RCA 1906A computers, commented, "You should know what that would amount to."[7]

[6] *San Jose Mercury,* June 27, 1971, Jan. 9, 1972; *Los Angeles Times,* Jan. 19, 1971.

[7] *Barron's Weekly,* Jan. 4, 1971. For further information on computers, see Susan L. M. Huck, "Calculation: Giving Ourselves the Business," *American Opinion,* Dec. 1970, and Ivan Berenyi, "Computers in Eastern Europe," *Scientific American,* Oct. 1970.

CHAPTER TWELVE
Congress and the Bureaucrats

If the American people lose their freedom any time in the near future, it will not be as a result of Communism but from the bureaucratic excesses of giant government.
BARRY GOLDWATER, U.S. Senator from Arizona, October 1972

Congress is a body of elected representatives of the people. It has the power of investigation, impeachment, and subpoena, the power of persuasion, and, above all else, the power to raise its voice and be heard. Yet Congress has apparently abandoned principle for special-interest pleading in the case of our subsidy of the Soviet military-industrial complex.

A few courageous congressmen and senators spoke out and conducted hearings in the fifties and sixties. One by one, White House heat, business lobbying, and vested-interest pressure forced them to give up. In some cases, like that of former Congressman John G. Schmitz of California, they were singled out for "special treatment." Thus, the thundering conservative big guns of the sixties have become the collectivized yes-men of the early seventies.

So far as the bureaucracy is concerned, the problem yet to be faced by Congress has three major elements:

1. The Departments of State and Commerce have, over a period of almost fifty years and especially since the early

1930s, expedited the export of military goods and related technology to the Soviet Union.

2. Both the Korean and Vietnamese wars were fueled on both sides by previously exported Western—mainly U.S.-origin—technology.

3. There have been continuing and largely successful attempts by the bureaucracy to conceal information concerning this massive technical transfer and its subsequent military utilization by the Soviets.

Congressional Attempts to Prevent Military Assistance to the Soviet Union

From just before the Korean War until the 1960s, Congress attempted to restrict the export of goods with military potential to the Soviet Union. The Export Control Act of 1949, replaced by the Export Administration Act of 1969, provided for restrictions on materials whose export might have an adverse effect on national security. Section 3 (a) provided that rules and regulations were to be established for denial of exports, including technical data, to any nation "threatening the national security of the United States," if the President determined that such export made "a significant contribution to the military or economic potential of such nation."

This power was administered by the Department of Commerce for most exports, by the Department of State for munitions, and by the Atomic Energy Commission for nuclear materials.

The Mutual Defense Assistance Control Act of 1951 (known as the Battle Act) is a multinational approach to the same end. The Battle Act represents an attempt to prevent export from Western countries of strategic items that have the capability of strengthening the military power of the Soviet Union. The Battle Act provides for United States participation in the coordination of these national controls through an informal international committee (CoCom). Essentially, the act provides a link with U.S. strategic trade controls established under the Export Control Act of 1949.

The Battle Act forbids U.S. aid to any country that knowingly permits the shipment of strategic items to the Soviet bloc when such items are listed for embargo by the administrator of the act; that is, by the State Department. The U.S. State Department has never requested the President to apply sanctions under Section 103 (b) of the Battle Act, although there have been scores of violations. The Battle Act has been violated from its inception. It has never provided an effective restraint to the export of strategic goods from the West to the Soviet Union. The State Department has never attempted to fully apply its provisions. Lax administrative actions and gross administrative ignorance concerning the technical capability of the USSR and its use of Western processes and technologies have been major contributory causes to its failure.

An excellent example of the failure is the supply of transportation equipment to the Soviet Union and the subsequent use of this equipment against the United States and its Asian allies in the Vietnamese War. Whereas the Export Control Act of 1949 and the Battle Act of 1951 include an embargo on "transportation materials of strategic value," an analysis of the merchant vessels utilized by the Soviet Union to carry armaments to South Vietnam and the vessels leased by Poland to Red China for similar purposes indicates that such ships and technology were acquired *after* the passage of the relevant export control acts.

Of ninety-six ships used by the Soviets on the Haiphong run, twelve have not been identified. Of the eighty-four ships positively identified, only fifteen were even partly built in Soviet yards. The other sixty-nine, all tankers and cargo ships, were built outside the USSR. Of these sixty-nine ships, only thirteen were built before the Battle Act embargo of 1951: *In other words, fifty-six were built after the embargo and outside of the USSR.* Six of the thirteen built before 1951 are Lend-Lease ships.

The most important component of a ship is its main engine.

Of the eighty-four identified ships on the Haiphong run, only one has a main engine possibly designed and manufactured in the Soviet Union. Larger marine diesel engines, up to 9,000 brake horsepower (the largest made in the USSR), are of Burmeister & Wain design. Although Denmark is a member of NATO and supports the NATO objective of an embargo on war materials to the Soviet Union, the Burmeister & Wain firm was allowed (in 1959) to make a technical-assistance agreement for manufacture of the B & W series of large marine diesel engines at the Bryansk plant in the USSR.

No meaningful distinction can be made between technology exports to the USSR and those to the other East European bloc countries. Political differences among Communist nations have not led to reductions in intrabloc trade or intrabloc technological transfers. Indeed, and paradoxically, the Western reaction to polycentralism in the form of "more trade" has led to an increased transfer of Western technology to the Soviet Union. Processes and products embargoed for direct shipment to the Soviets are transferred to the Soviet Union indirectly through East European Communist countries.

As the acquisition of Western technology is a prime objective of all Communist nations, one effect of the West's response to its own interpretations of differing forms of communism in Eastern Europe has been to provide a more effective economic basis for fulfillment of Soviet foreign policy objectives.

The Bureaucrats' View of "Peaceful Trade"

The State and Commerce departments have consistently rejected the argument that "peaceful trade" can assist Soviet military objectives. For example, a 1969 State Department leaflet asserts (under the heading "US exports do not help Hanoi"):

> Over two thirds of our exports to the Soviet Union and East Europe are foodstuffs and raw materials for consumption within their economies. There is no

evidence that our exports of such goods to these countries release resources for manufacturing war materials
for North Vietnam.[1]

What is wrong with this statement?

The Soviet Union needs—and receives—U.S. technology, not
"foodstuffs and raw materials." The bureaucracy may claim
U.S. wheat does not go to Vietnam and Cuba, but it avoids the
crucial point that export of our wheat to the Soviets releases
Soviet wheat for export to Hanoi. No economist will deny that
our technical transfers release Soviet domestic resources for
armaments production. The State Department assertion is therefore a compound of distortion and ignorance.

These unsubstantiated distortions are given to Congress as
verifiable truth. For example, Edwin M. Martin, Assistant
Secretary of State for Economic Affairs, made the following
statement to Congress in 1961: "I don't think there is con-
vincing evidence that the net advantage to the Soviet Union of
the continuation of trade is a major factor—or a particularly
significant factor in the rate of their overall economic development in the long term."[2]

There is also confusion concerning the Soviet practice of
copying. For example, the following exchange took place before a congressional committee in 1961:

> *Mr. Lipscomb:* Does the Department of Commerce feel
> that Russia has developed a great deal of their agricul-
> tural equipment from prototypes obtained both legally
> and illegally from the United States?
> *Mr. Behrman:* No sir, I don't think that the evidence
> we have indicates that the equipment that they them-

---

[1] U.S. Dept. of State, Public Information Series P-310-369 (Washington, D.C., 1969).

[2] Edwin M. Martin, Assistant Secretary of State for Economic
Affairs, before the House Select Committee on Export Control,
Dec. 8, 1961.

selves produce copies—that they produce copies of equipment which we have supplied.[3]

Even well-informed members of Congress have taken positions directly opposed to the evidence. Senator Jacob Javits of New York comments: "Trade with the West as a general matter, must necessarily be a marginal factor in the performance and potentialities of the Soviet economy."[4]

There exist, presumably unknown to Senator Javits and the others quoted above, three volumes of detailed evidence that totally refutes these statements.[5]

A popular book in the 1930s was *You Can't Do Business with Hitler!* The moral and national-security arguments in this book apparently apply only to Hitler's brand of totalitarianism. There is extraordinary inconsistency in the treatment of Hitlerian totalitarianism and Soviet totalitarianism. Indeed, there is some direct evidence and a great deal of indirect evidence that the policymakers in Washington do not view the Soviet Union as a totalitarian power at all. At the end of World War II, the conclusion of an interagency committee on German industry, with members from the State and Commerce departments, was as follows:

> The Committee is unanimously of the opinion that the major force for war represented in a motor vehicle industry is its availability as a major machine shop aggregation, under able management and engineering, which can be turned, by conversion, to production of

[3] U.S. House of Representatives, Select Committee on Export Control, Investigation and Study of the Administration, Operation and Enforcement of the Export Control Act of 1949, and Related Acts (H.R. 403), 87th Cong., 1st sess., Oct. 25, 26, and 30, and Dec. 5, 6, 7, and 8, 1961, p. 403.

[4] *Congressional Record,* Senate, Vol. 112, pt. 9 (89th Cong., 2nd sess.), May 24, 1966, p. 11233.

[5] Antony C. Sutton, *Western Technology and Soviet Economic Development* (see Bibliography).

an extremely wide variety of military products. Its role as a producer of combat and military transport vehicles ranks second in significance.[6]

Yet *today* State and Commerce argue vehemently that the export of equipment for a motor vehicle industry is "peaceful trade"—*even when military vehicles produced by previously exported technology are photographed in Vietnam and Cuba.* Obviously, no amount of hard evidence can shake these people from their illusions. The policymakers are locked onto an image of totalitarianism which, to them, is morally and strategically acceptable.

U.S. assistance to the Marxist brand of totalitarianism is not limited to the Soviet Union. In 1971 for example, the State Department attempted to help Allende, the Marxist president of Chile, to purchase aircraft and paratroop equipment in the United States *(Indianapolis News,* July 1971). Three months later Allende attempted to impose complete Marxist control in Chile. At the time of this writing the rising Chilean middle class is protesting, and we may yet see a civil war in that country. Once again the State Department wants to help a Marxist clique to impose its rule on an unwilling population.

The current assertion that we should exchange our technology for Soviet raw materials will not stand penetrating analysis. Soviet raw materials only become competitive to our enormous low-grade domestic reserves if extraction is subsidized by U.S. loans and guarantees—again to the disadvantage of the American taxpayer. From the national security viewpoint the "exchange" is absurd. Once our technology is passed to the Soviet Union it cannot be reclaimed, it becomes an integral part of their military industrial operations. But Russian raw material supplies, developed with our assistance, can be cut off any time the Soviets wish. In other words, once again our

[6] Foreign Economic Administration, *Study by Interagency Committee on the Treatment of the German Automotive Industry from the Standpoint of International Security* (Washington, D.C., 1945).

policymakers have exchanged something for nothing and charged it to the American taxpayer and citizen.

The State Department and Military Intelligence Information

It would seem elementary that State Department officials would forward incoming reports with military information to military intelligence. Yet reports containing military information from one of the few Americans with full direct knowledge of Soviet military construction in the Five-Year Plans were buried in the department's files. The informant was an American engineer named Zara Witkin, a former Communist, who held one of the most important jobs in the Soviet Union of the early 1930s, for he was charged with integrating the First and Second Five-Year Plans and supervising "special-unit" or military construction.

This is the brief life of incoming Warsaw Report No. 130 reporting an interview with Witkin and containing hard information, of direct use to U.S. military intelligence, on the location of Soviet weapons plants:

> Received Washington, D.C., 4 P.M. January 8, 1934.
> Received Eastern European Affairs Department, January 9, 1934, marked "NO DISTRIBU-TION."
> Received Assistant Secretary of State (Moore), January 16, 1934.
> Received Division of Protocol and Conferences, February 6, 1934.
> FILED, February 8, 1934.

In brief, the report was marked "NO DISTRIBUTION" and filed within four weeks of receipt.

The life of Warsaw Report No. 136 was even shorter. Also containing military information, the report was received and filed *within four days* of receipt:

Received Washington, D.C., 11:30 A.M. January 23, 1934.

Received Eastern European Affairs, January 24, 1934, Marked "NO DISTRIBUTION."

Received Assistant Secretary of State, January 26, 1934.

FILED, January 27, 1934.

The State Department's "Exchange" Program

Even in a seemingly innocuous academic exchange program we find clear military advantages granted to the USSR.

In the three years 1965 to 1967, a total of 162 Americans went to the USSR and 178 Soviets came to the United States under the State Department's exchange program. The totals are roughly in balance but the fields of research are extraordinarily out of balance. Most of the Soviet nationals (139 out of 178) came to the United States to do research in engineering and physical sciences, while most of the Americans (153 out of 162) worked in the fields of history, social science, and literature.

While forty-six Soviets studied chemistry and metallurgy in the United States, not a single American had the opportunity to study chemistry or metallurgy in the USSR. While forty-eight Soviets studied engineering (mechanical, electrical, and materials science) in the United States, only two Americans were able to study engineering in the Soviet Union. While twenty-seven Soviet physicists came to the United States, only two American physicists went to the USSR, and so on.

On the other side of the research coin, while eighty-three Americans studied history, only twelve Soviets studied history in the United States. While thirty-four Americans studied Russian literature, the Soviet Union neglected to send even one Russian literator. And while eleven Americans studied the Russian language, only one Russian came to study English. For further details see Table 12.1.

TABLE 12.1

Americans in Soviet Union		Soviets in United States	
History	83	Chemistry and Metallurgy	46
Literature	34	Engineering (all types)	48
Language	11	Physics and Mathematics	27
Political Science,			
Law, Education	19		
	147		121
	(out of 162)		(out of 178)

Source: Exchanges with the Soviet Union and Eastern Europe (U.S. State Dept., 1967).

The State Department's July–December 1964 report on the exchange program takes note (p. 8) of this unusual imbalance:

As in previous years, most of the Soviet students (13 of 20) were in the physical sciences and technology. The Americans, with the exception of one physicist, were enrolled in the humanities, social sciences, and linguistics.

The Soviets send their people to acquire the fruits of American technology, while denying Americans the opportunity to examine any Russian technological advances. The program totals are kept roughly in balance by sending Americans to study history and literature. There is nothing mutual about the exchange of a historian or an economist for an engineer—*if the engineering topic has military applications.*

Thus, typical Americans going to the Soviet Union had the following subjects:

Joel Spiegelman of Brandeis University at Moscow Institute of Music, "Keyboard Music of the 18th Century in Russia."
George P. Majeska of Indiana University at Leningrad State University, "Russian Travelers in Byzantium."
Henry R. Huttenback of Louisiana State University at Moscow State University, "Research on the History

of the Zemsky Sobor during the reign of Ivan IV."
Byron Lindsey of Cornell University at Moscow State
University, "Structural Analysis of Chekhov's Stories."

Research undertaken by Soviet nationals in the United States
had distinct relevance to the Soviet missile program. Indeed,
the State Department's "bridges for peace" seems in some in-
stances more like "bridges for war."
For example:

Vadim I. Alferov of the Institute of Mechanics of
Moscow State University at Massachusetts Institute of
Technology, "Characteristics of the Discharge in a
Gas Flow of High Velocity."
Victor Ye. Anisimov of Voronesh State University at
University of Nebraska, "Processes of Depositing
Dielectric, Semiconducting, and Metallic films in
Conditions of Low-temperature Plasma of Gaseous
Discharge."
Vladimir N. Filimonenko of Novosibirsk Institute of
Electrical Engineering at Brown University, "Quanti-
tative Dependence between Phase Composition, Micro
and Macrostress in the Surface Layer and Mechanical
Properties of Hard Alloys."
Nikolai I. Khvostov of Moscow Institute of Energy at
University of Michigan, "State of the Boundary Layer
in Nozzles at Large Mach Numbers."

The last topic listed above is "State of the Boundary Layer
in Nozzles at Large Mach Numbers." Even this sketchy title
suggests a topic with distinct relevance for aerodynamics and
rocket technology. "Exchange," according to any dictionary, is
the "mutual giving and receiving of equivalents." Administration of this principle of equivalency requires exchange of a
Soviet musician for an American musician, a Soviet electrical
engineer for an American electrical engineer, a historian for a
historian, and so on.

The "exchange" program would then promptly evaporate! Why? Because while the Soviets are more than willing to send engineers to work in *our* engineering research laboratories, they are completely unwilling to allow American engineers to work in *theirs*. That's espionage! (If Soviets work in research labs here, it is called a "peaceful exchange.")

Breakdown of the State Department Facade

From time to time, under assault from persistent questioners, the bureaucratic facade of the State Department has broken down. Witness how a congressional counsel demolished a confident but erroneous claim by an Assistant Secretary of State. In 1961, the Senate Committee on the Judiciary was interested in determining the nature of a Yugoslav "guarantee" that U.S. strategic-materials imports would not be shipped on to the Soviet Union. Philip H. Trezise, then Acting Assistant Secretary of State (in 1972 the "Acting" was dropped)[7] was asked a simple question by Mr. Sourwine, Counsel for the Committee:

Mr. Sourwine: Do you have any form of control or agreement with Poland or Yugoslavia with regard to possible transshipments from them to the rest of the Soviet bloc?

Mr. Trezise: Yes, we do.

Mr. Sourwine: Is this in the form of a treaty?

Mr. Trezise: No!

Mr. Sourwine: Is it in the form of an executive agreement?

Mr. Trezise: No, it is not.

[7] See State Department *Biographic Register*. Philip H. Trezise has a long and interesting career in the State Department, including major positions in the Far East Division, Intelligence, Policy Planning, and Economic Affairs. In 1965 Trezise received the President's Award for Distinguished Federal Civilian Service.

Mr. Sourwine:	Well, what kind of an agreement can we have with a foreign nation if it is neither a treaty nor an executive agreement?
Mr. Trezise:	Mr. Sourwine, on this point, we have a whole series of understandings, agreements, arrangements with all the countries which come under the purview of the Battle Act.
Mr. Sourwine:	Leave out understandings and arrangements, because they are not agreements.
Mr. Trezise:	That is right.
Mr. Sourwine:	What kind of agreement can we have with a foreign country that is neither a treaty nor an executive agreement?
Mr. Trezise:	In the Yugoslav case, we have the assurance of the Yugoslav Government that it will not transship. We have received this from high officials of the Yugoslav Government.
Mr. Sourwine:	This is just their personal agreement or is it binding on their Government?
Mr. Trezise:	They commit the good faith of their Government.
Senator Keating:	Is it a letter or a document or what?
Mr. Trezise:	In the Yugoslav case it was an oral statement.
Senator Keating:	Made by whom?
Mr. Trezise:	I have a—made by an official of the Yugoslav Government. I am afraid Senator, I do not have the individual. I imagine the Foreign Minister.

Trezise was then asked to submit a written statement containing the name of the Yugoslav official who had given the undertaking. A letter was later transmitted to the committee, but *without the name* of the "official of the Secretariat of Foreign Affairs" who allegedly made the statement.

The State Department has many failings, but incompleteness of reporting from the field is not one of them. It is inconceivable that any Yugoslav official made an agreement with a U.S. official who did not report the agreement back to Washington.

There are two alternatives in the Trezise case. Either there was no such agreement—oral or written—concerning transshipment of U.S. strategic goods to the Soviet Union and Secretary Trezise was untruthful before a congressional committee, or the Yugoslav official was of such low rank that to give his name would reveal Trezise's testimony to be misleading.

The actions of the State Department in connection with the so-called Genocide Convention suggest once again its complete lack of interest in the welfare of U.S. citizens. The genocide treaty awaits ratification by the United States. The effect of this treaty, if signed, will be to allow an American citizen to be sent arbitrarily out of the country for trial before an international criminal tribunal (in defiance of the Sixth Amendment to the Constitution). Of course one of the first signatories to this international treaty was the Soviet Union and not surprisingly the State Department is a strong supporter of U.S. signing. The Soviet Union broke its solemn word, as given in the convention, by its 1968 invasion of Czechoslovakia and its present treatment of Jews and Baptists—but this has no effect at all on the State Department mystics.

A letter from David M. Abshire, Assistant Secretary for Congressional Relations, to Senator J. W. Fulbright (March 26, 1971) states, "We are looking forward to prompt and favorable action on the Genocide Convention by the Committee and the Senate as a whole."

The sneaker in the innocuous sounding treaty is that "mental harm" is considered a crime and is not defined. Therefore, criticism of the internal practices of the Soviet Union, for example, could constitute a criminal offense, for which an American could be transported forcibly out of the United States for trial before an international tribunal. It is for this that the State Department is "looking forward to prompt and favorable action."

Of course, to suggest to the State Department, or to supporters of Senators Church, Javits, and Fulbright, that we should haul Kosygin and Brezhnev before an international tribunal for their persecution of Russian Jews, Baptists, and intellectuals would cause these gentlemen to shiver in their little cotton socks. Such conventions are not usually applied to the Soviet Union or other totalitarian countries.

Furthermore, when it comes to helping out the Soviet Union, the State Department has no hesitation in breaking United States laws. This practice goes back before the export control laws—indeed into the 1920s.

The Farquhar plan in the 1920s for development of the Donetz Basin in the USSR required a railroad survey. H. G. Kelley, formerly president of the Grand Trunk Railroad, and his associate C. H. Gerber, were selected in 1925 to go to the Soviet Union and examine existing facilities.[8] Kelley was a Canadian citizen, though a resident of the United States. He could not, therefore, be issued a passport by the U.S. government. On the other hand, he wanted to return to the United States from the Soviet Union as a nonquota alien. The Farquhar Papers detail the efforts made by the State Department to issue a passport to Kelley.

Through a firm of Washington lawyers, a plan was devised under which the State Department would certify a permit to be issued by the U.S. Department of Labor to Kelley, enabling him to re-enter the United States as a nonquota alien. The Department of Labor's thirty-day requirement was waived by use of a letter from Chief Justice Taft and the lawyers assured Farquhar, "If this plan does not prove to be satisfactory, Mr. Olds [State Department] assures me that the Department will try to find some other way in which the desired result can be accomplished."[9]

This document was taken to the German Embassy to obtain a transit visa. The embassy refused to recognize its validity and

---

[8] Based on Percival Farquhar Papers, Hoover Institution, Stanford University.

[9] Farquhar Papers, Folder 6, Box 4.

suggested that a passport was required. The State Department then prepared a "certificate" enabling Kelley to return to the United States from the Soviet Union. Under U.S. law, the department is not permitted to give an alien a passport or a document "in lieu of a passport."

Kelley then went to the Soviet Union, made his railroad survey, wrote his report, and returned to the United States.

The State Department's Policy of Misinformation

The State Department has a disgraceful record of attempting to black out information and present a false picture of historical events.

Historians trusted to present a version of history favorable to the Establishment, are given a relatively free run of classified files. Thus Theodore Sorensen and Arthur M. Schlesinger, Jr., were given access to the Vienna Conference transcript, which is not likely to be made available elsewhere until 1984. In the early 1950s, under Secretary of State Dulles, Republican promises to change the situation turned to dust, as did President Nixon's promise two decades later to reform and clean out the State Department. Under John Foster Dulles, Dr. G. Bernard Noble, a Rhodes scholar and inveterate enemy of any attempt to change the Establishment's party-line, was promoted to take charge of the Historical Office. Two historians, Dr. Donald Dozer and Dr. Bryton Barron, who protested the official policy of distorting information and suppressing historical documents were railroaded out of the State Department. Dr. Barron, in his book, *Inside the State Department*,[10] specifically charged the department with responsibility for the exportation of military technology to the Soviet Union, and listed four examples of highly strategic tools whose export to the USSR was urged by officials of the State Department:

[10] Bryton Barron, *Inside the State Department* (New York: Comet Press, 1956).

1. Boring mills essential to the manufacture of tanks, artillery, aircraft, and the atomic reactors used in submarines.
2. Vertical boring mills essential to the manufacture of jet engines.
3. Dynamic balance machines used for balancing shafts on engines for jet airplanes and guided missiles.
4. External cylindrical grinding machines which a Defense Department expert testified are essential in making engine parts, guided missiles, and radar.

Bryton Barron concludes:

> It should be evident that we cannot trust the present personnel of the Department to apply our agreements in the nation's interest any more than we can trust it to give us the full facts about our treaties and other international commitments.

Breathtakingly inaccurate are the only words that can describe State Department claims regarding our military assistance to the Soviet Union. The general State Department line is that the Soviets have a self-developed technology, that trade is always peaceful, that we have careful controls on the export of strategic goods, and that there is no conceivable relationship between our exports to the Soviet Union and Soviet armaments production.

Some examples will make the point:

> *Ambassador Trezise:* We, I think are sometimes guilty, Senator, of a degree of false and unwarranted pride in our industrial and technological might, a kind of arrogance, if you will.... we are ahead of the Soviet Union in many areas of industry and technology. But a nation that can accomplish the scientific and technological feats the Soviet Union has accomplished in

recent years is clearly not a primitive, mud-hut economy. . . . It is a big, vigorous, strong, and highly capable national entity, and its performance in the space field and in other fields has given us every indication that Soviet engineers, technicians, scientists, are in the forefront of the scientists, engineers, technicians of the world.

Naturally Trezise did not submit evidence to back his sweeping claims. Indeed he *could* not, for there is no such evidence.

The following assertion by Trezise conflicts with the evidence presented in this book:

> *Senator Muskie:* So that the urge toward increased trade with Eastern European countries has not resulted in a weakening of the restrictions related to strategic goods?
> *Ambassador Trezise:* I think that is an accurate statement, Senator.
> Now we have, we think, quite an effective system of handling items which are in the military area or so closely related thereto that they become strategic item by everybody's agreement.

The State Department is unable even to learn from its own files. There are hundreds of documents going back to the time of the Revolution testifying to Soviet reality: that the Soviet government has always been a brutal totalitarian regime with hostile intent abroad and a persecution complex towards its own citizens. One example will illustrate the case. U.S. State Department File 861.5017 Living Conditions/302 is an interview with Dr. Louis Lefrak on July 22, 1931 (that is, midway in the American program to build up the Soviet military-industrial complex). Dr. Lefrak was "a practising physician of New York City who visited Russia recently. Dr. Lefrak, who is of Russian Jewish origin, returned to Russia with a feeling of great friendliness and sympathy for the Soviet regime, but in view of his experience and observations is very much embittered against it."

The accompanying State memorandum records Dr. Lefrak's experience and says that he "broke down under the nervous strain of recalling the sights he had witnessed."*

President Kennedy gave up fighting the State bureaucracy. President Johnson enlarged it under the illusion it could solve his problems. President Nixon made some ineffectual stabs at reform and reduction, then he too gave up. At appropriations time, Congress takes a few jabs and may slice a few dollars from a budget here and a budget there. In the final analysis, neither the Executive Branch nor the Congress has attempted to come to grips with the problem.

Why not?

Probably because for both the Executive and the Congress, there are more politically rewarding tasks. Moreover, many elected officials may be afraid of the power wielded by the bureaucrats. Finally, the bureaucrats do contribute to the wheeling and dealing inherent in political operations.

The Washington bureaucracy is obviously out of control and out of step. It neither protects nor preserves the United States and its citizens. Indeed it harasses and betrays them. It is persistently and pervasively untruthful and evasive in its dealings with the public, the independent researcher, and Congress.

The time has come to call a halt. Our military exports to the Soviet Union constitute an excellent justification for congressional action.

---

* The final lines of the State Department report remind us of a recent book by Herman Dinsmore, *All the News That Fits.* The State report concludes, "His [Dr. Lefrak's] original views of friendliness towards Russia were based on the articles published in the *New York Times,* which he now described as misleading." This was 1931, but even today the *New York Times,* in quest of its own fantasies of a world order, continues to print "misleading" information.

The State Department budget should be halved within three years. This would increase, not reduce its efficiency. The Department of Commerce budget should be reduced by 90 percent within three years, on the grounds that too close a relationship between the business and political worlds creates major policy problems. However, personnel cuts should be made from the top downwards. It is the top bureaucratic layers, the most powerful layers, that have to be completely eliminated by forced retirement. The lower layers may, and probably do, contain untapped talent and fresh ideas.

CHAPTER THIRTEEN

Why National Suicide—Some Answers

Q: Is there danger of this country's helping the Russians build a war potential that might be turned against the interests of the free world?

A: Under the circumstances, we might be very foolish not to accept business which could create jobs in the United States, when refusing to sell to the Soviet Union would in no way deter their progress.

MAURICE H. STANS, investment banker and former Secretary of Commerce, in reply to U.S. NEWS & WORLD REPORT, December 20, 1971

During the half-century since 1917, the United States and its allies have developed and maintained an enemy so powerful that an annual defense expenditure of $80 billion is now required. This policy has already cost 100,000 Americans and countless allies killed in Soviet-supplied wars in Korea and Vietnam. We have now embarked on the next fateful stage—to bring the Soviet military-industrial complex into the age of the computer.

"Strategic" goods, it is argued in Washington, are not licensed for export to the Soviets. Those who attempt to question this assertion have been called extremists, screwballs, and probably worse.

To argue that we have *not* militarily assisted the Soviet Union is a negative hypothesis. A negative hypothesis can be completely refuted simply by providing evidence to the contrary; in this case, that we *have* militarily assisted the Soviet Union. We have presented in this book substantial evidence that Soviet military capabilities depend on our assistance. The Establishment's hypothesis is invalid. It now remains to examine some of the more plausible reasons for this long-term policy of national suicide.

A Wise and Deliberate Policy Aimed at Creating a Peaceful World

It has been widely and profusely asserted that general economic assistance to the USSR is justifiable and advantageous as it will bring the Soviet Union into the family of freedom-loving, civilized nations. This argument assumes that the Soviet Union is totalitarian and that we *do* provide economic assistance. On the other hand, no one, to this writer's knowledge, has argued that export of military capabilities to a statist regime will create a more peaceful world, and *that* is precisely the point at issue in this book.

It could be argued that military assistance is a by-product of our technical and economic assistance (this is the implicit argument in the CED report discussed in Chapter One), and that this economic assistance will mellow the Soviets. The fact that must be faced, however, is that this policy has been pushed periodically since 1917. It is a failure. It has built the Soviet military-industrial complex.

Soviet actions make it abundantly clear that the USSR is governed by a brutal totalitarian regime. Those that keep such statist regimes in business have been adequately described by Lysander Spooner, one of the least known but most important political theorists of the nineteenth century, as "among the greatest villains that the world has ever seen."

Subthemes on the basic argument of "peaceful trade" as a

civilizing influence can also be identified. It is argued that the Soviet Union is thus made dependent on the United States, or that we need Soviet natural resources as ours are running out, or that technology is an exchange and we gain from Soviet technology. None of these assertions can be supported.

The Soviet Union is dependent on the United States, but this dependency has not prevented wars, nor will dependency ever keep a statist regime from going to war. Second, the fear-tactic "natural resources are running out" argument reveals a kindergarten knowledge of economics. Shortages are impossible under a free-market system. As fossil fuels become exhausted, the price of these fuels rise; ultimately, it pays to utilize atomic energy or some other fuel. Of course, and perhaps not unexpectedly, we find upon investigation that there is no substance to the idea of resources scarcity. In 1972 the U.S. Geological Survey reported that the United States had identified reserves of 3,200 *billion* tons of coal, 2,900 *billion* barrels of petroleum, and a possible 6,600 *trillion* cubic feet of natural gas. So much for fossil fuels "running out." Once again the mystics ignore the evidence and prattle or peddle their fantasies.

Why then do U.S. companies want to go into Siberia to develop Russian resources if the same resources are available in the United States? Obviously, because the Washington altruists are going to provide American tax monies to promote the project.

Further, if a peaceful world is indeed the objective and this objective is held to be worthy and justifiable, why is censorship and classification of information necessary? Obviously our policies will not stand the harsh light of day.

Even further, why is it necessary to draw policymakers from the same limited pool of expertise and common prejudice with off-limits signs posted for outsiders? We expect conservatives and libertarians to be rejected as key advisers. But what about all the other elements in the advisory spectrum? Why, for example, did Lyndon Johnson refuse the counsel of Hans Morgenthau, a controversial left-liberal perhaps, but an influential figure in the development of international political policy? Is it because

Morgenthau, like the conservatives and the libertarians, is out-side the Establishment? Policymakers, it seems, are in practice drawn only from a narrow self-perpetuating clique, whose mem-bers, after periodic elections, put the Republican and Demo-cratic labels in four-year storage. We note that Henry Kissinger pops up under Presidents Kennedy, Johnson, *and* Nixon—and *always* in foreign policy.

Even after the Vietnam fiasco, the Establishment is still able to claim the loyalty of this closed, self-perpetuating circle. Un-fortunately, this bipartisan group has given the United States a long series of bloody wars and catastrophic international problems. Regrettably, its members must be described as a circle of professional mystics—not as rational policymakers act-ing in the national interest of the United States.

An Accident—The Establishment Did Not Know It Was Helping the Soviets

The hundreds of examples cited here are not accidents. Many individual congressmen and persons outside government have attempted to stop the export of military goods to the Soviet Union. Samuel Gompers tried in the 1920s. U.S. Navy officers risked court-martial in the 1930s in their effort to stop Presi-dent Franklin D. Roosevelt from approving the sale of military equipment to the Soviets. The Senate investigated the "machine tools" case in 1945–46 when Commerce officials tried to send tank-gun milling equipment to the Soviet Union. Warnings were raised in the 1950s by Congressman Lipscomb and others about the results of building up Soviet military strength. In the 1960s individual American firms and engineers protested against the export of ball bearings processing equipment which could *only* be used to process bearings for Soviet missile-guidance sys-tems. In the 1970s the voices are quieter, but they are still protesting.

Are we to believe that Mr. Nicholaas Leyds, general manager of Bryant Chucking Grinder Company of Springfield, Vermont, does not know that his grinding machines are used to process the races for ball bearings for missile-guidance systems? When Bryant has sold the same machine to the U.S. government—for the same purpose? Or that the Hammer family does not know the results of its fifty-year-plus association with the USSR?

In 1919 Dr. Julius Hammer was a member of the Executive Committee of the Communist party of the United States and in 1972 Armand Hammer (his son and early business partner) is described as America's "No. 1 Capitalist."

It is not an accident. Some groups somewhere have always known the exact end-uses of the exported equipment. They have been brazen enough to persist in building up the Soviet military-industrial complex while pleading "civilizing the Bolsheviks" (1918) and "peaceful trade" (1972).

Our Policy Is Pragmatic. It Is Not Consistent with Any Long-run Objectives at All

One can develop a strong argument that pragmatism is the basic and underlying reason for our military assistance to the USSR. In other words, our international policies are not decided according to any firm principles or long-run objectives, but are formulated on a day-by-day, ad hoc basis, subject to shifting and often random political and economic pressures. In other words, our foreign economic policy is something like a cork bobbing around in the Potomac.

Senator Mansfield recently claimed that in his thirty years in Washington, he had never seen a policy question decided on the basis of principle. Not many would want to oppose that claim. The inference is that our foreign economic policy is determined by political trade-offs, political pull, political debts, and political aspirations within a framework determined by current, immediate, or pressing military and economic factors. The time framework is yesterday (in the past) and the next election (in the future).

This "explanation" would account for most of the phenomena described in this book if we could not also identify presidential actions with long-run objectives. We must distinguish between political claims of long-run objectives—made for the benefit of voters—and real intent. Is President Nixon's "new world order" a public relations gimmick or a long-run objective? President Roosevelt's secret military agreement with the Soviets in 1938 clearly fulfilled no internal political ambitions because it was kept absolutely secret until the 1950s. The agreement specifically states common long-run purposes with the Soviet Union. It was known to only four persons in the United States.

While State Department efforts to conceal information may be due to no more than the unwillingness of bureaucratic officials to expose themselves to congressional fire, it must be recognized that at the same time these bureaucrats have consistently, over a period of decades, allowed the export of goods with military potential to the USSR. This can be interpreted as a long-run policy distinct from, indeed in opposition to, congressional directives.

On the basis of the evidence so far, it is difficult to draw an immediate conclusion. Now that our military assistance to the Soviets has been identified, the picture should clarify. If we continue to build the Soviet military-industrial complex, then obviously there is some long-run hidden objective; hidden, that is, from the American public. If we now finally act in our own national self-interest and cut off military assistance to the USSR, then pragmatism would be acceptable as an explanation for former actions. In sum, the test of the pragmatism hypothesis is in future action.

Our Foreign Policy Is Based on Mysticism and Altruism

To subsidize the Soviet military-industrial complex must appear to most readers to be irrational and inconsistent with national self-interest. Is there any evidence that our policies are founded on mysticism, that is, on fantasy based on implicit or explicit rejection of empirical evidence and rationality? Or are our policies founded on international altruism—the very opposite of national self-interest?

Certainly our Washington planners have never learned the hard way that national policy cannot be based on altruism and mysticism. Henry Kissinger has never been on the receiving end of a bullet. *Indeed, in most cases policymakers have never undertaken any occupation where the cost of a wrong decision fell upon their own shoulders—and that may be one of the major problems.*

Mr. Kissinger's words are those of a fluent mystic. The following extract is from the conclusion of his book *Nuclear Weapons and Foreign Policy* (p. 431):

> A statesman must act as if his inspirations were already experience, as if his aspirations were truth. He must bridge the gap between society's experience and his vision, between its tradition and its future.

Note the words "act as if." Act "as if" fantasy were reality is the clear implication. Act "as if" objectives (whatever they may be) are always moral.

In other words, anything is real if you wish it to be, and anything is moral if you want it to be.

This kind of mysticism enables policymakers to accept anything as reality and any goal as moral—even their wildest fantasies, and even if a few hundred-thousand people are killed.

This is the moral quagmire and epistemological wilderness in which we find ourselves today. It may explain at least part of the problem.

A Conspiracy to Create a One-World Collectivist State

The argument put forth in several dozen books, including Gary Allen's *None Dare Call It Conspiracy,* Dan Smoot's *Invisible Government,* and Phoebe Courtney's *Nixon and the CFR,* is that there exists an operating conspiracy for world control. This conspiracy allegedly involves an alliance between international bankers and international Communist forces. It is argued by these authors that the Council on Foreign Relations and its counterpart organizations in other countries play a central role in this international alliance.

Conspiracy is a word that evokes immediate, hostile reaction from the academic and media worlds. It was a commonplace enough word in the nineteenth century, but today it is about as popular as a skunk in the bedroom. This emotional climate is compounded by the practical difficulty of proving that *any* conspiracy exists.

There are at least two problems. The first is similar to that of price conspiracy under the Sherman Act; that is, if all firms have a conspiracy to fix prices, you cannot, by just looking at patterns of prices, tell if the single price is the result of a price conspiracy or of pure competition in the marketplace. The international Communist–international banker *association* for which evidence does exist may therefore have a nonconspiratorial explanation; it may be a problem of market expansion.

Secondly, circumstantial evidence cannot be used to *prove* conspiracy. Proof requires detailed evidence of deliberate actions undertaken with illegal or immoral intent. This evidence, even if it existed, would be difficult, perhaps almost impossible, to obtain.

We can, however, rephrase the question. Are there any events related to our assistance to the Soviet Union that may point in the direction of secret, organized, concerted political action by specific groups?

The answer to this more limited question is: Yes! There does appear to be some evidence pointing in that direction. We have cited FDR's secret military information agreement with the Soviet Union in 1938. Knowledge was restricted to four persons on each side, and all the Americans were in the Executive Branch. Moreover, continued classification of the Operation Keelhaul file by the Department of the Army suggests a concerted series of actions to keep the file from public knowledge. Chapter Three suggests further cases. These are straws in the wind.

The attention of conspiracy theorists is centered upon the Council on Foreign Relations, and it is a fact, for whatever it is worth, that many of the persons cited in this book—from quite different fields of endeavor—are members of this organization. For example, Philip H. Trezise of the Department of State; Victor F. Weisskopf, concerned with the transfer of atomic equipment in the Atomic Energy Commission; Peter G. Peterson, Secretary of Commerce and prominent in recent assistance to the Soviets; Eugene W. Rostow, national security adviser under President Johnson; Donald Douglas, Jr., an industrial member; Charles W. Yost, head of Munitions Control in State back in the 1930s; and so on. There are common patterns of participation in the council and in actions to assist the Soviet Union. It may be, however, that these gentlemen are members of CFR because they hold important positions, not that they hold important positions because they are members of CFR. There is a problem of causality. The question obviously requires thorough investigation (this would be a simple research task).

The *Washington Post* review of Allen's *None Dare Call It Conspiracy,* by Nicholas von Hoffman (Sept. 13, 1972), is interesting as an incisive review of the so-called right by a so-called left-liberal. Hoffman slashes Allen, but does not condemn him. Hoffman points out—quite correctly—that the merits of the Federal Reserve System have not been debated for decades, noting that when someone with a conspiracy argument questions the merits of the FRB, "... he's called 'simplistic' and dismissed as a fringe 'screwball.' " Hoffman suggests a variation to the Allen "conspiracy" explanation; that is, "The radical left explanation that Nixon is a one worlder because international monopoly capitalism can't tolerate excessive national sovereignty is more plausible."

Neither Hoffman nor anyone else has yet pointed out in this regard that in science the "simplistic" answer is the more acceptable answer—the simple explanation is to be preferred over the complex one, providing it covers all the facts.

Finally, Hoffman suggests that the ideas of "Allen and his friends" provide a corrective to current thinking because "they are talking about the uses of power, money and politics in ways we can learn from."

To sum up, the existence of a conspiracy has not been proven. On the other hand, as Nicholas von Hoffman says, these ideas are based on facts usually pushed under the rug, and we had best take a look at them and investigate. Can we explain our military assistance to the Soviet Union in terms of American international bankers unwilling to allow too much American national sovereignty? This is a shattering hypothesis. International bankers also have sons and friends who get caught up in war. No law of physics known to the author states that the Chase Manhattan Bank is immune from nuclear fallout or has a private built-in antimissile defense. The history of the Nazis and the Bolsheviks shows that bankers get put up against a wall and shot along with those who are not bankers.

Nothing in history, then, suggests that bankers do not act in their own rational self-interest. While all this does suggest that the international-banker hypothesis is not supportable, the horrific human cost of our international policies and the tissue-paper-thin justifications for our suicidal actions demand investigation of all possibilities.

Radical means to get to the root of something. Any theory tendered by both the radical right and the radical left—and this conspiracy theory is—demands the most thorough empirical investigation, because all you have left in the middle is the Establishment, and the Establishment would have a vested interest in keeping mum.

Is It Treason?

Does this sequence of events and actions fall within the meaning of treason?* Specifically, does military aid to the Soviet Union constitute "adhering to their enemies, giving them Aid and Comfort"?

* "Treason against the United States shall consist only in levying War against them, or in adhering to their enemies, giving them Aid and Comfort..." Article III, Section 3 of the Constitution of the United States.

There is little question but that the Soviet Union is an enemy of the United States, and has been during the half-century since the Bolshevik Revolution. The Soviet Union has directly and indirectly caused the deaths of over 100,000 American citizens. This constitutes enmity in full measure, even apart from the continuing self-declared hostility of the Soviets to the United States.

Do the actions described in this book constitute "adhering" to these enemies, "giving them Aid and Comfort"?

The actions do not legally constitute treason. The Constitution defines the term strictly, for the intention of the framers, with good reason, was to deny Congress the right to interpret treason too freely. Moreover, the body of relevant case law is not substantial. The Cramer and Haupt cases after World War I suggest that both intent to commit treason and overt treasonable acts are required, in addition to thorough proof. While the actions described here could be interpreted as giving immediate "Aid and Comfort" to the Soviet Union, there is no specific evidence of intent, and intent is a vital requirement. Idiocy, inefficiency, intellectual myopia, and so on, do not suggest intent.

What Is to Be Done?

When the hard-working, long-suffering, overtaxed American citizen learns about our military assistance to the Soviet Union, a country directly responsible for fomenting the wars and supplying the arms to kill 100,000 of his fellow Americans and countless allies and Russians, he will be entitled to feel an overwhelming sense of betrayal. He is already pushed around by the insolent bureaucratic establishment, socially engineered by the educational establishment, sneered at by the academic establishment, and it could be that the fact of military assistance to our enemies will be the final straw to destroy his faith in the American system.

Policymaking circles in the United States have tragically

failed to grasp certain essential empirical truths about our world. Leaving aside the reasons for this failure, what are the fundamentals that must form the bedrock of any policy of rational self-interest and of a world at peace?

First, altruism has no usefulness for policymaking. Nothing can be done for society or for world peace by indiscriminate giving away of the taxpayers' earned wealth. Altruism is plunder. The wealth so freely scattered is earned by someone, a "someone" who has no influence over policies except to pay the bills. Our policies are based on international altruism. They are also fraudulent policies of plunder. They are impractical and a demonstrated failure.

Second, statist systems originate conflict. Whether it is Hitler's Germany or Brezhnev's Russia, statism generates conflict. Therefore, statist systems cannot be treated with in the same manner as nonstatist systems. Those who want to find accommodations with statism will sooner or later be faced with the choice of fighting or surrendering. That is the clear and irrefutable lesson of history.*

The inclination to compromise, which makes for success in American-style politics, has a fatal flaw: that appointive policymakers also attempt to use compromise, rather than principle, in international agreements with statist systems. They have been caught with their pants down every time. Where these appointed policymakers are also businessmen with the overall objective of expanding overseas markets, national-security factors obviously receive short shrift.

Third, statist countries cannot generate innovation. They cannot develop military-industrial complexes without assistance from nonstatist countries. "Peaceful trade" is the carrier of technical innovation; this is the only means statist systems have to generate military production.

---

* This section is not intended to be critical of, or in opposition to, revisionist historical interpretations. However, the reconciliation of these statements and revisionist arguments would take considerable space and is not germane to our discussion.

Fourth, it follows that if we provide the means for construction of statist military-industrial complexes (either Hitler's or Brezhnev's), then we shall pari passu encourage the inherent conflict-generating proclivities of these state machines.

The empirical and logical interconnections of these fundamental observations have been ignored by the policymakers.

The essential problem for the man in the street, who pays the tax bills and gets killed in the resulting wars, is that policymaking is in the hands of a self-perpetuating circle which rejects reason and accepts altruism in lieu of national self-interest. Whether the explanation of our suicidal national policy be pragmatism, accident, mysticism, incompetence, or conspiracy is not fully known: it may be a blend of all these elements. But the result is plainly horrific: lost lives, a mounting burden of taxes, and a rapid decline in constitutional guarantees.

Let's face it, Congress has done nothing to clean out the paper-shuffling, policy-waffling bureaucrats. The way to get rid of pro-Communists and suicidal mystics in government is to abolish government jobs and it will take a major taxpayers' revolt to achieve *that* goal. We can't even get rid of five tea-tasters.

The Establishment is not going to draw in fresh thinking. It cannot tolerate new ideas and new evidence. In the author's own brief experience it has been made amply clear that it cannot even tolerate the slightest criticism or deviation from established dogma. It is too far down the road in pursuit of bankrupt objectives.

On the other hand, a Freedom of Information Act with real teeth would go far to ensure accountability for policies. There is no valid reason in a free society why *all* government papers should not be declassified after three years.

The root of the problem is the policymaking alliance of business and state, which is insulated from the electorate.

Congress must publish the names and corporate affiliations of all lobbyists and other persons who have previously influenced it to relax the export control laws, together with the inducements and arguments offered.

Congress should further require the Department of Commerce to publish each month a full, detailed list of all exports to Communist countries, together with the names of the firms involved, brief technical descriptions, and a departmental statement that the exports cannot be used for military purposes against the United States.

The long-run objective must be to dismantle the insolent, ineffective Washington bureaucracy, to disseminate political power, and divest big business of its influence on policymaking. Instead of being gathered in Washington, power must be dispersed—genuinely dispersed—and immoral policies will be dispersed in its wake.

If the reader thinks these proposals are drastic, he should pause and reflect on the argument—and more importantly, the evidence—in this book. Any group of men that can knowingly bring about the tragic situation described is capable of any irrational or self-perpetuating or appeasing policy. The taxpayer now supports an $80-billion-a-year defense budget against an enemy we built ourselves, and now it is seriously proposed in Washington that we expand this hostile military-industrial complex. Even further, the American taxpayer is to lend the funds and then guarantee the loans for this suicidal proposal. Our policy is a reductio ad absurdum.

We have no choice. If the individual citizens and the Congress of the United States fail in this task, then over the ashes and ruins of our cities and our bodies, the coroner could read the cause of death as National Suicide.

APPENDIX A

Some Background Information about
National Suicide

This book was not originally intended for publication by a trade publisher for general public distribution. The research work was originally oriented to an academic examination in order to complete a previously published three-volume study of our technical assistance to the Soviet economy.

In 1971 the author asked the Department of Defense to declassify sufficient material to write a fourth volume, detailing our military assistance to the Soviet Union. It was suggested that openly available data were insufficient to make the case in exhaustive detail, although there were probably sufficient data to make a general case.

The Defense Department was at first most responsive and requested full details of the proposed research. A statement of the required information was submitted. No reply was received from DOD. Five months later an inquiry was submitted concerning the status of the request, and at that point the request for declassification was politely but firmly rejected.

The full-scale academic project remains then as it was in 1971; dormant. It *is* quite possible to write a detailed one- or two-volume work but this cannot be done until government files are made available to nongovernmental researchers.

The exchange of correspondence between the author and DOD is printed below in full:

July 16, 1971

The Hon. Melvin R. Laird
Secretary of Defense
The Pentagon
Washington D.C. 20301

Dear Mr. Laird:

The undersigned is author of a three volume study entitled WESTERN TECHNOLOGY AND SOVIET ECONOMIC DEVELOPMENT. Two volumes have already been published . . . and the third volume will be published later this year. The study details our enormous technical and economic assistance to the Soviet Union.

I am now considering an additional fourth volume tentatively entitled:
WESTERN TECHNOLOGY AND THE SOVIET MILITARY-INDUSTRIAL COMPLEX

The intent will be to detail in precise technical terms the use made of our technology by the Soviets to develop and maintain a credible military capability.

Administration support for the British computer sale has convinced me that our assistance is virtually unknown and that such a volume is vitally necessary.

I have no doubt that I could raise private funds to make such a book possible. On the other hand only a limited amount of data is available to me (particularly for the period after 1945) and perhaps hardly sufficient to convince the skeptics of the extraordinary assistance we provide our enemies.

Would, therefore, the Department of Defense consider declassification and making available to me, either on loan or for later deposit at the [name of library], sufficient technical material to make a comprehensive and unassailable argument?

In the event consideration of my request is possible I would be more than happy to submit a list of the material required.

With best wishes and appreciation for any assistance it may be possible to grant me,

I am,
Very sincerely,
Antony C. Sutton

DIRECTOR OF DEFENSE RESEARCH AND ENGINEERING
WASHINGTON, D.C. 20301

8 Sep 1971

DEAR MR. SUTTON:

Your request to Secretary Laird for technical material concerning the Soviet Union has been referred to my office. I will be happy to evaluate your request, or to have the appropriate DoD organizations evaluate it when you submit a list of the material that you require.

As you may know, we are conducting a thorough study of the U.S. and USSR capability for defense research and development, which includes an evaluation of transfer of technology. During the course of this net assessment, there is a systematic and continuous effort to declassify all pertinent information, based on an assessment of the benefit which such data might give to a potential enemy. As a result there is a data base available on this subject.

I suggest that you contact Dr. N. F. Wikner, my Special Assistant for Threat Assessment, for further information.

Sincerely,
/s/ E. RECHTIN
FOR JOHN S. FOSTER, JR.

September 15, 1971

Dr. N. F. Wikner
Special Assistant for Threat Assessment
Director of Defense Research and Engineering
Department of Defense
The Pentagon
Washington D.C. 20301

DEAR DR. WIKNER:

I am in receipt of a letter from the office of the Director of Defense Research and Engineering (signed Eberhardt Rechtin) in regard to an inquiry made by me to the Secretary concerning technical information for a projected book
WESTERN TECHNOLOGY AND THE SOVIET ARMAMENTS INDUSTRY.

In response to this letter, which suggests that I should contact you, I enclose:

    a. a list of the information desired
    b. a very approximate and preliminary outline of the structure of the book.

I shall, of course be more than happy to clarify any points that may arise in consideration of my request.

With best wishes,

                        Very sincerely,
                        ANTONY C. SUTTON
                        Research Fellow

DETAILS OF INFORMATION REQUESTED
The information required is as follows:

a) Detailed technical and engineering data on Soviet weapons systems from 1945 to date, in the form of technical handbooks or reports (maintenance or servicing handbooks are adequate but less valuable). In Russian or English with diagrammatic layouts, cutaways, technical specifications of materials used and metallurgical analyses.

These are needed for the production models in each weapons series from 1945 to date. For example, MEDIUM TANKS: data is needed on the T 34, T 54 and T 62; but data is *not* needed on development models, such as T 44 or variants of main production models such as T 34/76B (a turret variant of the main production model T 34).

The weapons spectrum for which this range of data is required are the production models of:

tanks (heavy, medium and light), armored cars, self propelled guns, trucks and tractors, guns of all types (from tank guns down to hand guns), ammunition, planes, naval craft, rocket launchers, missiles. In other words the standard models in the broad weapons spectrum.

I am not interested in the more esoteric weapons under development (such as lasers), or weapons developed and abandoned, but only those systems which constitute (or have historically constituted) the *main* threat to the Free World.

b) A detailed listing of the inputs required to manufacture each of the above Soviet weapons including if possible the chemical or physical specifications of material inputs, quantities of inputs per weapon, and model numbers and types of equipment.

Categories (a) and (b) are required in order to determine *how* Soviet weapons are manufactured and *what* material inputs are used.

c) Reports or raw data on the use by the Soviets of Western technology in weapons systems and general military production. Equipment rosters of Soviet armament plants, i.e. their machinery inventories, (these will identify use of Western machines).

d) Reports or raw data on Soviet manufacture of propellants, explosives, military clothing and instrumentation and computers; the process used, outputs, names of plants.

For example: I would like to know the types of explosives produced by the Soviets and either the chemical analysis or sufficient information to determine an approximate analysis. I am not interested in the military aspects i.e. the explosive force or characteristics of the explosion, only *what* is being produced and *how* it is being produced.

e) Material on the conversion of a civilian industrial base to a military base; the U.S. experience in World War II and Korea; the problems of conversion, time required, adaptability of a civilian plant to military output.

f) Details of the important Export Control cases (both under the Export Control Act and CoCom in Paris) where DOD has argued against export of technology or equipment items to the Soviet Union or to other countries where there was a possibility of transfer to the USSR. These would include for example, the Transfermatic Case of 1961 and the Ball Bearings case of about the same date. From the mid 1950's down to the present time.

g) Equipment lists (by model number, not necessarily quantities) of North Viet and Viet Cong forces.

In general I am *not* interested in the quantitative aspects (i.e. how many they have of a particular weapon) nor in military characteristics (i.e. ballistic properties, operating characteristics etc.).

On the other hand I am interested in qualitative aspects, particularly knowing *how* weapons are produced and the material and equipment inputs used to produce these weapons. Whether the weapons and materials produced are militarily or economically efficient is of little concern for this study.

February 18, 1972

Dr. N. F. Wikner
Special Assistant for Threat Assessment
Director of Defense Research and Engineering
Washington D.C. 20301

DEAR DR. WIKNER:

This refers to my letter of September 15, 1971 concerning my request for technical information on the transfer of technology to the Soviet Union.

My understanding is that the Department has a suitable data base and that according to Mr. Eberhardt Rechtin's letter of September 9: "there is a systematic and continuous effort to declassify all pertinent information."

Accordingly I submitted with my letter a detailed statement of the information desired.

In the absence of any reply or acknowledgement from the Department in the elapsed five months, would it now be accurate for me to assume that there is no desire to pursue the question further?

Sincerely,
ANTONY C. SUTTON

OFFICE OF THE DIRECTOR OF DEFENSE RESEARCH AND
ENGINEERING
WASHINGTON, D.C. 20301

13 March 1972

DEAR MR. SUTTON:

This is to acknowledge your letter of 18 February 1972 as well as your previous correspondence, particularly that of 15 September 1971 which included a listing of material that you would like information on. The scope of the material that you desire is not directly available to this office in an unclassified form. A considerable amount of work will be required to obtain the information, and I will have to suggest that the burden of doing this research is yours.

It is difficult to know where to suggest you begin your research work into this interesting matter, but it may be helpful for you to contact the Foreign Science & Technology Center, Department of Army, Federal Building, 2020 7th Street N.E., Charlottesville, Virginia 22901, Colonel Garth Stevens (703-296-4012). I regret I cannot be of detailed assistance to you, but I think that this would be a fruitful research project for you to pursue.

Sincerely,
N. F. WIKNER
Special Assistant
(Net Technical Assessment)

APPENDIX B

Testimony of the Author
Before Subcommittee VII of the Platform
Committee of the Republican Party
at Miami Beach, Florida,
August 15, 1972, at 2:30 P.M.

This appendix contains the testimony presented by the author before the Republican Party National Security Subcommittee at the 1972 Miami Beach convention. The author's appearance was made under the auspices of the American Conservative Union; the chairman of the subcommittee was Senator John Tower of Texas.

Edith Kermit Roosevelt subsequently used this testimony for her syndicated column in such newspapers as the *Union Leader* (Manchester, N.H.). Both major wire services received copies from the American Conservative Union; they were not distributed. Congressman John G. Schmitz then arranged for duplicate copies to be hand-delivered to both UPI and AP. The wire services would not carry the testimony although the author is an internationally known academic researcher with three books published at Stanford University, and a forthcoming book from the U.S. Naval Institute.

The testimony was later reprinted in full in *Human Events* (under the title of "The Soviet Military-Industrial Complex") and *Review of the News* (under the title of "Suppressed Testimony of Antony C. Sutton"). It was also reprinted and extensively distributed throughout the United States by both the American party and the Libertarian party during the 1972 election campaign.

The following is the text of this testimony as it was originally presented in Miami Beach and made available to UPI and AP:

The Soviet Military–Industrial Complex

The information that I am going to present to you this afternoon *is* known to the Administration.

The information is probably *not* known to the Senator from South Dakota or his advisers. And in this instance ignorance may be a blessing in disguise.

I am not a politician. I am not going to tell you what you want to hear. My job is to give you facts. Whether you like or dislike what I say doesn't concern me.

I am here because I believe—and Congressman Ashbrook believes—that the American public should have these facts.

I have spent ten years in research on Soviet technology. What it is—what it can do—and particularly where it came from. I have published three books and several articles summarizing the work.

It was privately financed. But the results have been available to the Government. On the other hand I have had major difficulties with U.S. Government censorship.

I have 15 minutes to tell you about this work.

In a few words: there is no such thing as Soviet technology.

Almost all—perhaps 90–95 percent—came directly or indirectly from the United States and its allies. In effect the United States and the NATO countries have built the Soviet

Union. Its industrial *and* its military capabilities. This massive construction job has taken 50 years. Since the Revolution in 1917. It has been carried out through trade and the sale of plants, equipment and technical assistance.

Listening to Administration spokesmen—or some newspaper pundits—you get the impression that trade with the Soviet Union is some new miracle cure for the world's problems.

That's not quite accurate.

The idea that trade with the Soviets might bring peace goes back to 1917. The earliest proposal is dated December 1917— just a few weeks after the start of the Bolshevik Revolution. It was implemented in 1920 while the Bolsheviks were still trying to consolidate their hold on Russia. The result was to guarantee that the Bolsheviks held power: they needed foreign supplies to survive.

The history of our construction of the Soviet Union has been blacked out—much of the key information is still classified— along with the other mistakes of the Washington bureaucracy. Why has the history been blacked out?

Because 50 years of dealings with the Soviets has been an economic success for the USSR and a political failure for the United States. It has not stopped war, it has not given us peace. The United States is spending $80 billion a year on defense against an enemy built by the United States and West Europe. Even stranger, the U.S. apparently wants to make sure this enemy remains in the business of being an enemy.

Now at this point I've probably lost some of you. What I have said is contrary to everything you've heard from the intellectual elite, the Administration, and the business world, and numerous well-regarded Senators—just about everyone.

Let me bring you back to earth.

First an authentic statement. It's authentic because it was part of a conversation between Stalin and W. Averell Harriman. Ambassador Harriman has been prominent in Soviet trade since the 1930's and is an outspoken supporter of yet more trade. This is what Ambassador Harriman reported back to the State Department at the end of World War II:

"Stalin paid tribute to the assistance rendered by the United States to Soviet industry before and during the War. Stalin* said that about two-thirds of all the large industrial enterprises in the Soviet Union has been built with the United States' help or technical assistance."

I repeat: "two-thirds of all the large industrial enterprises in the Soviet Union had been built with the United States' help or technical assistance."

Two-thirds.

Two out of three.

Stalin could have said that the other one-third of large industrial enterprises were built by firms from Germany, France, Britain and Italy.

Stalin could have said also that the tank plants, the aircraft plants, the explosive and ammunition plants originated in the U.S.

That was June 1944. The massive technical assistance continues right down to the present day.

Now the ability of the Soviet Union to create any kind of military machine, to ship missiles to Cuba, to supply arms to North Vietnam, to supply arms for use against Israel—all this depends on its domestic industry.

In the Soviet Union about three-quarters of the military budget goes on purchases from Soviet factories.

This expenditure in Soviet industry makes sense. No Army has a machine that churns out tanks. Tanks are made from alloy steel, plastics, rubber and so forth. The alloy steel, plastics and rubber are made in Soviet factories to military specifications. Just like in the United States.

Missiles are not produced on missile-making machines. Missiles are fabricated from aluminum alloys, stainless steel, electrical wiring, pumps and so forth. The aluminum, steel, copper wire and pumps are also made in Soviet factories.

In other words the Soviet military gets its parts and materials

* He, in original.

from Soviet industry. There is a Soviet military-industrial complex just as there is an American military-industrial complex.

This kind of reasoning makes sense to the man in the street. The farmer in Kansas knows what I mean. The salesman in California knows what I mean. The taxi driver in New York knows what I mean. But the policy makers in Washington do not accept this kind of common sense reasoning, and never have done.

So let's take a look at the Soviet industry that provides the parts and the materials for Soviet armaments: the guns, tanks, aircraft.

The Soviets have the largest iron and steel plant in the world. It was built by McKee Corporation. It is a copy of the U.S. Steel plant in Gary, Indiana.

All Soviet iron and steel technology comes from the U.S. and its allies. The Soviets use open hearth, American electric furnaces, American wide strip mills, Sendzimir mills and so on— all developed in the West and shipped in as peaceful trade.

The Soviets have the largest tube and pipe mill in Europe— one million tons a year. The equipment is Fretz-Moon, Salem, Aetna Standard, Mannesman, etc. Those are not Russian names.

All Soviet tube and pipe making technology comes from the U.S. and its allies. If you know anyone in the space business ask them how many miles of tubes and pipes go into a missile.

The Soviets have the largest merchant marine in the world— about 6,000 ships. I have the specifications for each ship.

About two-thirds were built outside the Soviet Union.

About four-fifths of the engines for these ships were also built outside the Soviet Union.

There are no ship engines of Soviet design. Those built *inside* the USSR are built with foreign technical assistance. The Bryansk plant makes the largest marine diesels. In 1959, the Bryansk plant made a technical assistance agreement with Burmeister & Wain of Copenhagen, Denmark, (a NATO ally), approved as peaceful trade by the State Dept. The ships that carried Soviet missiles to Cuba ten years ago used these same Burmeister and Wain engines. The ships were in the POLTAVA class. Some have Danish engines made in Denmark and some have Danish engines made at Bryansk in the Soviet Union.

About 100 Soviet ships are used on the Haiphong run to carry Soviet weapons and supplies for Hanoi's annual aggression. I was able to identify 84 of these ships. None of the main engines in these ships was designed and manufactured inside the USSR.

All the larger and faster vessels on the Haiphong run were built outside the USSR.

All shipbuilding technology in the USSR comes directly or indirectly from the U.S. or its NATO allies.

Let's take one industry in more detail: motor vehicles.

All Soviet automobile, truck and engine technology comes from the West: chiefly the United States. In my books I have listed each Soviet plant, its equipment and who supplied the equipment. The Soviet military has over 300,000 trucks—all from these U.S. built plants.

Up to 1968 the largest motor vehicle plant in the USSR was at Gorki. Gorki produces many of the trucks American pilots see on the Ho Chi Minh trail. Gorki produces the chassis for the GAZ-69 rocket launcher used against Israel. Gorki produces the Soviet jeep and half a dozen other military vehicles.

And Gorki was built by the Ford Motor Company and the Austin Company—as peaceful trade.

In 1968 while Gorki was building vehicles to be used in Vietnam and Israel further equipment for Gorki was ordered and shipped from the U.S.

Also in 1968 we had the so-called "FIAT deal"—to build a plant at Volgograd three times bigger than Gorki. Dean Rusk and Walt Rostow told Congress and the American public this was peaceful trade—the FIAT plant could not produce military vehicles.

Don't let's kid ourselves. *Any* automobile manufacturing plant can produce military vehicles. I can show anyone who is interested the technical specification of a proven military vehicle (with cross-country capability) using the same capacity engine as the Russian FIAT plant produces.

The term "FIAT deal" is misleading. FIAT in Italy doesn't make automobile manufacturing equipment—FIAT plants in Italy have U.S. equipment. FIAT *did* send 1,000 men to Russia for erection of the plant—but over half, perhaps well over half, of the equipment came from the United States. From Gleason, TRW of Cleveland and New Britain Machine Co.

So in the middle of a war that has killed 46,000 Americans (so far) and countless Vietnamese with Soviet weapons and supplies, the Johnson Administration doubled Soviet auto output.

And supplied false information to Congress and the American public.

Finally, we get to 1972 under President Nixon.

The Soviets are receiving now—today, equipment and technology for the largest heavy truck plant in the world: known as the Kama plant. It will produce 100,000 heavy ten-ton trucks per year—that's more than ALL U.S. manufacturers put together.

This will also be the largest plant in the world, *period*. It will occupy 36 square miles.

Will the Kama truck plant have military potential?

The Soviets themselves have answered this one. The Kama truck will be 50 per cent more productive than the ZIL-130 truck. Well, that's nice, because the ZIL series trucks are standard Soviet army trucks used in Vietnam and the Middle East.

Who built the ZIL plant? It was built by the Arthur J. Brandt Company of Detroit, Michigan.

Who's building the Kama truck plant? That's classified "secret" by the Washington policy makers. I don't have to tell you why.

The Soviet T-54 tank is in Vietnam. It was in operation at Kontum, An Loc, and Hue a few weeks ago. It is in use today in Vietnam. It has been used against Israel.

According to the tank handbooks the T-54 has a Christie type suspension. Christie was an American inventor.

Where did the Soviets get a Christie suspension? Did they steal it?

No, sir! They bought it. They bought it from the U.S. Wheel Track Layer Corporation.

However this Administration is apparently slightly more honest than the previous Administration.

Last December I asked Assistant Secretary Kenneth Davis of the Commerce Department (who is a mechanical engineer by training) whether the Kama trucks would have military capability. In fact I quoted one of the Government's own inter-agency reports. Mr. Davis didn't bother to answer but I did get a letter from the Department and it was right to the point. Yes! we know the Kama truck plant has military capability, we take this into account when we issue export licenses.

I passed these letters on to the press and Congress. They were published.

Unfortunately for my research project, I also had pending with the Department of Defense an application for declassification of certain files about our military assistance to the Soviets.

This application was then abruptly denied by DOD.

It will supply military technology to the Soviets but gets a little uptight about the public finding out.

I can understand that.

Of course, it takes a great deal of self confidence to admit you are sending factories to produce weapons and supplies to a country providing weapons and supplies to kill Americans, Israelis and Vietnamese. In writing. In an election year, yet.

More to the point—by what authority does this Administration undertake such policies?

Many people—as individuals—have protested our suicidal policies. What happens? Well, if you are in Congress—you probably get the strong arm put on you. The Congressman who inserted my research findings into the Congressional Record suddenly found himself with primary opposition. He won't be in Congress next year.

If you are in the academic world—you soon find it's OK to protest U.S. assistance to the South Vietnamese but never, never protest U.S. assistance to the Soviets. Forget about the Russian academics being persecuted—we mustn't say unkind things about the Soviets.

If you press for an explanation what do they tell you?

First, you get the Fulbright line. This is peaceful trade. The Soviets are powerful. They have their own technology. It's a way to build friendship. It's a way to a new world order.

This is demonstrably false.

The Soviet tanks in An Loc are not refugees from the Pasadena Rose Bowl Parade.

The "Soviet" ships that carry arms to Haiphong are not peaceful. They have weapons on board, not flower children or Russian tourists.

Second, if you don't buy that line you are told, "The Soviets are mellowing." This is equally false.

The killing in Israel and Vietnam with Soviet weapons doesn't suggest mellowing, it suggests premeditated genocide. Today—*now*—the Soviets are readying more arms to go to Syria. For what purpose? To put in a museum?

No one has ever presented evidence, hard evidence that trade leads to peace. Why not? Because there *is* no such evidence. It's an illusion.

It is true that peace leads to trade. But that's not the same thing. You first need peace, then you trade. That does not mean if you trade you will get peace.

But that's too logical for the Washington policy makers and it's not what the politicians and their backers want anyway.

Trade with Germany doubled before World War II. Did it stop World War II?

Trade with Japan increased before World War II. Did it stop World War II?

What was in this German and Japanese trade? The same means for war that we are now supplying the Soviets. The Japanese Air Force after 1934 depended on U.S. technology. And much of the pushing for Soviet trade today comes from the same groups that were pushing for trade with Hitler and Tojo 35 years ago.

The Russian Communist Party is not mellowing. Concentration camps are still there. The mental hospitals take the overload. Persecution of the Baptists continues. Harassment of Jews continues, as it did under the Tsars.

The only mellowing is when a Harriman and a Rockefeller get together with the bosses in the Kremlin. That's good for business but it's not much help if you are a G.I. at the other end of a Soviet rocket in Vietnam.

I've learned something about our military assistance to the Soviets.

It's just not enough to have the facts—these are ignored by the policy makers.

It's just not enough to make a common sense case—the answers you get defy reason.

Only one institution has been clearsighted on this question. From the early 1920's to the present day only one institution has spoken out. That is the AFL-CIO.

From Samuel Gompers in 1920 down to George Meany today, the major unions have consistently protested the trade policies that built the Soviet Union.

Because union members in Russia lost their freedom and union members in the United States have died in Korea and Vietnam.

The unions know—and apparently care.

No one else cares. Not Washington. Not big business. Not the Republican Party.

And 100,000 Americans have been killed in Korea and Vietnam—by our own technology.

The only response from Washington and the Nixon Administration is the effort to hush up the scandal.

These are things not to be talked about. And the professional smokescreen about peaceful trade continues.

The plain fact—if you want it—is that irresponsible policies have built us an enemy and maintain that enemy in the business of totalitarian rule and world conquest.

And the tragedy is that intelligent people have bought the political double talk about world peace, a new world order and mellowing Soviets.

I suggest that the man in the street, the average taxpayer-voter thinks more or less as I do. You do not subsidize an enemy.

And when this story gets out and about in the United States, it's going to translate into a shift of votes. I haven't met one man in the street so far (from New York to California) who goes along with a policy of subsidizing the killing of his fellow Americans. People are usually stunned and disgusted.

It requires a peculiar kind of intellectual myopia to ship supplies and technology to the Soviets when they are instrumental in killing fellow citizens.

What about the argument that trade will lead to peace? Well, we've had U.S.-Soviet trade for 52 years. The 1st and 2nd Five Year Plans were built by American companies. To continue a policy that is a total failure is to gamble with the lives of several million Americans and countless allies.

You can't stoke up the Soviet military machine at one end and then complain that the other end came back and bit you. Unfortunately, the human price for our immoral policies is not paid by the policy maker in Washington. The human price is paid by the farmers, the students and working and middle classes of America.

The citizen who pays the piper is not calling the tune—he doesn't even know the name of the tune.

Let me summarize my conclusions:

One: trade with the USSR was started over 50 years ago under President Woodrow Wilson with the declared intention of mellowing the Bolsheviks. The policy has been a total and costly failure. It has proven to be impractical—this is what I would expect from an immoral policy.

Two: we have built ourselves an enemy. We keep that self-declared enemy in business. This information has been blacked out by successive Administrations. Misleading and untruthful statements have been made by the Executive Branch to Congress and the American people.

Three: our policy of subsidizing self-declared enemies is neither rational nor moral. I have drawn attention to the intellectual myopia of the group that influences and draws up foreign policy. I suggest these policies have no authority.

Four: the annual attacks in Vietnam and the war in the Middle East were made possible only by Russian armaments and our past assistance to the Soviets.

Five: this worldwide Soviet activity is consistent with Communist theory. Mikhail Suslov, the party theoretician, recently stated that the current detente with the United States is temporary. The purpose of the detente, according to Suslov, is to give the Soviets sufficient strength for a renewed assault on the West. In other words, when you've finished building the Kama plant and the trucks come rolling off—watch out for another Vietnam.

Six: internal Soviet repression continues—against Baptists, against Jews, against national groups and against dissident academics.

Seven: Soviet technical dependence is a powerful instrument for world peace if we want to use it.

So far it's been used as an aid-to-dependent-Soviets welfare program. With about as much success as the domestic welfare program.

Why should they stop supplying Hanoi? The more they stoke up the war the more they get from the United States.

One final thought.

Why has the war in Vietnam continued for four long years under this Administration?

With 15,000 killed under the Nixon Administration?

We can stop the Soviets and their friends in Hanoi anytime we want to.

Without using a single gun or anything more dangerous than a piece of paper or a telephone call.

We have Soviet technical dependence as an instrument of world peace. The most humane weapon that can be conceived.

We have always had that option. We have never used it.

APPENDIX C

Specifications of the Ninety-six Soviet Ships Identified Transporting Weapons and Supplies to North Vietnam, 1966–1971

Name of Soviet ship	Gross Registered Tonnage	Soviet Register No.	HULL CONSTRUCTION Date	HULL CONSTRUCTION Place	Type of Engine	Brake Horsepower (b.h.p.)	Western-Design Origin and Place of Manufacture	Model No.
1. Ala-Tau	7,153	127	1943	United States	Steam	—	United States	—
2. Aleksandr Grich	10,741	4753	—	Yugoslavia	(Diesel)	—	Yugoslavia under Burmeister & Wain license	—

3. Amursk	3,170	216	1960	USSR	Diesel	2,000	Skoda, Czechoslovakia	(480 series)
4. Anapka	3,330	225	1963	Finland	Diesel	2,900	A/S Burmeister & Wain, Denmark	550-VT2BF-110
5. Aniva	3,360	250	1963	Finland	Diesel	2,900	A/S Burmeister & Wain, Denmark	550-VT2BF-110
6. Argus	829	277	1961	USSR	Diesel	1,000	Alco (U.S.) design in USSR	D 50
7. Arkhangel'sk	5,659	302	1953	Finland	Diesel	4,000	Maschinenfabrik Augsburg-Nürnberg A.G., West Germany	K7Z 78/140
8. Arktika	2,900	285	1936	United Kingdom	Steam	—	United Kingdom	—
9. Bakuriani	—	—	1943	(Not identified—probably U.S. Lend-Lease)				
10. Balashikha	10,985		(Not identified)	USSR	Diesel			
11. Baltiysk	5,585	378	1955	Finland	Diesel	4,000	Maschinenfabrik Augsburg-Nürnberg A.G., West Germany	K7Z 78/140
12. Batumi	6,236	404	1931	Denmark	Diesel	—	A/S Burmeister & Wain, Denmark	674-VT2BF-150
13. Baymak	795		(Not identified)				(Not identified)	
14. Belgorod Dnestrovskiy	11,011	4776	1965	USSR	Diesel	7,000	Bryansk, USSR under Burmeister & Wain license	774-VT2BF-160
15. Berezovka	10,996	5450	1967	USSR	Diesel	9,000	Bryansk, USSR under Burmeister & Wain license	674-VT2BF-160
16. Biysk	10,684	5147	1964	Denmark	Diesel	—	A/S Burmeister & Wain, Denmark	874-VT2BF-160
17. Bratstvo	12,285	5154	1963	USSR	Steam	13,000	Sulzer Gebruder, Switzerland	—

ENGINE DATA

Name of Soviet ship	Gross Registered Tonnage	Soviet Register No.	HULL CONSTRUCTION		Type of Engine	Brake Horsepower (b.h.p.)	Western-Design Origin and Place of Manufacture	Model No.
			Date	Place				
18. Brasov			(Identified as Rumanian)					
19. Braslav	3,170	550	1961	USSR	Diesel	2,000	Skoda, Czechoslovakia	(430 series)
20. Bryanskiy Rabochiy	11,089	569	1964	USSR	Diesel	7,000	Bryansk, USSR under Burmeister & Wain license	774-VT2BF-160
21. Buguruslan	8,229	577	1958	USSR	Diesel	2,000	Skoda, Czechoslovakia	(430 series)
22. Chapayevsk	2,603	4594	1957	Poland	Steam	2,000	Poland, under Sulzer license	—
23. Chelyabinsk	3,359	4602	1960	East Germany	Diesel	—	Görlitzer, East Germany	—
24. Dimogorsk	8,843	974	1961	Poland	Diesel	7,800	Holland, under Sulzer license	—
25. Dmitriy Guliya	10,741	4846	—	Yugoslavia	(Not identified—probably B & W)			
26. Galich	1,248	802	1963	Hungary	Diesel	1,000	Lang, Hungary	—
27. Glukhov	1,248	850	1963	Hungary	Diesel	1,600	Lang, Hungary	—
28. Gornoaltaysk	3,725	878	1963	East Germany	Diesel	4,000	East Germany, under M.A.N. license	K6Z 57/80
29. Ignatiy Sergeyev			(Not identified)					
30. Ingur	4,084	1190	1961	West Germany	Diesel	7,250	Maschinenfabrik Augsburg-Nürnberg A.G., West Germany	K8Z 70/120

31. Ivan Babushkin	1,700	1132	1956	Belgium	Diesel	4,560	Sulzer Gebruder, Switzerland	RD-56
32. Izhma	3,357	1158	1959	East Germany	Diesel	—	Görlitzer, East Germany	—
33. Kamchatka	3,725	1265	1964	East Germany	Diesel	4,000	East Germany, under M.A.N. license	K6Z 57/80
34. Kapitan Vislagovskiy			(Not identified)					
35. Kapitan Yeslobokov			(Not identified)					
36. Kaunas	8,229	1329	1956	USSR	Diesel	4,000	Skoda design made in USSR	(430 series)
37. Kirovsk	5,518	1364	1957	Finland	Diesel	6,300	Finland, under Sulzer license	—
38. Komsomol	8,229	1422	1957	USSR	Diesel	4,000	Skoda design made in USSR	(430 series)
39. Komsomolets Ukrainy	8,229	1428	1959	USSR	Diesel	4,000	Skoda design made in USSR	(430 series)
40. Kosmonaut	10,658	1454	1963	Denmark	Diesel	12,600	A/S Burmeister & Wain, Denmark	684-VT2BF-180
41. Kostroma	8,299	1459	1955	USSR	Diesel	4,000	Skoda, Czechoslovakia	(430 series)
42. Krasnopolye			(Not identified)					
43. Kura	3,382	1543	1919	United States	Steam	—	United States	—
44. Kuibyshev	6,403	1535	1919	United States	Steam	—	Hoover, Canada	—
45. Lazarev	3,359	1562	1960	East Germany	Diesel	—	Görlitzer, East Germany	—
46. Leninogorsk	9,935	1600	1958	Poland	Diesel	8,000	Fiat, Italy	—
47. Magnitogorsk	6,339	1668	1932	United Kingdom	Steam	—	Central, United Kingdom	—

ENGINE DATA

Name of Soviet ship	Gross Registered Tonnage	Soviet Register No.	HULL CONSTRUCTION		Type of Engine	Brake Horsepower (b.h.p.)	Western-Design Origin and Place of Manufacture	Model No.
			Date	Place				
48. Malaya Vishera	3,114	1680	1963	USSR	Diesel	2,000	Skoda, Czechoslovakia	(430 series)
49. Manych	1,083	1686	1949	Hungary	Diesel	—	United States	Lend-Lease
50. Medin (Medyn)	10,107	—	1965	Poland	Diesel	9,000	Poland, under Sulzer license	—
51. Metallurg Kurako	12,285	1780	1960	USSR	Steam	13,000	USSR	—
52. Mezhdurechensk	10,107	4927	1965	Poland	Diesel	9,000	Poland, under Sulzer license	—
53. Mikhail Frunze	6,799	1818	1922	Germany	Steam	—	Krupp, Germany	—
54. Michurin	4,441	1821	1923	United Kingdom	Diesel	—	United States	Lend-Lease
55. Minsk	8,430	1799	1963	Poland	Diesel	9,600	Poland, under Sulzer license	RD-76
56. Molodechno	8,229	1836	1956	USSR	Diesel	4,000	Skoda design made in USSR	(430 series)
57. Molodogvardekets	647	—	1960	Poland	Steam	—	Poland, under Sulzer license	—
58. Mozdok	10,107	1831	1964	Poland	Diesel	9,600	Poland, under Sulzer license	RD-76
59. Nagayevo	3,359	1905	1960	East Germany	Steam	—	Görlitzer, East Germany	—
60. Netushe			(Not identified)					
61. Nikolay Chernyshevskiy	1,849	1972	1955	Belgium	Diesel	4,560	Sulzer Gebruder, Switzerland	RD-56
62. Nikolay Ostrovskiy	1,849	1969	1955	Belgium	Diesel	4,560	Sulzer Gebruder, Switzerland	RD-56

Name								
63. Nikolayevsk	4,870	1961	1962	East Germany	Diesel	4,000	East Germany, under M.A.N. license	—
64. Orekhov	11,087	2069	1963	Japan	Diesel	12,000	Japan, under Burmeister & Wain license	874-VT2BF-160
65. Partizanskaya Slava	10,881	5492	1967	USSR	Diesel	9,000	Bryansk, USSR under Burmeister & Wain license	674-VT2BF-160
66. Pavlovsk	11,089	2127	1964	USSR	Diesel	9,000	Bryansk, USSR under Burmeister & Wain license	774-VT2BF-160
67. Perekop	11,089	2172	1963	USSR	Diesel	8,750	Bryansk, USSR under Burmeister & Wain license	774-VT2BF-160
68. Polotsk	9,500	2232	1963	USSR	Diesel	8,750	Bryansk, USSR under Burmeister & Wain license	674-VT2BF-160
69. Pos'yet	3,455	2251	1961	East Germany	Diesel	—	Maschinenfabrik Augsburg-Nürnberg A.G., West Germany	K6Z 57/80
70. Poti	8,229	2253	1954	USSR	Diesel	4,000	Skoda design made in USSR	(430 series)
71. Pridneprovsk	11,089	2268	1964	USSR	Diesel	8,750	Bryansk, USSR under Burmeister & Wain license	774-VT2BF-160
72. Pula	11,287	2360	1964	Yugoslavia	Diesel	—	Yugoslavia under Burmeister & Wain license	874-VT2BF-160
73. Revda	3,359	2394	1959	East Germany	Diesel	—	Görlitzer, East Germany	—

ENGINE DATA

Name of Soviet ship	Gross Registered Tonnage	Soviet Register No.	HULL CONSTRUCTION		Type of Engine	Brake Horsepower (b.h.p.)	Western-Design Origin and Place of Manufacture	Model No.
			Date	Place				
74. Samuil Marshak	10,409	—	1966	Poland	Diesel	9,600	Poland, under Sulzer license	RD-76
75. Saransk	3,359	3018	1959	East Germany	Diesel	—	Görlitzer, East Germany	—
76. Sevastopol	7,176	3052	1943	United States	Steam	2,500	Iron Foundry, United States	Lend-Lease
77. Simferopol	9,344	3119	1968	Poland	Diesel	9,600	Poland, under Sulzer license	RD-76
78. Sinegorsk	3,359	3122	1960	East Germany	Diesel	—	Görlitzer, East Germany	—
79. Solnechnogorsk	9,935	3218	1958	Poland	Diesel	—	Fiat, Italy	—
80. Sovetsk	9,344	3193	1962	Poland	Diesel	9,600	Poland, under Sulzer license	RD-76
81. Suchan	7,176	4301	1943	United States	Steam	—	Hendy, United States	Lend-Lease
82. Tashkent	6,456	4337	1914	United States	Diesel	—	Maryland, United States	Lend-Lease
83. Tungus	7,194	4412	1943	United States	Diesel	—	Williamette, United States	Lend-Lease
84. Turkistan	3,359	4420	1959	East Germany	Diesel	—	Görlitzer, East Germany	—
85. Timlat	1,309	—	1960	Hungary	Diesel	1,000	Lang, Hungary	—
86. Uritsk	5,628	4481	1958	East Germany	Diesel	4,700	East Germany, under M.A.N. license	K7Z 70/120

87. Ussuriysk	9,501	4487	1960	Denmark	Diesel	—	A/S Burmeister & Wain, Denmark	874-VT2BF-160
88. Ustilug	5,628	4488	1960	East Germany	Diesel	4,700	East Germany, under M.A.N. license	K7Z 70/120
89. Vaykan			(Not identified)					
90. Vereya (Vereia)	9,437	—	1965	East Germany	Diesel	4,700	East Germany, under M.A.N. license	K7Z 70/120
91. Vladivostok	4,722	—	1960	USSR	Diesel	8,300	East Germany, under M.A.N. license	K6Z 57/80
92. Voykov	7,176	—	1943	United States	Diesel	—	Hendy, United States	Lend-Lease
93. Yasnogorsk			(Not identified)					
94. Yasnomorsk	3,359	4757	1960	East Germany	Diesel	—	Görlitzer, East Germany	—
95. Zaysan	3,359	1073	1960	East Germany	Diesel	—	Görlitzer, East Germany	—
96. Zeya	1,248	1107	1962	Hungary	Diesel	1,000	Lang, Hungary	—

Sources: Grateful acknowledgement is made to Joseph Gwyer of Washington, D.C., for information on Soviet ships used on the Haiphong run.

Specifications taken from: Registr Soiuza SSR. *Dopolneniia i izmeneniia k registrovoi knige morskikh sudov soiuza SSR, 1964–1965.* No. 1. Moscow, July 1966.

—————. *Registrovaia kniga morskikh sudov soiuza SSR 1964–1965.* Moscow, 1966.

SELECTED BIBLIOGRAPHY

Dallin, David J. *Soviet Espionage*. New Haven: Yale University Press, 1956.

——, and Nicolaevsky, B. I. *Forced Labor in Soviet Russia*. London: Hollis & Carter, 1947.

Evans, Medford. *The Secret War for the A-bomb*. Chicago: Henry Regnery Co., 1953.

Goodsmit, S. *ALSOS*. New York: Schuman, 1947.

Hutton, J. B. *The Traitor Trade*. New York: Obolensky, 1963.

Jordan, George Racey. *From Major Jordan's Diaries*. New York: Harcourt, Brace & Co., 1953.

Keller, Werner. *Are the Russians Ten Feet Tall?* London: Thames & Hudson, 1961.

Kilmarx, R. A. *A History of Soviet Air Power*. New York: Frederick Praeger, 1962.

Kubek, Anthony. *How the Far East Was Lost*. Chicago: Henry Regnery Co., 1963.

Mallan, Lloyd. *Russia and the Big Red Lie*. New York: Fawcett, 1959.

Milsom, John. *Russian Tanks 1900–1970*. Harrisburg, Pa.: Stackpole Books, 1971.

Sutton, Antony C. *Western Technology and Soviet Economic Development, 1917 to 1930*. Stanford: Hoover Institution, 1968.

——. "Some Aspects of Trade, Western Technology and Soviet Military Capability." In *Export Expansion and Regulations*. Hearings before the Subcommittee on International Finance of the Committee on Banking and Currency, U.S. Senate, 91st Cong., 1st sess., 1969.

——. "Soviet Export Strategy." *Ordnance* (Nov.–Dec. 1969).

——. "The Western Origins of Soviet Marine Diesel Engines." *U.S. Naval Institute Proceedings* (Jan. 1970).

———. "Soviet Merchant Marine." *U.S. Naval Institute Proceedings* (Jan. 1970).

———. *Wars and Revolutions: A Comprehensive List of Conflicts, with Fatalities, Part I, 1820–1900*. Stanford: Hoover Institution, 1971.

———. *Western Technology and Soviet Economic Development, 1930 to 1945*. Stanford: Hoover Institution, 1971.

———. *Western Technology and Soviet Economic Development, 1945 to 1965*. Stanford: Hoover Institution, 1973.

———. *The Soviet Merchant Marine*. Annapolis: U.S. Naval Institute, forthcoming.

Tokaev, Colonel G. A. *Stalin Means War*. London: George Weidenfeld & Nicolson, 1951.

U.S. Senate. *Export of Ball Bearing Machines to Russia*. Committee of the Judiciary, 87th Cong., 1st sess. Washington: Government Printing Office, 1961.

U.S. Senate. *Export of Strategic Materials to the U.S.S.R. and Other Soviet Bloc Countries*. Hearings before the Subcommittee to Investigate the Administration of the Internal Security Act and other Internal Security Laws, 87th Cong., 1st sess., Part 1. Washington, 1961.

U.S. Senate. *Proposed Shipment of Ball Bearing Machines to the U.S.S.R.* Committee of the Judiciary (Feb. 28, 1961). Washington, 1961.

U.S. State Dept. Decimal File.

U.S. State Dept. *Report on War Aid Furnished by the United States to the U.S.S.R.* Washington: Office of Foreign Liquidation, 1945.

Vladimirov, Leonid. *The Russian Space Bluff*. London: Tom Stacey Ltd., 1971.

INDEX